Secrecy and
INSURGENCY

Secrecy and INSURGENCY

Socialities and Knowledge Practices in Guatemala

SILVIA POSOCCO

THE UNIVERSITY OF ALABAMA PRESS
Tuscaloosa

Manufactured in the United States of America

Typeface: Minion

Cover photograph: Petén, Guatemala, 2000; courtesy of the author
Cover design: Erin Bradley Dangar/Dangar Design

∞
The paper on which this book is printed meets the minimum requirements of American National Standard for Information Sciences—Permanence of Paper for Printed Library Materials, ANSI Z39.48-1984.

Library of Congress Cataloging-in-Publication Data

Posocco, Silvia.
Secrecy and insurgency : socialities and knowledge practices in Guatemala / Silvia Posocco.
pages cm
Summary: "This title deals with the experiences of guerrilla combatants of the Fuerzas Armadas Rebeldes (Rebel Armed Forces) in the aftermath of the peace accords signed in December 1996 between the Guatemalan government and guerrilla insurgents. Drawing on a broad field of contemporary theory, the author presents a vivid ethnographic account of secrecy as both sociality and a set of knowledge practices. Informed by multi-sited anthropological fieldwork among displaced communities with experiences of militancy in the guerrilla organization Fuerzas Armadas Rebeldes, the book traces the contours of dispersed and intermittent guerrilla social relations, unraveling the gendered dimensions of guerrilla socialities and subjectivities in a local context marked by violence and rapid social change"— Provided by publisher.
Includes bibliographical references and index.
ISBN 978-0-8173-1359-3 (hardback) — ISBN 978-0-8173-8698-6 (e book)
1. Guerrillas—Guatemala—Social conditions. 2. Secrecy—Social aspects—Guatemala. 3. Fuerzas Armadas Rebeldes (Guatemala) 4. Guatemala—History—Civil War, 1960–1996—Peace. 5. Ethnology—Guatemala. I. Title.
F1466.7.P67 2013
972.8105'31—dc23

2013019835

This book is dedicated to the memory of the *compañeras* and *compañeros* who died during the Guatemalan conflict and to those who sustain the struggle by different means in civilian life.

El trabajo se dedica a la memoria de las compañeras y los compañeros que fallecieron en el conflicto armado en Guatemala y a todas/os las/os que siguen luchando en la vida civil.

Nosotros estamos y no estamos
We are there, but we are not there
—Luis Augusto Turcios Lima, FAR Comandante, 1967

Hay cosas que no se saben, y nosotros nunca las dijimos.
There are things that are not known, and that we never told.
—FAR Comandante, 2000

¡Las preguntas no son las indiscretas, si no las respuestas!
Questions are never indiscreet, but answers are!
—FAR Comandante, 2000

Contents

Illustrations

TABLES

FIGURES

MAPS

Acknowledgments

The research presented in this book benefited from the generous support offered by the Society for Latin American Studies, the University of London Central Research Fund, and the London School of Economics. Reflections on the field of performativity theory were assisted by a jointly awarded research grant from the British Academy.

Henrietta L. Moore, Sylvia Chant, Rachel Sieder, and Nigel Rapport commented on the text at different stages. I am grateful for their suggestions. I would like to thank Henrietta L. Moore in particular for her unwavering support over the years. Special thanks also to Joseph B. Powell for expert editorial guidance and encouragement and to two anonymous readers for their painstakingly detailed reading of the manuscript. Chapter 3 was greatly enriched by the generous comments offered by Sarah Pinto; I am grateful for her thoughtful engagement with my arguments. The map of Petén was drawn by Mina Moshkeri. Thanks also to Dan Waterman, Crissie Johnson, Carol Connell, Latasha Watters, Kathy Cummins, Erin Bradley Dangar, and Susan Harris at the University of Alabama Press for editorial, design, and indexing support.

I acknowledge the support offered over many years by Italo Posocco, Anna Spedicato, Paolo Spedicato, Laura Posocco, Marco Posocco, Romana Molinari, Elio Giammarioli, Simon Phillips, Ellen Abdulla, Lilach Hazan, JongMi Kim, Pam Brown, and, most recently, Anabeatriz Alarcón Posocco.

My greatest debt is to many individuals and communities in Guatemala. I hope that the book may go some way toward reciprocating their kindness.

Brief sections of Chapter 2 and Chapter 6—short ethnographic fragments, without arguments—are excerpted from Posocco, Silvia (2008), "Zoning: Environmental Cosmopolitics in and around the Maya Biosphere Reserve, Petén, Guatemala," *Nature and Culture*, Vol. 3, No. 2: 206–24, doi: 10.3167/

nc.2008.030204, and Posocco, Silvia (2011), "Ethnography and Incommensurability in the Aftermath of Insurgency," *Cultural Dynamics*, Vol. 23, No. 1: 57–72, respectively. They are reproduced here with kind permission of the publishers.

Acronyms

ALMG	Academia de Lenguas Mayas de Guatemala (Guatemalan Maya Languages Academy)
CEH	Comisión de Esclarecimiento Histórico (Commission for Historical Clarification)
CIA	United States Central Intelligence Agency
CONAP	Consejo Nacional de Áreas Protegidas (National Council of Protected Areas)
COPMAGUA	Coordinación de Organizaciones del Pueblo Maya de Guatemala (Coordination of Organizations of the Pueblo Maya of Guatemala)
CPR	Comunidades de Población en Resistencia (Communities of Population in Resistance)
EGP	Ejército Guerrillero de los Pobres (Guerrilla Army of the Poor)
FAR	Fuerzas Armadas Rebeldes (Rebel Armed Forces)
FGEI	Frente Guerrillero Edgar Ibarra (Guerrilla Front Edgar Ibarra)
FRG	Frente Republicano Guatemalteco (Guatemalan Republican Front)
FYDEP	Empresa Nacional de Fomento y Desarrollo de Petén (National Enterprise of Fomentation and Development of Petén)
JPT	Juventud Patriótica del Trabajo (Workers' Patriotic Youth)
MINUGUA	Misión de Verificación Naciones Unidadas Guatemala (United Nations Verification Mission in Guatemala)
MR-13	Frente Rebelde Alejandro de León Aragón 13 de Noviembre (Rebel Front Alejandro de León 13th November)

NASA	United States National Aeronautics and Space Administration
ORPA	Organización del Pueblo en Armas (Organization of People in Arms)
PAC	Patrullas de Autodefensa Civil (Civil Patrols)
PGT	Partido Guatemalteco del Trabajo (Guatemalan Workers' Party)
PUR	Partido Unión Revolucionaria (Revolutionary Unity Party)
RBM	Reserva de la Biósfera Maya (Maya Biosphere Reserve)
URNG	Unidad Revolucionaria Nacional Guatemalteca (Guatemalan National Revolutionary Unity)
USAID	United States Agency for International Development

Secrecy and INSURGENCY

Introduction

When I arrived in Guatemala in October 1999, the country was in the grip of the electoral campaign for the first "free and democratic" national elections since the signing of the Guatemalan Peace Accords between the Guatemalan government and the umbrella guerrilla organization Unidad Revolucionaria Nacional Guatemalteca (Guatemalan National Revolutionary Unity; URNG) on 29 December 1996. Peace negotiations were punctuated by innumerable setbacks,[1] but eventually they culminated in a series of successive Peace Agreements.[2] The Guatemalan Peace Accords nominally ended a period of thirty-six years of *conflicto armado interno*, or internal armed conflict.

This book is an ethnographic exploration of histories of violence and socialities of secrecy in Petén, northern Guatemala, in the aftermath of the Peace Accords signed in 1996 by the Guatemalan government and guerrilla insurgents. Informed by multi-sited anthropological fieldwork among displaced communities with experiences of militancy in the guerrilla organization Fuerzas Armadas Rebeldes (Rebel Armed Forces; FAR), the book traces the contours of dispersed and intermittent guerrilla social relations, unraveling the gendered dimensions of guerrilla socialities and subjectivities in a local context marked by violence and rapid social change.

An ethnography of "secrecy" understood as an ensemble of social relations and knowledge practices in post–Peace Accords northern Guatemala, this book begins by charting shifting governmentalities in Petén in the twentieth century. It offers a detailed analysis of the operations of early colonization initiatives; state-sponsored violence, insurgency, and state repression in the 1980s; and, most recently, the rationalities of government linked to global/local environmental conservation. Human trafficking, illegal logging, illicit trades in ancient Maya antiquities, and, increasingly, the drug trade are social, political, and economic processes of great contemporary significance in the region. The book demonstrates how the region of Petén, produced as marginal and peripheral in the anthropological imagination and ethnographic record (Schwartz 1990), was throughout the twentieth century embedded in rationalities of rule significantly tied to broader processes of social change and profoundly rooted in local histories and relations.

By focusing on an elusive constituency of guerrilla combatants and sympathizers in the immediate aftermath of the Peace Accords–sanctioned dispersal of the insurgent movement, the book deals with a complex set of secret socialities and relations captured at the point of dissolution. In an ethnographically nuanced account, the book traces the emergence of processes of incitement and replication of ambivalence in social relations, highlighting their gendered dimensions and articulations. It illustrates the relations between plural histories of violence and the complex production of secrecy through negative and positive forms of sociality. It considers guerrilla ethics and aesthetics of sociality and how these were established and maintained through generation and circulation of "guerrilla substance," the latter understood by the insurgents to consist of "arms," "supplies," and "combatants." Finally, the book discusses guerrilla gendered embodiments and subjectivities, as these emerged in the context of ethnographic encounters. Drawing specifically on the partiality inherent in the ethnographic encounters (Clifford 1988) and on the multiple, complex, and partial scales of guerrilla secrecy, the book asks what might be adequate theoretical, hermeneutic, and representational frames to apprehend and represent multiple shifts in perspectives.

The book argues that to offer an account of secrecy in postwar Guatemala means moving between different orders of connection between the partiality of socialities and knowledge practices. The book shifts between an ethnographic accounting of socialities and subjectivities tied to experiences of political mobilization and militancy in the Guatemalan insurgency, and the analysis of the knowledge practices that order and govern the ethnographic endeavor, casting a skeptical eye over those "artifacts of rhetoric" that are social wholes figured in terms of "cultures," "societies," "social groups," "individuals," or "subjects" (Thornton 1988).

Gender and Secrecy: Catachresis and Partiality as Pre-theoretical Commitments

The book is situated in the field of the ethnography of relational categories.[3] This approach is concerned with people's understandings and figurations, as well as with the analytical models for apprehending and representing social and cultural realities that are available to the ethnographer and her interlocutors. In this view, pre-theoretical commitments and analytical presuppositions, rather than implicit or occluded from view, can be elicited, foregrounded, and made to yield important insights. For example, the relational category of "gender" is neither understood as an intrinsic property of subjects and bodies, nor taken to refer to cultural elaborations of naturally occurring differences. Rather, from this perspective, "gender" is a form of relational categorization as well as an analytics. This point is cogently developed by Marilyn Strathern (1988) in relation to Melanesian ethnography, for which she argues that gender ought not to be figured in terms of binary oppositions or as the property of univocally gendered individuals. Rather, the model of the person as individual does not hold in relation to the Melanesian material whose analysis Strathern is concerned with. Instead, a multiplicity of gendered processes of "partibility" becomes apparent and holographic and fractal configurations of multiply gendered persons, processes, relations, and bodily substances emerge. The person is also reconfigured accordingly as "dividual"—a figure that encompasses plurality—rather than "individual." This radical reconfiguration opens up the analytical terrain, so that "gender" may refer to a range of relations and social forms—not all dependent on the human scale—in which gender is articulated and conjured up. Drawing on this set of propositions, the book suggests the eliciting of "gender" in a range of constructs, socialities, relations, and subjectivities. Rather than understanding "gender" as having to do with "men" and "women"—or even with their relations—"gender" here is a concept-metaphor (Moore 2004; 2007) activated in relation to a different set of scales of relations and knowledge practices, such as "secrecy," "violence," "partiality," "excess," and so on. This does not mean that historical subjects are absent from my account. On the contrary, the analysis that follows privileges ethnographic exchanges, rendered in vivid vernacular,[4] in which subjects deflect interlocution or open up in dialogue. It does mean, however, that constructs such as "men" and "women," insofar as they relate to "gender," are taken to be catachrestic, that is, to be concept-metaphors with no adequate referent, and thus open to resignification at every turn and with every reinscription. When "gender" itself is understood to be catachrestic, an important consequence of this is that it might at times appear as not having much to do with "men" and "women" at all. This decoupling might initially appear as a loss, but it does also present a new range of phenomena as amenable to description and analysis.

One such phenomenon is secrecy. A focus on secrecy as a set of relations *and* knowledge practices also produces a range of revelations, the most notable of which relates to how the social and cultural field saturated by secrecy is made to appear as a site of ever-increasing partiality. The partiality of the social field engendered by secrecy requires that an explicit effort be made to apprehend and represent shifts in perspective, while also raising questions concerning the presuppositions that may make partial subjectivities and socialities amenable to experience, reflection, and representation. The work of foregrounding questions of partiality, relationality, and relativization in the analysis of gender and secrecy produces a form of destructuring and decentering. Such an analysis eschews strong metaphysical claims to delineate fictionalized experiences of reality instead. Defying "strong thought," scientism, objectivity, realism, and representationalism, this perspective makes explicit the artifice of ethnography and of the analytical and interpretative work of social and cultural analysis more generally.[5] In other words, this approach is as concerned with giving an account of the veracity and materiality of the ethnographic encounter, as much as with the task of bringing into view the labor of fabrication that coincides with it, and with ethnographic analysis and interpretation. Such a concern with "fabrication," which one could rephrase in Nietzschean terms as "fabling," is deeply analytical. As Rapport (1997, 658) notes, the challenge here lies in the task of maintaining "a sense of the *provisional* and *tentative* nature" in the accounts of social and cultural analysis, as much as in attending to "the continual *overflowing* of extant analytical categories" (Rapport 1997, 658; my emphasis). I explicitly inscribe provisionality and tentativeness within an analysis of secrecy in the aftermath of the Peace Accords in northern Guatemala, as they inform the contingency of the ethnographic accounting presented in the book. Overflow and excess are also important. In the chapters that follow, I hope to be able to show that the ethnographic subjects that emerge through this account continuously spill over. They overflow in and through their names and the "epistemic murk" (Taussig 1987, 121) of subjectivities and sociality marked by experiences of the conflict.[6] They pour out of their own accounts, and by doing so, they tell tales of how they have exceeded their own frames as much as the frames others impose upon them. Along with the ethnographer, they conjure up further analytical categories and relations, making sense of complex encounters and experiences. Overflow of subjectivities and socialities often occurs through refusal, restraint, and negative relationalities, that is, through social relations articulated through avoidance, deflection, and negation. The book is thus born out of an attempt at *apprehending* the constant shifting of positions thus engendered and *representing* the shifts of positions throughout.

This double emphasis on provisionality and tentativeness, overflow and excess, apprehension and representation is underpinned by a range of pretheoretical commitments and alignments, that is to say, by a set of presuppositions that ought to be accounted for and made explicit.

Performativity and Deconstruction: Theoretical Idioms of Post-plurality

In the book I propose that frames of analysis, theoretical propositions, and ethnographic accounts ought not to be understood, in a narrow sense, as amorphous descriptions. Rather, I suggest that they are inextricably tied to practices of signification through which objects, subjects, and relations are "conjured up." This point has been made with great flair by Marilyn Strathern with regard to, inter alia, anthropological and feminist accounts of Melanesia, English kinship, and attitudes to biotechnology and bioscience. Strathern shows that the act of description may be figured as underpinned by knowledge practices that open up, rather than define, relations. Merographic knowledge practices (Strathern 1992a), for instance, conjure up relations between parts and wholes, and in the process, reconfigure entities. By the same token, ethnographic description is not inert, but generative and imaginative. Descriptions come into being through specific knowledge practices, for example, "contextualization," "comparison," "enumeration," and so on. In turn, knowledge practices have epistemological dimensions whose effects can be traced, unpacked, and elucidated. Furthermore, descriptions—including those offered by ethnography—are always reinscriptions, as much as "conceptualization is inevitably reconceptualization" (Strathern 1992b, 75), that is to say, knowledge practices of recontextualization and resignification. One way to figure this multiple articulatory movement is through the theoretical idiom of performativity, according to which words (Austin 1962), language (Derrida 1970; 1972; 1974; Felman 1983), and/or discourse (Barad 2003; Butler 1990; 1993) are not governed by representationalism, that is, they are not, strictly speaking, representations of the world ordered by a stable and direct relation of correspondence between signifier and signified. Rather, they constitute a doing that by far exceeds the accounts of representationalism. Performativity theory was popularized by Judith Butler (1990; 1993; 1997) in the 1990s. However, the term and the theoretical propositions captured by it have multiple genealogies pointing to philosopher J. L. Austin's classic text *How to Do Things with Words* (1962). At its most general, performativity is a notion that seeks to capture a seemingly simple idea, that is, that discourse may not be a description but a doing, and that therefore discursive practices may participate in enacting the objects they purport to reference. In this view, any representation or description is not an inert rendition of an empirically ascertainable and ontologically distinct reality. Rather, it is constitutive of the reality or object it seeks to represent or describe. Austin makes this point in his much quoted discussion of the utterance "I do" in the context of the marriage ceremony, in which he notes that the utterance does not constitute a description of a state of affairs, but rather may accomplish the marriage itself. While not all utterances may be "happy" performatives that accomplish a deed—I may, indeed, be already married, and the utterance "I do" may make me into a bigamist, Austin (1962) notes—Derrida in *Limited Inc.* (1972) contends that this performative dimension may not be discrete to selected types of utterances but that all language may be performative. This genealogy of theorizing informs very directly the contemporary permutations of performativity theory in gender studies and social and cultural theory, principally through the influential restaging of Austinian and Derridean questions in the work of Judith Butler (1990; 1993; 1997).

My emphasis on the act of "conjuring up" aims to make the performative dimensions of ethnography explicit, that is, knowledge practices of description are highlighted as not mere representations, but rather *qua* practice, as a doing through which contexts, subjects, relations, and knowledge are brought into being. This performative dimension, with the possibility of resignification that it entails, signals a distancing from pluralist knowledge practices intent on tracking the multiplication of different and yet unitary and internally coherent entities, be they societies, cultures, or individual subjects. Post-plurality here refers to the emergence of the conditions of possibility for thinking beyond potentially infinite and distinct partial perspectives, as well as a distancing from the knowledge practice of enumeration of the internally coherent and bounded components of multiplicity. Post-plurality therefore denotes the task of apprehending and representing constant shifts of partial perspectives in anti-foundational terms, without having to rely on assumptions of coherent wholes and unitary subjects.

As pointed out by Moore (1999), the advent of deconstruction, poststructuralism, and postmodernism is associated with a "crisis of representation" in social and cultural analysis, and specifically with a progressive polarization of terms according to dyads such as objectivism/subjectivism and empiricism/social constructionism. The crisis of representation has brought about "an insistence on partiality and partialness of all interpretations, and a profound questioning of the assumptions and techniques used to develop and convey cultural representations and interpretations"

(Moore 1999, 5). Further, Moore notes an increasing awareness of the "multiple models and/or discourses within cultures, societies or sets of people," highlighting that social and cultural analysis has "only recently begun to discuss and to document the existence of multiple models, and to look at the variation that exists within cultures as well as between them" (Moore 1994, 34). In this sense, a post-plural splintering of the "object/subject" of study coincides with a new recognition of complexity and the progressive erosion of assumptions of coherence, completeness, and wholeness. Further, postmodern and deconstructionist-informed debates have engendered an emphasis on the researcher's role "in knowledge construction, the importance of positionality, and the partialness of all interpretations" (Moore 1999, 8) and an increased alertness as to the performative character of debates and recurrent representational crises themselves, that is, in sum, of the post-plural conditions in which ethnographic analysis emerges. In the context of the analysis presented in this book, post-plurality is not exclusively derived by the idioms of fragmentation and resignification of social and cultural theory. Post-plurality also emerges out of the distinct historical conjuncture of post–Peace Accords Guatemala.

Such a historically located post-plurality marked by histories of violence and conflict constitutes a challenge to certain genres of ethnographic accounting. It is my contention that in studies of those social contexts marked by multiple histories of conflict and cultures of secrecy, there may be serious impediments to ethnographic "thick description" (Geertz 1973, 3–30). In his seminal essay "Thick Description: Toward an Interpretive Theory of Culture," Clifford Geertz (1973, 3–30), following the work of analytic philosopher Gilbert Ryle, considers the example of two boys rapidly contracting the eyelids of their right eyes. The thin description of the natural experimental sciences would describe the boys' activity in terms of a rapid eyelid contraction of their right eyes. Conversely, thick description entertains the possibility that the contraction of the boys' right eyelids might amount to a meaningful gesture. Insofar as this is the case, the ethnographer is not just engaged in observation. Rather, she engages in an effort of interpretation that considers whether twitches may in fact be winks, and if so, what winks may be about, what they may mean in any specific context and social interaction.[7]

With regard to the challenges inherent in ethnographic thick description, whether an "ethnographic effect" may connote my experience of fieldwork in post–Peace Accords Petén, northern Guatemala, this is grounded in the intuition that the thickness of the ethnography may be its very thinness. As Strathern explains, "[t]he ethnographic moment is a relation in the same way as a linguistic sign can be thought of as a relation (joining signifier and signified). We could say that the ethnographic moment works as an example of a relation which joins the understood (what is analyzed at the moment of observation) to the need to understand (what is observed at the moment of analysis). The relation between what is already apprehended and what seems to demand apprehension is of course infinitely regressive, that is, slips across any manner of scale (minimally, observation and analysis each contains within itself the relation between them both). Any ethnographic moment, which is a moment of knowledge or insight, denotes a relation between immersement and movement" (Strathern 1999, 6).

A key ethnographic effect suggests that the ethnographic analytics of thick description may be undergirded by and predicated upon pre-theoretical commitments to holism as well as representationalism. These are presuppositions that may be ill-suited to an engagement with socialities and knowledge practices elicited in a context marked by violence, conflict, and secrecy—and, crucially, predicated upon partiality, dissimulation, and deflection. Violence, conflict (Daniel 1997; Das et al. 2000), and secrecy (Barth 1975) raise profound issues of epistemology, that is, they explicitly and very directly trouble the status of knowledge claims. It may be argued that thick description may accommodate omissions and absences in the analysis and in the interpretative framework—here including the ethnographer's as much as her interlocutors' lacunae. Refusals, absences, and silences may be described in the "thick" form they take and in the "thick" ethnographic encounters they connote. Here I define the analytical and theoretical task as one grounded in a critical analysis of the knowledge practices of "centering," "contextualization," and "intelligibility-creation" taking place in and through social and cultural analysis, and the descriptions they engender. Further, I suggest that processes of "decentering," "out-contextualization," and "unintelligibility-creation" may be as important. Through an analysis of secrecy as sociality and knowledge practice, it may therefore be possible to think of the ethnographic enterprise in performative terms and recast description within a performative and post-plural horizon. In the account of secrecy as relation and knowledge practice that I am concerned with here, performativity comes into being and is effectuated in and through a complex agentic territory, characterized by overt and covert injunctions to secrecy. Interlocutors often place these injunctions upon the ethnographer, as they demand that degrees of confidentiality be respected. On the other hand, notably in research on violence and conflict, demands to secrecy often involve a simultaneous commitment to telling.[8] It is within this complex predicament that the urgency of secrecy, with the telling that is involved, emerges. Performative rearticulation may also engender self-discipline and suppression, though they are not exclusively that. The resulting description has a component of rhetorical and epistemological departure from Geertzian thick description in the sense that it is inscribed within an ethnography of secrecy and conflict that is self-consciously complicit with that secrecy-imbued and violence-marked ethnographic encounter willed by the ethnographer, but fully driven by the agentic "object/subject" of study and the performative nexus established in specific ethnographic encounters and exchanges. The routes and structures of these demands for secrecy may be highlighted in ethnographic analyses. Such descriptions thus also depend on established practices of concealment and camouflage (Pitt-Rivers 1954), but go beyond these as they aim to self-consciously and reflexively explore the complexity of refusal and nescience, as well as negative and positive relationalities and socialities. In my definition, and for the purpose of the present analysis, ethnographic enquiry implies a taciturn and tergiversating mode of disclosure that recognizes the ambiguities, evasions, and equivocations that are an important part of cultural translation and cultural analysis. This form of description does not dispel but acknowledges the possibility that the thickness of ethnography may be its very thinness. Through such a description, it is possible to highlight that keeping secrets at times involves telling, telling may be an opaque form of concealment, and silences may be oblique narrative modes. More fundamentally, ethnographic description performatively opens itself up, and does not forestall what is the impending prospect of recontextualization and resignification. As inquiry into post-plural subjects and relations, it nevertheless requires an account of the sociohistorical conditions of its emergence.

Revelation and Dénouement

On 26 April 1998 the Human Rights Office of the Archbishop of Guatemala published its report *Guatemala: Never Again* (ODHAG 1998). In four volumes, the report detailed the findings of research conducted in the dioceses of the Catholic Church across the country. It focused on detailed analysis of approaches, methods, and techniques of violence and terror, and the histories of insurgency and counterinsurgency. In the fourth tome, it named the victims of the conflict. Grounded in interviews with more than fifty thousand people, the *Guatemala: Never Again* report attributed the great majority of violations to a succession of Guatemalan governments, Guatemalan state forces, and the Army. On 28 April 1998, two days after the release of the report, Bishop Juan Gerardi, the man who had been its driving force, was assassinated.

In 1999 the United Nations–sponsored Commission for Historical Clarification (Comisión de Esclarecimiento Histórico, CEH) published the report *Guatemala: Memory of Silence* (CEH 1999). The document was produced in collaboration with the warring parties. Again, the conflict appeared in all its dazzling organizational detail, stern linear periodization, and chilling causal certitude. Unlike the report of the Human Rights Office of the Archbishop of Guatemala (ODHAG 1998), however, in the Commission for Historical Clarification report, anodyne prose and methodical revelation were featured alongside systematic omission. The "memory of silence" would not provide information on the grounds of which criminal prosecutions might be undertaken. The names of victims and perpetrators would not be disclosed, and impunity would be assured.[9]

The Past in the Present

The Unidad Revolucionaria Nacional Guatemalteca (Guatemalan National Revolutionary Unity; URNG) was established on 7 February 1982. It brought together the four insurgent organizations operating in the country, namely the Ejército Guerrillero de los Pobres (Guerrilla Army of the Poor; EGP), the Organización del Pueblo en Armas (Organization of People in Arms; ORPA), the Partido Guatemalteco del Trabajo (Guatemalan Workers' Party; PGT), and the Fuerzas Armadas Rebeldes (Rebel Armed Forces; FAR). The history of guerrilla organizing in Guatemala, however, had begun more than twenty years previously. The first embryonic and yet foundational rebellion took place on 13 November 1960, when discontented Army officers sought to mobilize elements of the Guatemalan Army and stage an insurrection (CEH 1999, Volume I, Item 124; Handy 1984, 230). Among them were Marco Antonio Yon Sosa, known as "El Chino," Alejandro de León, Luis Trejo, and Luis Turcios Lima. The latter, while an officer of the Guatemalan Army, had been sanctioned for publicly criticizing Army corruption and mistreatment and had been sent to the military base of Poptún, Petén. On 12 November 1960, however, Turcios Lima was in Guatemala City and joined the rebellion (Fernández 1968). The officers were unable to mobilize large numbers of sympathizers in the Army ranks, and sought refuge in El Salvador (Fernández 1968).

On 26 February 1962 the insurgents released a declaration in which they identified as the Frente Rebelde Alejandro de León Aragón 13 de Noviembre (Rebel Front Alejandro de León 13 November; MR-13). New guerrilla actions followed and slowly proliferated. In 1962, a guerrilla column appeared in the western region of Huehuetenango. The local population apprehended the insurgents and turned them in to the Army (CEH 1999, Volume I, Item 125). Meanwhile, members of the PGT (Partido Guatemalteco del Trabajo; Guatemalan Workers' Party) and PUR (Partido Unión Revolucionaria; Revolutionary Unity Party) assembled Frente 20 de Octubre (Front 20 October). Many were killed in a confrontation with the Army. Among the survivors was Rodrigo Asturias, known by his nom de guerre Gaspar Ilom, who would later be co-founder and leader of the Organización del Pueblo en Armas (ORPA) (CEH 1999, Volume I, Item 128).

Electoral fraud and intimidation marred the national elections of 1961. Civil unrest followed, with mass mobilization and protests in Guatemala City led by students and unions. Unable to regain control of the capital, President Ydígoras Fuentes greatly extended the mandate of the Army. According to the Commission for Historical Clarification, such episodes of popular mobilization and the increasing prominence of the Army were decisive factors in the establishment of the military confrontation that was to grip the country for over thirty years (CEH 1999, Volume I, Item 127). Students responded by assembling the guerrilla group Movimiento 12 de Abril, and although the organization was short-lived, many of its members would join the insurgent organization that was born in 1962. In December 1962, the PGT (Partido Guatemalteco del Trabajo) called upon the guerrilla groups MR-13, Movimiento 20 de Octubre, and Movimiento 12 de Abril to devise a common strategy. At the meeting it was decided that the four organizations would seek to overthrow the government through armed struggle. The Fuerzas Armadas Rebeldes (Rebel Armed Forces; FAR) were born (CEH 1999, Volume I, Item 128; Handy 1984). FAR would be responsible for military aspects of the struggle and PGT would continue to lead political fronts.

The leader of MR-13, Marco Antonio Yon Sosa, with Rodolfo Payeras, César Montes, Luis Turcios Lima, and many others converged in the newly established FAR. FAR guerrilla operations took place in the eastern *departamentos* of Zacapa and Izabal,[10] but by 1963 internal conflicts between FAR and the Trotskyist group close to MR-13 increased (CEH 1999; Turcios Lima 1968). Following substantive disagreements as to the aims, objectives, and methods of the struggle, MR-13 and FAR split. Despite the schism, in 1965 FAR regrouped, headed by Luis Turcios Lima. FAR now encompassed members of the Juventud Patriótica del Trabajo (JPT; Workers' Patriotic Youth) and Frente Guerrillero Edgar Ibarra (FGEI). An ambitious military guerrilla campaign followed, but during intense activities, Comandante Turcios Lima was killed in a car accident (CEH 1999, Volume I, Item 145; Fernández 1968). He was twenty-five years old.[11]

Yon Sosa and Turcios Lima lived on in the memories of the ex-combatants I met in Petén. They were revered figures. Two FAR guerrilla columns operating in and across Petén during the 1980s and 1990s were named after them, and the political program published by FAR in 1988 featured a photograph of a young Turcios Lima on its cover (FAR 1988). Following the death of Turcios Lima, Camilo Sánchez had been in command of FAR, but in August 1968 Sánchez was captured and command was handed over to Pablo Monsanto (CEH 1999, Volume I, Item 146). Pablo Monsanto was to head FAR until December 1996. In 1968, FAR attempted to make a way into the *departamento* of Alta Verapaz, but the population did not respond positively. The following year, FAR attempted to reach Alta Verapaz and El Quiché from Petén, again with limited success. The northern *departamento* of Petén thus became their base and key area of operations. Until 1979, FAR did not engage in public operations and concentrated its efforts on organizing support among *campesinos* in Petén and among students and workers in the capital (CEH 1999, Volume II, Item 248-9).[12]

Between 1971 and 1979 ORPA underwent a process of organization that resulted in a public declaration of its existence on 18 September 1979 and subsequent operations in the *departamentos* of San Marcos, Sololá, Quetzaltenango, and Chimaltenango (CEH 1999, Volume II, Item 261-4). The EGP was founded on 19 January 1972 by Rolando Morán, who had been militant in previous guerrilla efforts and grew to control large areas of the *departamento* of Quiché. The PGT, FAR, EGP, and ORPA had different approaches to the struggle. FAR, EGP, and PGT declared a Marxist Leninist orientation, with FAR and EGP closer to orthodox Marxism (CEH 1999, Volume II, Item 236). The operations of both FAR and EGP were informed by the *foquista* theory of revolution of Guevara and Debray (Vinegrad 1998), according to which guerrilla struggle would proceed through the establishment of *focos*, that is, groups of committed vanguard revolutionaries who could lead the struggle by fomenting widespread popular insurrection. However, FAR was distinctive in its hermetic hierarchical structures and militaristic leanings, when compared with the EGP's emphasis on mass participation (CEH 1999). ORPA, on the other hand, placed emphasis on the racist structure of Guatemalan society rather than on class-based analysis and was less militaristic in orientation (CEH 1999, Volume II, Item 237). Since 1982, the four guerrilla organizations operated under the aegis of the Unidad Revolucionaria Nacional Guatemalteca (URNG). Nevertheless, each maintained its distinctive identity, in terms of area of influence, organizational structure, military operations, and political organizing. In the period after the Peace Accords, the sense of belonging to FAR was very much felt by the ex-combatants I met in Petén, where I conducted most of my fieldwork.

The first document related in earnest to the Peace Accords was signed in 1991 in Querétaro, Mexico. The document bore the signatures of Comandante Gaspar Ilom (ORPA), Comandante Rolando Morán (EGP), and Comandante Pablo Monsanto (FAR). Carlos Gonzales of the PGT also signed all subsequent Accords. The four leaders underwrote the Accords by their respective noms de guerre, but by December 1996, when the final Peace Agreement was drawn, they signed the document with their civilian names. Their noms de guerre were given in brackets (Guatemalan Peace Accords 1996, 293). As established in the "Accord on the Basis for the Incorporation of the Guatemalan Revolutionary Unity to Legality" (Guatemalan Peace Accords 1996, 217–37), the URNG was thus set to transition from illegal and clandestine status to a legitimate political party. URNG leaders were turning from *comandantes guerrilleros* to party leaders and elected politicians. The process was fraught with difficulties for all URNG associates, and notably for ex-*guerrilleros/as* in the rural areas and the population who had actively supported the struggle, *las bases*. Many had undergone the process of demobilization as laid out in the Accords and overseen by the newly established United Nations Verification Mission in Guatemala (MINUGUA).

Demobilization

In February 1997, in preparation for demobilization procedures, the URNG handed over the names of 3,570 of its members, qualified as "*efectivos*," to the United Nations Mission (MINUGUA). Information concerning weapons of various kinds was also made available and the guerrilla voluntarily disclosed the location of land mines. MINUGUA proceeded to establish eight "concentration points" located in different areas of the country, where *guerrilleros/as* would gather to demobilize. Each "concentration point" benefited from a surrounding area of six kilometers in diameter where access by the Guatemalan Army was forbidden. Further, entrance to the "security areas" by the Guatemalan Police had to be cleared with the United Nations Military Observers. As stipulated by the "Agreement on Definitive Ceasefire" (Guatemalan Peace Accords 1996), the URNG had underwritten a commitment to present all its forces, including combatants, intelligence, logistics, and medical personnel, as well as its leaders, *el mando*. By 24 March 1997, the guerrilla forces had gathered at the "concentration points" for a

Table I.1: Demobilized Personnel of the URNG

Place	*Organization*	*Number*
Abejas (Quetzaltenango)	*Organización del Pueblo en Armas* (ORPA)	250
Sacol (Alta Verapaz)	*Fuerzas Armadas Rebeldes* (FAR)	642
Claudia I (Escuintla)	*Fuerzas Armadas Rebeldes* (FAR)	342
Claudia II (Escuintla)	*Organización del Pueblo en Armas* (ORPA)/ *Partido Guatemalteco del Trabajo*	224
Mayalán (Quiché)	*Ejército Guerrillero de los Pobres* (EGP)	428
Tzalbal (Quiché)	*Ejército Guerrillero de los Pobres* (EGP)	499
Tuluché I (Quiché)	*Ejército Guerrillero de los Pobres* (EGP)/ *Partido Guatemalteco del Trabajo* (PGT)	285
Tuluché II (Quiché)	*Ejército Guerrillero de los Pobres* (EGP)	258
Total	*URNG*	*2,928*

(Adapted from MINUGUA 1997, 11, Annex II, with the *departamentos* where the concentration sites were located indicated in brackets.)

total of 2,928 persons (MINUGUA 1997). As chronicled in their report, the United Nations Mission expressed disquiet, as 642 persons seemed not to have appeared. MINUGUA (1997, 4) reported that meticulous explanations were provided by the URNG to justify the low turnout, and their reasons were accepted. Table I.1 illustrates the numbers of combatants who demobilized in each location, with the guerrilla organizations noted.

Not all ex-*guerrilleros/as* I got to know during my fieldwork had reached the "concentration points" and formally demobilized. However, all of those who did demobilize concentrated in Sacol. Following disarmament procedures, the "concentration points" were turned into training camps. International organizations established literacy and health programs, as well as the somewhat euphemistically termed "professional training" schemes. The aim of the programs was to equip people with skills to facilitate their transition from clandestine combatants to civilian life. On 2 May 1997, a ceremony was held in Sacol to finalize the process of demobilization. As individuals left the "concentration points," they were issued identity cards and a "demobilization certificate" (*certificado de desmovilización*), commonly referred to by ex-combatants as *carnet de desmovilización*, or "demobilization card."

Many, however, did not know where to go next. Others, having gone back to their communities to be met by threats and hostility, returned to the "concentration points." MINUGUA thus set up four "refuges" (*refugios*) where these ex-combatants could stay on, receive further training, and organize a final resettlement (MINUGUA 1997). The ex-combatants I met in the field referred to these locations as *albergues*, or "hostels." From Sacol, they were moved to Papaljá, Cobán, Alta Verapaz. They remembered the months in temporary accommodation as times of extreme uncertainty, frustration, and fear.

No access to land or land tenure provision was made for ex-*guerrilleros/as*.[13] Ex-combatants who were able to establish contact with relatives joined their families. Some, however, considered that their only option was to cluster with fellow ex-combatants and purchase land at market price on which to settle. In 1999, in the aftermath of demobilization, FAR ex-combatants represented a dispersed constituency. They all held great hopes for the forthcoming elections.[14] Violence, intimidation, and vote rigging marred the electoral process in 1999. Nevertheless, they were declared overall "free and fair": the international community soon endorsed the electoral results. The Frente Republicano Guatemalteco (Guatemalan Republican Front; FRG) won the presidential race in the second round and Alfonso Portillo was elected president. General Efraín Ríos Montt, the man who had risen to power through a coup d'état in 1982 and was considered by many to be responsible for, and was later indicted for, the genocidal counterinsurgency campaigns mounted by the Guatemalan State and Army against the civilian population in 1982–1983 (CEH 1999), was installed in Congress. Ex-*comandantes guerrilleros* such as Pablo Monsanto won seats in Parliament; others worked for the party machinery in the capital. The majority of ex-combatants dispersed across the country. Many, but not all, of those who had been in the FAR ranks resettled in Petén.

Secrecy and Insurgency: Violence, Conflict, Ethnography

In 1999, the Commission for Historical Clarification's *Guatemala: Memory of Silence* (CEH 1999) seemed predicated on an ethos of disclosure. It endeavored to break the silence, bring to light the histories of the conflict, establish an archive of truth, and provide the basis for reconciliation. From its inception, however, the Commission for Historical Clarification relied extensively on concealment, as its mandate did not extend to provision of information that might be the ground for criminal prosecutions. As argued by Wilson (1998), Peace Accords–sanctioned interdiction of any linkage—between the findings of the Commission for Historical Clarification and the operations of the criminal justice system—produced a partial truth that, failing to be paired with the "other half" of prosecution procedures, was perhaps no truth at all. The report *Guatemala: Memory of Silence* (CEH 1999) may have broken the silence with regard to the histories of insurgency and the mechanisms of counterinsurgency, but at the same time it perpetuated the silence that would warrant impunity.

The ethos of partial disclosure of the Commission for Historical Clarification, as much as the program of open denunciation of the Office of Human Rights of the Archbishop of Guatemala's Report *Guatemala: Never Again* (ODHAG 1998), seemed at odds with my first experiences of fieldwork in Petén. Linear periodizations of the violence inflicted by the Guatemalan State against the insurgent and civilian populations, like those relating to guerrilla organizing, were also proving difficult to locate. Despite a general consensus on the accuracy of dates, places, and names where these were provided (CEH 1999; ODHAG 1998), in the early stages of fieldwork the disjunction between the accounts of the conflict offered in the Reports and people's own experiences and memories grew ever starker. To the extent that the Reports increasingly seemed partial accounts, the secret socialities of ex-*guerrilleros/as* and their experiences gradually emerged as predicated on a different and more profound partiality.

This book explores the multiple partialities engendered in the experiences of itinerant and multi-sited fieldwork in Petén, northern Guatemala, in an effort to represent social relations and subjectivities marked by histories of violence and socialities of secrecy. This is an account of the multiple partial perspectives that emerged in the course of my relations with the ex-combatants of the Fuerzas Armadas Rebeldes. Partialities of violence and secrecy trouble anthropological and popular representational practices (Daniel 1996; Das et al. 2000; Nordstrom and Robben et al. 1995). They require that researchers grapple with the culturally and historically specific effects of fear and terror (Taussig 1980) and related ambiguity and ambivalence. They present the ethnographer with the seemingly paradoxical task of denouncing violence and suffering, while refraining from disclosing individual identities, specific incidents, or deeds (Daniel 1996). Ethnographies of violence and conflict must simultaneously expose and conceal. They are inherently partial—peculiarly so.

In the book I strive to represent violent histories, secret socialities, and partial subjectivities as they unraveled in and through Petén. I do so through juxtaposition of different texts and experiences, and reflect on how the proliferation of perspectives thus engendered may be replicated in—and make a replica of—the ethnographic endeavor. While partial perspectives produced through ethnography constantly offset each other, I argue that knowledge practices should also continuously decenter and defer (in and through) ethnography's representational practices and theoretical models. In this sense, writing ethnography coincides with writing theory. Further, ethnographic juxtapositions represent a series of reflections on what knowledge practices do and how ethnographic writing and theoretical reflection may constantly "out-contextualize" each other.

Chapter 1 introduces "contextualization" as a key analytical strategy through which the "object/subject" of enquiry is produced, and illustrates how in the case of Guatemala "contextualization" has been realized through social scientific knowledge practices that have often relied on the intersection of notions of "indigeneity" and "place" in their context-making efforts. The preponderance of such tropes has produced accounts that are underpinned by nativism, but that often present an essentialist and ahistorical understanding of ethnic identity. If efforts to contextualize the Other produce a series of contextualizations, these can nevertheless be contrasted with knowledge practices that emerge in the accounts of the Guatemalan conflict and that disrupt essentialism to expose violent histories and the political economy of violence in the region. The chapter proposes that sensibility and awareness of knowledge practices of "contextualization" and "out-contextualization" and what they may entail can make an important contribution to understanding the plural histories and complex dynamics of violence and conflict in the region. I am interested in knowledge practices and the effects of out-contextualization in accounting for the relatively peripheral status the northern region of Petén has traditionally occupied in the national imagination and in scholarship on Guatemala, with Petén at once contextualized and out-contextualized as a distant peripheral region vis-à-vis metropolitan centers of governance. This attributed peripheral status has functioned as a very influential register of (out-)contextualization both nationally and transnationally, so the task is one of devising an alternative representational frame through which the context of "Petén" may emerge.

Chapter 2 explores the plural histories of violence, sovereignty, and governmentality as they played out in the region of Petén in the twentieth century. The chapter covers colonization strategies in the mid-twentieth century, the inception of violence, conflict, and insurgency, and, since 1990, the mentalities of rule linked to the inception and administration of the large conservation project of the Maya Biosphere Reserve. Plural histories and rationalities of rule are shown in their complex gendered logics and effects. Through textual juxtaposition and combining archival and ethnographic fragments, in this chapter the conflict is made to emerge surreptitiously, as it did during my fieldwork in people's own accounts.

Chapter 3 explores ex-guerrilla secrecy as it emerged in the course of my fieldwork. The chapter discusses practices of naming in the insurgency, and related partial socialities and relationalities. I argue that secrecy poses a challenge to representational practices, while also providing the opportunity for the articulation of knowledge that moves beyond simple enumeration of multiple perspectives to figure socialities, relationalities, and subjectivities marked by secrecy in post-plural scales.

Chapter 4 considers further articulations of secrecy and partiality, with specific reference to state violence and its effects on social relations and subjectivities. I refer to three stories that offer poignant analysis and exegesis of the arbitrary yet systematic operations of state actors as well as views about the complicity of agents of foreign power and their adverse effects on human creativity and ingenuity. I introduce the notion of "merography" (Strathern 1991) as a distinct form of connection between parts and wholes, while tracking ethnographically the insurgents' deployment of merographic connections in post-plural scales. Merography emerges as subjects' analogical ability to conjure up parts and wholes in complex ways, thus exemplifying the performative dimension of knowledge practices of the insurgency and of social and cultural analysis.

Chapter 5 focuses on multiple partial accounts of guerrilla life in Petén. In one account, the guerrilla was imagined as constituted by three substances, namely "combatants," "supplies," and "information." Further, food production, circulation, preparation, and consumption illustrated how guerrilla sociality and relationality may be articulated and constantly renewed. While these practices coincided with a moral order based on sharing, there existed moral orders based on distinct forms of relatedness. This point is made with reference to the short-lived practices of *matrimonios por las armas*, or "marriages by arms," as an example of how the guerrilla was envisioned through the idiom of family relations. The conclusion discusses combatants' experiences of the end of the conflict as coterminous with the dissolution of guerrilla moral orders.

Chapter 6 offers a reflection on the phenomenologies of guerrilla embodiment and subjectivity and argues for a conceptualization of "prosthetics" that may relinquish dependence from Cartesian-inspired dualisms and that may instead be grounded in multiple, complex, and performative experiences of ethnographic subjects' prosthetic embodiment. Drawing on in-depth interview material with individual ex-combatants, distinct gendered forms of "being in the world" are discussed, with a view to draw attention to the experiential and embodied quality of subjectivities and socialities in conflict. Further, I argue that in the course of specific ethnographic encounters and through specific prosthetic mediations, guerrilla and anthropological knowledge practices can be seen to temporarily supplement each other's prosthetic aesthetics. Through these exchanges the guerrillas and anthropology borrow each other's images to establish temporal, precarious, gendered partial connections.

Ethnographic Candor and Reticence

Fieldwork was itinerant and multi-sited (Marcus 1998), in my initial efforts to locate "the object/subject" of interlocution, and in the subsequent course that the agential "object/subject" determined I follow. During my eleven-month fieldwork between October 1999 and September 2000, I conducted a total of 121 interviews. Most of these were semi-structured interviews, and some were informal conversations. I attended meetings convened by women's groups, community groups, and indigenous rights groups, some of which I recorded with the permission of the organizers. All recordings were undertaken with subjects' explicit permission. I convened three meetings and recorded the proceedings with the permission of the participants. I also interviewed individuals who had held positions in the local government agency Empresa Nacional de Fomento y Desarrollo de Petén (National Enterprise of Fomentation and Development of Petén; FYDEP) prior to 1990 and got acquainted with non-governmental organizations that worked with returnees (COMADEP) and with the ex-combatants (Fundación Guillermo Toriello, ADEPAC, CIEP).

The total number of ex-*guerrilleros/as* interviewed was sixty-one, of which twenty-seven were women and thirty-four were men. Ages of ex-*guerrilleros/as* ranged from twenty to sixty-eight years old. All had been affiliated with the ex–Fuerzas Armadas Rebeldes. A small number had been involved in the organization since the 1960s. Many were sons and daughters of combatants killed in the conflict and whose families had a long history of *guerrilla* activism. The youngest interviewees may have not been active in military operations, but had lived a clandestine life with their older relatives. Some interviews were recorded following numerous informal conversations with the interviewees; some occurred through sheer serendipity. On one occasion, an individual agreed to speak to me in one capacity, but during the interview revealed his guerrilla affiliation and determined that the interview dealt with that, rather than with the issues we had previously agreed to discuss.[15] In addition to the ex-combatants with whom I conversed in an interview setting, I met and got to know many more, but did not record our conversations. Most Fuerzas Armadas Rebeldes ex-combatants who were interviewed identified as ladino,[16] but Mam, Q'eqchi', Achi', and Kaqchikel ethnicities were also represented among interviewees. Many other interviewees were not ex-combatants, but guerrilla sympathizers.

All names, pseudonyms, and nicknames that appear in the book have been changed. The practice of renaming subjects in order to protect their identities and ensure confidentiality is well established in traditions of anthropological inquiry and gender research. In the present research, however, renaming practices are grounded in understandings of "confidentiality" that are historically specific and culturally nuanced (Caplan 2003; Day 2007; Fluehr-Lobban 2003). The renaming practices I deploy are intended to graft onto the complex naming practices used by subjects themselves. As discussed at length in the book, *guerrilleras* and *guerrilleros* often had numerous names, pseudonyms, and nicknames. They named and renamed themselves, and each other, for multiple purposes, and I rename them accordingly. Many of the names and pseudonyms featured in the book are drawn from the novels of José Flores (Flores 1995; 1997a; 1997b; n.d.). "José Flores" is the pseudonym for the writer of four novels that deal with the civil conflict; specifically, with experiences of the Fuerzas Armadas Rebeldes in Petén. Numerous apocryphal stories about José Flores circulated among URNG associates in Guatemala City in 1999–2000. Some involved tropes of gender and other reversals, but none dared to question the veracity of the writer's accounts. José Flores, his own vivid narrative, the stories about him, and rumors about his sources, captured and shaped my "ethnographic imagination" (Comaroff and Comaroff 1992; Moore 1994). Many of the individuals who are featured in the book thus bear the names of the characters of José Flores' novels.

Nicknames (*apodos*), on the other hand, often involved capturing a trait of the person and were metaphorical and allegorical. Some were secret in the sense that they were known only to those involved in the guerrilla organization. Some became public to the extent that individual combatants were known to communities by their nicknames and not by their pseudonyms. Some were long-lived, others transient, others still survived only in the memory of the nickname holder. In my account, I have changed all the nicknames except those bestowed upon me. To do this, I have had to conjure up new ones. I have tried to maintain a sense of the metaphorical, allegorical, and ironic associations and emphases featured in the original nicknames. Any exoticizing effect, however, is fully unintended and may be an unwelcome product of a representational strategy that seeks to establish sufficient distance between the original nickname and its reworking in the book while maintaining a connection with the landscape the combatants inhabited. I have also been consistent when referring to individual biographies and have refrained from creating composite characters imagined as the synthesis of different individual experiences. Where subjects appear composite, on whatever level, this is not as a result of montage, or any other textual technique.

Itinerant and multi-sited fieldwork in as large a region as Petén (36,000 square kilometers), could not strive, or indeed wish, to cover the "vastness" through which this territory is and has been imagined. I traveled across Petén following the routes of guerrilla secrecy. I visited some communities regularly, others sporadically or only once. I never got to many of the places and the people I wanted to reach. On occasions, I reached villages to find that those I wanted to meet had left a few hours prior to my arrival. They were not expected to return any time soon, as they had set out to reach the United States/Mexican border. Nevertheless, some communities had the kindness to welcome me on a regular basis and endure my questions. To them, I promised to give full anonymity. I am aware that, a good number of years following our first encounter, conditions have changed and the visibility of some of these communities and subjects has since increased. Nevertheless, and for the purpose of the present analysis, I consider the first agreement between us as binding. Thus, no geographical or other details are given when discussing particular settlements. This does not mean that particular communities were not instrumental to the present research, or that their distinctiveness and individuality (Rapport 2003) will not transpire through the text, just that I am reticent about revealing their identities.

Heteroglossia and Note on Transcription

Guatemala is a multicultural and multilingual country. The official language is Spanish, but there exist numerous Maya and non-Maya languages spoken in the country (COPMAGUA 1995; Tzian 1994 cited in CEH 1999, footnote 5, Appendix 9, Chapter 1). Although the exact number of languages is disputed, the Academia de Lenguas Mayas (ALMG) notes the existence of twenty-two Maya languages spoken in Guatemala, each with relative subgroups.[17] To these are added Xinca and Garífuna. Equally disputed is the number of indigenous languages spoken in the region of Petén. As a receptacle of migratory population displaced from other areas of the country, Petén is linguistically as well as culturally diverse. Itza' and Mopan speakers have traditionally been considered autochthonous to the region, the former usually said to be located around Lake Petén Itzá in central Petén and the latter in and around the town of San Luis in southern Petén (Reina 1964; 1967a; 1967b; Reina and Schwartz 1974; Schwartz 1971; 1983; 1990). Despite their long-standing presence in southern Petén, Q'eqchi' speakers on the whole are not considered native to Petén by non-Q'eqchi' persons. Many of them nevertheless are, and consider themselves to be, from this region. Further, they are no longer confined to the southern lowlands. Q'eqchi' speakers are increasingly settling in eastern, western, and northern Petén. The linguistic makeup of the region is yet more complex when one considers populations deemed to be "internally displaced" ("*desplazados internos*") and those returning from exile in Mexico ("*retornados*"). In these communities, many Maya languages are represented, including K'iche', Mam, Kaqchikel, Q'eqchi', Poqomchi', and Q'anjob'al. In turn, Spanish monoglots who identify as ladino feature regional accents, inflections, and lexical variations.

The material featured in the book was gathered for the most part in Spanish. This includes interviews and conversations with polyglots whose first language was not Spanish. Being already proficient in Guatemalan Spanish, while in Petén I studied Q'eqchi' using available textbooks and dictionaries. While I was never fluent in the language, I experimented with gathering material in Q'eqchi' and briefly collaborated with Q'eqchi' speakers for translation of selected texts. Due to ethical questions, I resolved to discontinue collaboration with translators, although the experiment was important in terms of language training and, more importantly, the establishment of long-term friendships. In the course of the research, material on Q'eqchi' culture and practices was gathered mostly in Spanish, or, when working in Q'eqchi', translations were produced on the day of the conversations and in collaboration with the interviewees.

For Q'eqchi' words, I follow the orthographic rules endorsed by the ALMG. Where quoted authors do otherwise, I retain their respective orthographic choices. Although this may appear confusing at times, I think it would be unwise to collapse histories of orthographic usage and instead retain a sense of changes in orthography over the years, as these are implicated in broader shifts in conceptualization of, and struggles over, the meanings attached to "indigeneity" in the country. Thus, insistence on contemporary conventions is part of ever more politicized expressions of indigeneity (CEH 1999; COPMAGUA 1995; Wilson 1995). The new orthography developed by the ALMG aims to provide an orthographic system common to all Maya languages spoken in the country. It aims to reduce dependence from Spanish and is linked to efforts made by indigenous rights groups to include indigenous languages in school curricula, and to establish schools in which learning occurs in indigenous languages as first languages, with Spanish as a second language. I support this wholeheartedly and in the text that follows, where quoted authors render the ALMG-endorsed orthography of *Q'eqchi'* (Siebers 1999; Wilson 1995) as *Kekchi* or *K'ekchi*, be it in works published prior to (Adams 1965) or following (Pedroni 1990; Ruiz Puga 1994; Schwartz 1990) the establishment of the new standard orthography, differences are maintained, specifically to reflect the time of their production or evasion of ALMG-endorsed conventions.

On occasions, conversations that were held in Spanish between myself and subjects whose first language was an indigenous language featured peculiar syntactic structures. Rather than considering the syntax of sentences in Spanish unsteady or inexact, I strive to reproduce the shifts in syntax in my English translations as well as the distinctive expressive styles of individual speakers. Spanish lexicon is also variable in a multicultural and multilingual region such as Petén. This is the case not only among Maya language polyglots, but also among Spanish monoglots who come from different regions of the country. I strive to give a sense of such variations in my English translation. Further, I indicate Q'eqchi' or Spanish terms in brackets where I feel there are subtleties of tone, reference, or inflection that may be lost in translation.

Individuals with different biographies, but with a history of militancy in the Fuerzas Armadas Rebeldes, shared a common lexicon. I consider some of these terms and idioms to be so imbued with the shared experiences of struggle as to be untranslatable. For instance, Fuerzas Armadas Rebeldes combatants, militants, and sympathizers referred to each other as *compañeros*, and *compañeras* for the feminine inflection. Similarly, when ex-*guerrilleros/as* referred to their experiences of clandestine life, they often said they were *en la montaña*. This expression complements and exceeds the meaning of being *en la selva*, that is, in the forest. It stands for clandestine life in the guerrilla in general, with all the phenomenological specificities of the case. I hope the book as a whole may give a sense of what it may have meant to be a *compañera* and to live a clandestine life *en la montaña*.

The chapters that follow feature juxtapositions of different texts. The analysis of field notes and secondary sources is provided in the main text, with no indentation, as is the analysis of interviews. All materials in the main text contain my own analysis and interpretation. Interviews that were tape recorded were transcribed. Transcripts of speech are clearly marked by indentation.

1
The Problem of Context

> Interpretation and contextualization involve the making of connections. What context does is to define where and which connections are made, and where disconnections, ruptures and discontinuities begin.
> —Roy Dilley, *The Problem of Context*, 1999, 37

Introduction

This chapter explores traditions of social and cultural analysis in and about Guatemala,[1] and key knowledge practices related to this field. The aim is to examine a range of trajectories in social, cultural, and historical research and highlight the influential and rich reservoir of ideas for the production and figuring of the Guatemalan context historically, both nationally and transnationally. The emphasis is on the processes through which the object of study may be said to emerge in and through specific epistemological propositions and methodological operations.

Many traditions of social and cultural enquiry that developed in the late nineteenth century and early twentieth century are epistemologically grounded in the contextualization of knowledge (Strathern 1995a; 1995b) and have provided interpretations of local cultures through contextualization. In turn, disciplinary and interdisciplinary interpretative efforts have become context-dependent (Dilley 1999, 1–2), to the extent that a strictly a-contextual social and cultural analysis now appears improbable (see, for example, Moore 2004). Analytical strategies of contextualization are, however, inextricably tied to systems of representation. In representation, "context" is produced as an object of scrutiny through specific analytical operations (Dilley 1999, 3; 2002; Strathern 1987, 276; 1995d, 160).

Furthermore, context-making practices can be considered in relation to other analytical operations and associated key concept-metaphors (Moore 2004). "Culture," for instance, may be amenable to multiple genealogies (Knauft 1996; Kuper 1999). Historically it has been premised on contextualization understood through cultures imagined as local, integrated, and coherent wholes (Dilley 1999, 3; Moore 1999). Through a multiple and multiplier effect, contextualization has highlighted the local quality of Western presuppositions and produced, in this relational dimension, knowledge of, and about, ethnocentrism (Dilley 1999; Strathern 1987; 1995b).[2] For example, Dilley argues that "[e]ver since Malinowski, anthropologists have chanted the mantra of 'placing social and cultural phenomena in context,' an analytical strategy adopted to throw light on . . . and make some sort of authentic sense of, ethnographic material" (Dilley 1999, 1). The question of contextualization is clearly not discipline-specific. Rather, it reflects a transdisciplinary problem (Dilley 1999, 5–6), insofar as invoking and producing "context" is an analytical strategy to make sense of data generally (Castree 2005; Dilley 1999). Castree (2005) views a range of approaches to contextualization as part of a specific "epistemology of particulars," which, in the field of human geography he is concerned with, has sought to engage and negotiate two distinct and contrasting approaches, namely: "On the one side, a nomothetic perspective presumes an ontological regularity in both pattern and process between different contexts. On the other side, an idiographic worldview accents the contingent and enduring differences that make 'context' no mere 'modifier' of ostensibly general processes" (Castree 2005, 541). In this account, contextualization emerges as a knowledge practice located at the epistemological fault line where claims to particularity and generality are made, and where a number of questions concerning the possibility and feasibility of abstraction emerge. An "epistemology of the particular" (Castree 2005), then, does not dispel, but rather, forcefully recenters "philosophical-cum-theoretical" issues (Castree 2005, 544) concerning how "context" is produced as an object of enquiry, and what ontological, epistemological, and methodological implications might follow from such framings.

Thus, although context-making as process and practice has been assumed to be a transparent and unproblematic source of authenticity of phenomena and/or interpretations, assumptions about the "positivity" of context (Fabian 1999) and the transparent quality of "culture" have been the subject of increased critical scrutiny in recent years, through, inter alia, epistemological and methodological critical reflection (Castree 2005; Dilley 1999; Strathern 1988), critiques of representational practices (Clifford 1988; Clifford and Marcus 1986), and analyses informed by feminist (Haraway 1989; Strathern 1988) and postcolonial (Asad 1973; Huggan 1994; Mignolo 2000; Prakash 1992; 1994) theory. Such interventions often link representational strategies to power, but the exercise is by no means exhausted. Neither is it exhaustible, when one considers that context- and culture-making have not been the exclusive prerogatives of social scientists. Rather, "context" and "culture," whether allied or discrete, are items of knowledge generated locally, with or without social scientists' presence (Strathern 1995c). Insofar as this applies to local uses of those "contexts" and "cultures" produced through social and cultural analysis, the possible deployments of such knowledge are "as always, already recontextualized" (Jaarsma and Rohatynskyj 2000; Strathern 1995b, 3). This adds a further dimension to local context- and culture-making, one in which the context-making practices of social and cultural analysis become entangled in complex ways. When viewed in this light, the field of social and cultural analysis expands to include discourses that may once have been its own, but are now, or indeed have always been, locally produced, reproduced, and consumed by multiple subjects and in multiple contexts. Such local appropriations of social scientific knowledge hold the potential to prospectively "out-contextualize" the researcher and her account (Strathern 1995b, 11).

This chapter investigates some key knowledge practices and representational frames that have produced the "context" of Guatemala. The focus is on a range of perspectives and strategies that are steeped in a range of traditions of social scientific enquiry and can be shown to have been an important site of articulation of debates over the status of indigeneity, and to have provided influential frames for contextualization of contemporary local and national configurations. Thus, analysis of the place accorded to ethnicity in social scientific literature on Guatemala is set against those ethnographic fragments that profoundly unsettle specific ways of analytically figuring links between ethnicity, settlement, and place (see, for example, Carmack 1979; 1995; Fischer and Hendrickson 2002; Nelson 1999, 121; Watanabe 1992). A critique of nativism—as an idiom or figuration for alterity—is accompanied by a reflection on context-making practices that bring tropes of violence and conflict into focus. I follow "violence" and "conflict" and their intersections with ethnicity and indigeneity in particular. I do this to consider how they may be made to connect or slip disjointedly from foreground to the background, in different times and political climates.

I strive to make the "contexts" of multiple conflicts emerge in a "spirit of calm violence" (Bhabha 1995), to reflect on the complex ways in which "violence" may mark the subject/object of enquiry in the realm of experience and representation. I am aware that neither the routes I trace through the literature, nor the deployments I make of ethnographic fragments, are innocent. Routes at once contextualize and out-contextualize my position vis-à-vis the "subjects"/"objects" of inquiry, namely "social scientific knowledge practices," "Guatemala," "conflict," and, progressively, "Petén" and "*la guerrilla*." When one considers previous framings of these issues (Fischer 1999; Hervik 2001; Smith 1990; Watanabe 1995a; Wilson 1995), it becomes clear that the experience of fieldwork is absolutely central and very directly informs the readings that I propose here, as I reveal investments in revisiting and reinventing the social scientific knowledge of Guatemala that I and others in the field consumed, to renew the relevance of tropes old and new. Thus, while ethnographic exchanges emerge as moments of recontextualization of social and cultural analysis, the experiences of fieldwork locate me vis-à-vis the literature, to point to the multiple out-contextualizations produced in the book.

History, Empire, Abjection

The history of Guatemala seems entangled in the histories of empires in (dis-)orderly ways. The Spanish Conquest in the sixteenth century inaugurated a long period of colonial domination that came to an end in the late nineteenth century. Following independence from Spain in 1821 and incorporation into the Mexican Empire the following year, Guatemala declared independence again, this time from Mexico, in 1824 and took up membership of the United Provinces of Central America (1823–1840). With the demise of the federation of Central American states, a series of liberal political reforms and laissez-faire economic policies assisted the recolonization of large areas of the country. German entrepreneurs invested in the lucrative coffee exports business in the western highlands,[3] while United States capital took control of the lowlands on the Pacific Ocean to the south and on the Caribbean Sea to the east. A largely United States–sponsored genocide waged by the Guatemalan State against the civilian and insurgent populations characterized the second half of the twentieth century. The conflict, or *La Violencia*,[4] officially came to an end in December 1996, when the Guatemalan government and the guerrilla umbrella organization Unidad Revolucionaria Nacional Guatemalteca (Guatemalan National Revolutionary Unity; URNG) signed the Guatemalan Peace Accords. In post–Peace Accords times, the multiple guises of empire are most immediately embodied in conditional foreign aid and unrestrained economic liberalization. The histories and destinies of most Guatemalans appear to have been and largely continue to be overdetermined, with manifold processes and factors conspiring to reconfigure conditions of exploitation and suffering over time.

Cumulative imperial agency seems to have defied the optimism of successive periodizations most apparent in local and national narratives of progress, of modernity, and, from the early 1960s to the mid-1990s, of revolution. In fact, the hopes invested in what appeared to be important dents into plural trajectories of domination were punctually shattered. The decade between 1944 and 1954 presented real possibilities to invert imperial logics, as the governments of Juan José Arévalo and Colonel Jacobo Árbenz encroached on United States interests in open defiance of the contemporary empire, or *imperialismo yanqui* (Yankee imperialism). Government-led expropriation and redistribution of land held by United States capital, in the form of the export-agriculture enterprise United Fruit Company (Schlesinger and Kinzer 1982), came to symbolize the possibility of interrupting imperial workings. In June 1954, however, the United States Central Intelligence Agency (CIA) designed and directed the overthrow of Jacobo Árbenz's government, and gave imperial agency a Guatemalan face (Cullather 1999).[5] Colonel Carlos Castillo Armas nominally headed the invasion of the country and dutifully executed orders issued directly by United States President Dwight D. Eisenhower. Castillo Armas' proximity to empire, however, swiftly led to his own personal demise. Discontented Army officers murdered him and consigned the country to over three decades of *conflicto armado interno*, or armed "internal" conflict (CEH 1999; Cullather 1999; Jonas 2000).

Periodically, extractive imperial agency has resurfaced to lay claims to land and labor, connote the present in spatial tropes of inclusion and exclusion, and qualify the violence in terms of internality. The genealogical character of empire in its recurrent violent reconfigurations has bolstered the agency of Guatemalan oligarchies as well as the insurrections and insurgencies of abject Guatemalans. Wedges in the narrative of apparent historical determinism, the insurgents of the second part of the twentieth century rose, seemingly from "within," to defy empire and "tomar el poder e instaurar un Gobierno Revolucionario, Patriótico, Popular, y Democrático que termine para siempre con la explotación, la opresión, la discriminación, la represión y la dependencia del extranjero," that is, "seize power and establish a Revolutionary, Patriotic, Popular, and Democratic Government that may put an end once and for all to exploitation, oppression, discrimination, repression, and dependency" (FAR 1988, 4; my translation). As many of the insurgents pointed out in the course of the ethnographic research presented in this book, and, more specifically, in the context of conversations during which they sought to make sense of the momentous events that had characterized their lives, their actions and reactions were incited by the unswerving, relentless, and unyielding agency of empire. Whether the agency of these genealogical subjects resided within or without was a question—in the ethnographic present—that directly engaged those who participated in the insurgency. Where the boundaries of insurgency and counterinsurgency actually lay is no less relevant to, albeit less explicitly, narratives of insurgency. Further, whether abject insurgency occupied a place within or outside the project of the nation is a question that still haunts the narratives of repression. There has never been any shortage of *enemigos internos*, or "enemies within," in Guatemala.[6]

Social, cultural, and historical processes through which dyads such as internal/external have been created, boundaries drawn, and subjects constituted deserve further attention. The theory of abjection elaborated by Julia Kristeva (1982) is pertinent. In Kristeva's formulation, the "abject" is a subject constituted through specific processes of expulsion and exclusion. Specifically, it is through disavowal and repudiation of elements of the self that the Other is constituted. Far from a coherent figure that is the defiled subject of exclusion external to the self, the abject, as Kristeva (1982) explains, is "neither subject nor object," that is to say, the abject marks the breaking down of categorical distinctions self/Other and internal/external and reveals those processes of constitution whereby elements of self are expulsed—"a confirmation of the fact that the subject can only be conceived of as a heterogeneous construction that is always already contaminated" (Sjöholm 2005, 97). Kristeva writes: "Along with sight-clouding dizziness, *nausea* makes me baulk at that milk cream, separates me from the mother and father who proffer it. 'I' want none of that element, sign of their desire, 'I' do not want to listen, 'I' do not assimilate it, 'I' expel it. But since the food is not an 'other' for 'me,' who am only in their desire, I expel *myself*, I spit *myself* out, I abject *myself* within the same motion through which 'I' claim to establish myself" (Kristeva 1982, cited in Butler 1990, 133).

Discourses concerning the sustained temporality of exploitation, the continuity of imperial domination, and the enduring relevance of imperial logics are master narratives of abjection that may broadly apply to the history of the country as a whole. However, the specificities of systemic control, recurrent imperialist *ingerencia* (interference), and, most importantly, of local discourses, representations, responses, and resistances have progressively been disentangled from the hegemonic histories of nation and empire.[7] What is at stake are multiple and complex articulations of abjection in the Guatemalan context, and the historically specific plurality of forms of "identity-differentiation" (Butler 1990, 134) thus engendered. At the heart of these efforts are signifiers of ethnicity and, more specifically, of indigeneity, *and* of gender. Social and cultural research is and has been in complex ways constitutive of and constituted by the multiple systems of representations through which "identity differentiation" and its (ethnicized and gendered) abjects have come into being in Guatemala.

Mestizaje, Blanqueamiento, and *Ladinización*

Projects of creation, normalization, and disciplining of difference have a long history in the country. Historiographical research points to the complex processes of construction of ethnicity, "race," and gender in Guatemala,[8] thus unsettling the presentist bias inherent in some accounts and complicating some of the assumptions on which Pan-Maya cultural/political activism is predicated. In some Latin American countries, notably Mexico, the postcolonial project of the nation was implicated in the ideology of *mestizaje*, that is, an apparently benevolent utopian vision of a "mix" of ethnic and racialized differences envisaged to deliver fusion and unity in shared sameness. As pointed out by Rowe and Schelling (1991, 18, cited in Radcliffe and Westwood 1993, 14), "*[m]estizaje*, a word denoting racial mixture, assumes a synthesis of cultures where none is eradicated. The difficulty with the idea of mestizajes is that, without an analysis of power structures, it becomes an ideology of racial harmony which obscures the actual holding of power by a particular group." In postcolonial Guatemala, the project of nation-building relied less heavily on narratives of mixing. Instead, it was profoundly influenced by debates in the 1920s and 1930s over the meanings, purpose, and status of *indigenismo* (Casaús Arzú 2005; see also Adams 2005). At the forefront of *indigenismo* was Antonio Goubaud Carrera (Goubaud 1964), the first Guatemalan anthropologist, who directed the state-funded Instituto Indigenista Nacional and whose work is discussed in more detail in the section "A 'Special Relation,'" below.

In view of this, the colonial systems of social, cultural, and racial differentiation, and related unequal power relations on which the historical process of *racialization* came to be articulated, clearly require careful unraveling. Furthermore, discourses that presented *mestizaje* as coterminous with a project of de-racialization of ethnic difference free of gendered implications (Nelson 1999, Chapter 6) and a leveling of inequality should be subjected to scrutiny. This is particularly important in Guatemala, where, as historian Taracena Arriola (1999) has poignantly argued, historiographical and genealogical research on colonial and postcolonial ideologies of "mixing" increasingly aims to clarify how exactly *mestizaje* may have produced the notion of "ladino." In contemporary usage, *ladino* has come to stand as a synonym of *mestizo*, or "mixed," and as a term that finds its Other in the category *indígena*, or "indigenous" (Dary 1994). It is therefore important to explore the historical routes through which contemporary binary understanding of ethnic difference—most obviously expressed in the ladino/*indígena* dyad—may have been produced (Morales 2000; Schackt 2000;

2002). The task also entails an analysis of the processes through which ladinos have emerged as historical subjects and agents, and *ladinización* (ladinoization) may have been presented as the paradigmatic process of formation of the modern Guatemalan nation in the twentieth century (Taracena Arriola 1999).

During the colonial period a strict racialized system of ethnic differentiation was established. In the groundbreaking and extremely influential book *La Patria del Criollo* (1970), historian Severo Martínez Peláez argued that ethnic and racial relations in Guatemala were grounded in the creation and subsequent recognition of three groups, namely Spaniards (*españoles*), indigenous (*indígenas*), and blacks (*negros*). Three further categories were soon fashioned and considered to arise from the ones noted above. *Mestizo* corresponded to the product of Spaniard and indigenous mixing. *Mulato* identified those of black and Spanish ancestry, while *zambo* marked those of black and indigenous descent. In point of fact, the establishment of colonial racialized taxonomies failed to order, discipline, and maintain sameness, inciting instead the production of ever more intricate representational orders of difference. *Mestizaje*, envisaged in the first place as a seemingly uncomplicated process of multiplication of *mestizos* through the "union" of Spaniards and indigenous populations, failed to deliver unmarked and undifferentiated singularity, belying instead increasing racialized, cultural, social and political diversity, and complexity. The gendered implications of the colonial and postcolonial projects of *mestizaje* have been cogently unraveled by Nelson, who has demonstrated the differential consequences of discourses of *mestizaje* for differently gendered and racialized subjects (Nelson 1999). Such was the complication and ever-widening differentiation inherent in *mestizaje* and specifically in the cross-articulation of *español, indígena, negro, mestizo, mulato*, and *zambo* that the colonial administration resorted to the demarcation of *castas*. Spaniard and indigenous populations were thus marked off from the newly fashioned categories of *pardo* and/or *ladino*. These *castas* referred to generalized racialized groups aimed at accommodating the proliferation of racialized difference spurred by foundational colonial racial orderings (Martínez Peláez 1970). Intended to be conveniently set against the populations marked as Spaniard and indigenous,[9] in the eighteenth century, *ladino* and *pardo* still retained marks of earlier racialized distinction, the former referring to those with acknowledged Spaniard ancestry and the latter marking off those considered to be of black descent. However, masking cultural and social complexities, the Spaniard/*ladino*/*pardo*/indigenous distinctions worked toward the erasure of ethnic and cultural differences among all groups, and notably among ladinos. Differentiation among ladinos increasingly distinguished between rural and urban populations, that is, between *ladinos rurales* (rural ladinos) and *capas medias urbanas* (urban middle strata) (Martínez Peláez 1970). At the heart of any *casta* demarcation was nevertheless an ingrained and virulent racialization. In 1820, facing increasing lax attitudes to the application of *casta* taxonomies, a document concerning the constitutional electoral system set out to clarify the distinctions in the following terms:

> White [*blanco*] with *indio* produces *mestizo*, and if the latter reproduces with white, *castizo* results, who if united with white will have offspring who may already *pass* as white. A white woman [*blanca*] with a black man [*negro*] produces *mulato*, and black and *indio* gives *zambo*. These are the qualified and commonly recognized races [*razas*] of the country. . . . Subsequent mixes [*mezclas*] of mixed persons [*personas mixtas*] are unending [*inacabables*] and unnamed [*innominadas*], but generally speaking all persons who are not pure Indians [*indios puros*] are named people of reason [*gente de razón*] or *ladinos* and whites are named Spaniards [*españoles*].[10]

The taxonomic order is predicated on practices of "recognition," which in turn open up the possibility of misrecognition and "passing."[11] Passing refers broadly to practices, techniques, or conditions of the self, identity, and/or subjectivity that are attributed to subjects who transverse social identifications to purposely adopt or inadvertently be assigned identities other than those conferred to them by socially enforced categorizations (Posocco 2004, 152). While passing may apply to any social taxonomy and dimension of difference, it is a term intimately linked to raciological orders and anxieties surrounding "whiteness." Processes of fabrication of whiteness, blackness, indigeneity, and their "unending" and "unnamed" permutations are clearly marked out in the passage above. While the possibility of upward mobility is less explicitly articulated, the demarcation of "people of reason" on the one hand and "pure indigenous" on the other hand suggests that a certain plasticity may apply to the realm of the former and less so ,if at all, to the latter.

Taxonomic plasticity and mobility aside, it is important to note that "passing" is nevertheless dependent upon normative claims to authenticity, and ostracism, repudiation, or violence may befall those deemed at any stage to be "inauthentic" (Ahmed 1999; Butler 1993; Posocco 2004). As argued by Butler (1993), whether passing entails any voluntarism on the part of subjects engaged in purposeful manipulations of social identities is open to question, as any transgression and subversion occur within a highly regulatory and normative terrain (Butler 1993; Posocco 2004). The latter position is endorsed by Ahmed (1999, 101), who notes that passing is consistently predicated upon—and enabled by—assumptions concerning the readability of the body and the visibility of identity. It is the existence of socially, historically, and culturally specific scopic regimes and related social taxonomies that creates the conditions of possibility for passing to occur. For subjects to "pass," there has to be a presumption of ontologies of the subject and of difference grounded in essentialism. When understood in these terms, rather than as the mimetic ability of the subject to adopt identities of choice, passing appears as a technique that is "exclusive and exclusionary," in that some subjects may *not* be able to pass (Ahmed 1999, 101), and identities may be predicated on grounds other than visibility. In Guatemala, these processes are often discussed in relation to the use of indigenous language and dress (see, for example, Hendrickson 1995; Otzoy 1996) whereby individuals' strategic negotiations of boundaries and markers of ethnic difference appear alongside less individualized cultural anxieties about authenticity in relation to ethnicity and gender (Nelson 1999; 2003) as well as a pervasive racial ambivalence (Hale 2006).

With the benefit of attributed "reason" in post-independence times, and throughout the nineteenth century, ladino constituencies rose to prominence in economic, political, and social arenas. Benefiting from increased access to land and trade, local ladino elites negotiated access to political space with the criollo population of Guatemala City.[12] In uneasy alliance with those whose power and influence were predicated on claims of direct Spaniard ancestry, namely the urban criollos, ladinos were increasingly defined in the negative as "nonindigenous" (Grandin 2000, 84; Taracena Arriola 1999, 346–9).

The complex liminal position of ladinos was also expressed in the racialized terms that continued to mark interethnic relations in Guatemala. As argued by Casaús Arzú (1995), urban criollos actively participated in the establishment of a pigmentocracy that would seek to "preserve" and "foster" whitening. As documented historically and ethnographically (Casaús Arzú 1995), criollo families actively sought to "preserve" whitening through endogamous practices that foreclosed unions with ladino families. They vigorously sought to "foster" whitening through endogamous marriage practices and exogamy aimed at incorporating German families into the lineage. Foreignness thus increasingly appeared as the quintessential repository of whiteness (Casaús Arzú 1995; Nelson 1999; Taracena Arriola 1999), and criollos were marked as whiteness bearers and producers. Ladinos, excluded

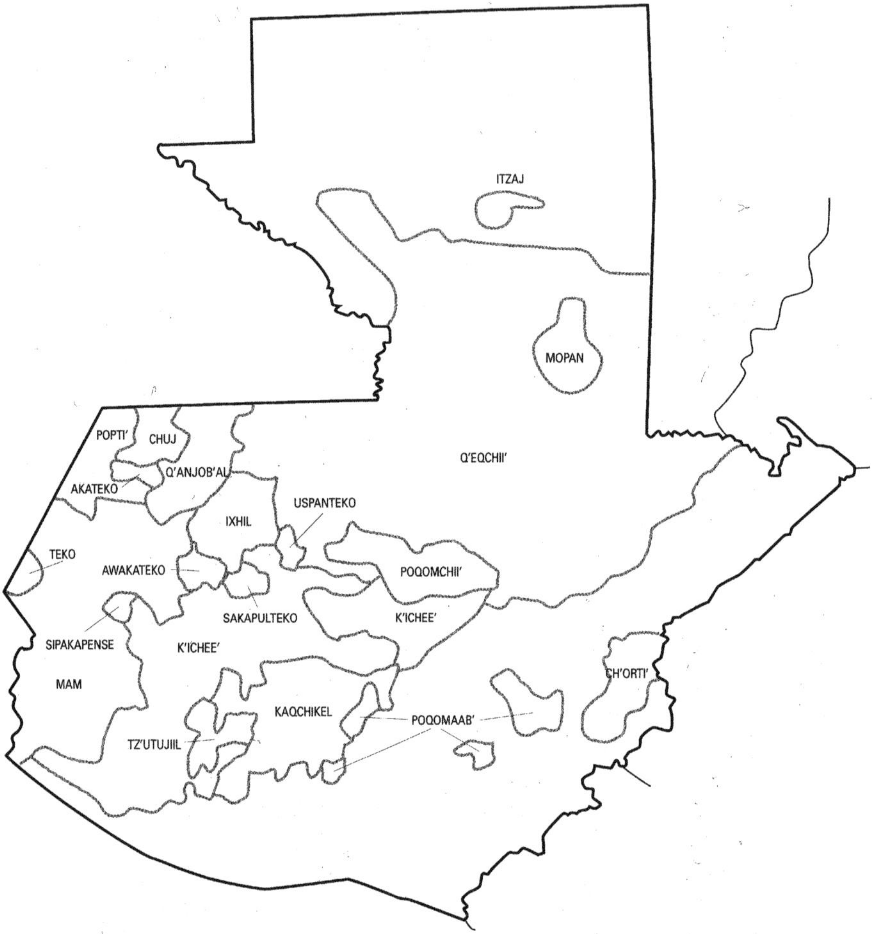

Map 1.1. Maya language map of Guatemala (Warren 1998, 14, reprinted with kind permission).

from whitening practices, relied on their nonindigenousness to stake their claims to power and influence. According to Casaús Arzú (1995), the project of *mestizaje* (mixing) was therefore undermined by the contemporary criollo project of *blanqueamiento* (whitening). In the nineteenth century, any project of *mestizaje*, if there was ever one in Guatemala, was truly defunct. The nation-state never really undertook a project of homogenization of difference, but instead actively pursued the whitening of criollos, and the separate and distinct whitening of ladinos, who may aspire to mold themselves in the image of the criollo elite, while always failing complete mimesis (Casaús Arzú 1995). As cogently argued by Taracena Arriola (1999, 346–9), ladino identity seems therefore never to have been directly predicated on criollo whiteness, but rather, on a sense of Hispanicized character, civilized conduct, and, most importantly, an inherent opposition to indigenous primitivism (see also Grandin 2000, 239). The process of ladinoization was therefore also summarily contradictory, and always haunted by ladinos' Other, that is, the indigenous. In the last instance, the various political, economic, and social projects pursued by the Guatemalan nation-state in different historical periods were consistently implicated in the creation, maintenance, and reinvention of difference, and never pursued homogenization. These genealogies of the ladino/*indígena* dyad inform the Guatemalan imaginaries of ethnic difference, and accounts offered by social and cultural analysis alike. They provide the conditions of possibility for the spatialization of that element that is not ladino. As apparent in linguistic maps of Guatemala, in which to each region there corresponds an indigenous language, what is increasingly marked out in contemporary Guatemala is indigeneity, in all its riveting diversity. The map of indigeneity is also a representation of the ambivalence inherent in ladino identity, as it is unclear whether it is its hegemonic character that makes it transparent, or whether it may be so ephemeral as to require its Other to be visibly marked in order to gain coherence and intelligibility.[13]

Ethnicity as *Telos*

Presence and absence, appearances and disappearances, and process of "identity differentiation" depend on systems of representation through which indigeneity has been articulated in Guatemala. In contemporary Guatemala, the Pan-Maya movement argues that the population of the country comprises four *peoples* whose histories and cultures are viewed as distinct, albeit intertwined (COPMAGUA 1995). The *Pueblo Maya*, estimated to amount to 60 percent of the population, is said to share a common ancestry in the ancient Maya civilization that inhabited the whole of Guatemala, the southern part of Mexico, eastern Belize, eastern Honduras, and northern El Salvador in pre-Columbian times. The Maya linguistic communities currently present in Guatemala are all viewed as part of the *Pueblo Maya*, namely Poqomchi', Achi', Q'eqchi', Ch'orti', Kaqchikel, Poqomam, Sipakapense, Tz'utujil, Mam, Ixil, Sakapulteka, Uspanteka, Awakateka, Chalchiteka, Akateka, Chuj, Jakalteka, Q'anjob'al, Tektiteka, K'iche', Itza', and Mopan (Cholsamaj Press, quoted in Nelson 1999; COPMAGUA 1995).[14] Prominent Maya intellectuals—such as Sam Colop, Demetrio Cojtí Cuxil, and Alberto Esquit

Choy, among others—have articulated a clear program for the Pan-Maya movement (see Fischer 2001; Fischer and McKenna Brown 1996; Gálvez Borrell and Esquit Choy 1997; Montejo 2005; Warren 1998). The program includes proposals to decolonize knowledge about the *Pueblo Maya*, develop an anti-colonial Maya consciousness, and establish political self-determination through decentralized forms of governance that may empower Maya constituencies. The *Pueblo Ladino*, approximately 39 percent of Guatemalans, is commonly identified as comprising the "Hispanicized" section of the population, who may more or less vocally acknowledge a direct Hispanic ancestry (COPMAGUA 1995; Dary 1994). Recent translations of *ladino* as "white" (Warren 1993, 51, note 4) imply a reference to the hegemonic status of ladino identity in the national context vis-à-vis Maya communities construed as marginalized minorities. While emphasizing the asymmetry inherent to Maya/ladino ethnic relations and highlighting the fact that the ruling economic and political oligarchy may or may not identify as ladino, this definition obscures the realities of exploitation, poverty, and political disenfranchisement faced by many rural and urban ladinos (Hale 2006). The *Pueblo Garífuna* is said to amount to about 1 percent of the population residing in the western department of Izabal, in the areas Livingstone and Puerto Barrios. Their presence can be traced back to the Garífuna migration from the Caribbean island of San Vincente to Guatemala in the late eighteenth century. Culturally, they regard themselves as encompassing Arawak, Caribe, and African traits (COPMAGUA 1995). Lastly, the *Pueblo Xinka*, reported as being in danger of extinction (Cholsamaj Press, cited in Nelson 1999), is said to have an unclear history yet to be unraveled.

In the context of contemporary multicultural and multilingual Guatemala, indigeneity, by virtue of its very existence, is often marked as oppositional (Warren 1998). After all, indigenous ethnicities are said to have withstood conquests; national ideologies of *mestizaje, blanqueamiento*, and *ladinización* (mixing, whitening, and ladinoization); the genocide of *La Violencia* (CEH 1999, Volume III, Chapter II); and multiple social, economic, and political inequities. Tropes of indigeneity and survival are prominently interlocked in contemporary articulations of Pan-Maya identities and politics (Fischer and McKenna Brown 1996; Warren 1998). Since the early 1990s, and most notably in post–Peace Accords times, the *movimiento Maya* has testified to the increasingly visible Pan-Maya activism and mass political mobilization. Social and cultural analysis has made important contributions to definitions of the status of indigeneity. Engaging with colonial, postcolonial, and neo-imperialist dynamics, it has produced a multiplicity of accounts that are intimately implicated in the delineation of teleologies of ethnicity. Interconnections between a multiplicity of unilinear teleological forms of historical discourse, in which history is prefigured as a process of purposeful development toward a final end, call for critical analysis.

A "Special Relation": The Chicago School and the Instituto Indigenista Nacional

In the aftermath of the 1944 revolution, the Guatemalan government of Juan José Arévalo established the Instituto Indigenista Nacional: "By means of the accord dated 29 August 1945, the Instituto Indigenista Nacional was founded in Guatemala City, with the objective of investigating and studying the very important problem of the indigenous (*problema del indígena*), with the aim to find, in collaboration with other institutions of the State, solutions to the different aspects of the problem" (Instituto Indigenista Nacional 1945, 9; my translation).

Two years after its creation, the Instituto Indigenista amended its constitution and expanded its mandate. In 1946 a comprehensive and empirically based study entitled *Distribution of the Contemporary Indigenous Languages in Guatemala* was published, authored by the Instituto's president Antonio Goubaud Carrera (Goubaud Carrera 1946). Goubaud Carrera trained in anthropology at the University of Chicago (Adams 2011; Gillin 1952). He graduated in 1943 and is held to be the "first professionally trained Guatemalan anthropologist" (Gillin 1952; Méndez-Domínguez 1975). In the introduction to the work, and in accordance with the aims of the Instituto, Goubaud Carrera noted the usefulness of a study focusing on "the geographical distribution of languages as they appear located today in the different regions of the country" (Goubaud Carrera 1946, 5; my translation). As with the ethos of the Instituto more broadly, the emphasis in Goubaud Carrera's study was both empirical and taxonomic. In point of fact, research at the Instituto was attuned to research strategies at Chicago University's anthropology department. The "special relation" (Méndez-Domínguez 1975, 541) that existed between the Chicago School and the Instituto Indigenista Nacional was largely based on research collaborations between Sol Tax, his Guatemalan research assistant and later researcher Juan de Dios Rosales (Rosales 1959), and Antonio Goubaud Carrera (Goubaud Carrera et al. 1944). Rosales, as well as Goubaud, had trained at Chicago (Méndez-Domínguez 1975). The collaboration between Sol Tax and the Guatemalan scholars of the Instituto Indigenista Nacional produced important ethnographic works that were to constitute the basis for future (re-)configurations of the ethnographic record.[15]

According to Méndez-Domínguez (1975), Sol Tax exerted great influence over his colleagues and was instrumental in setting the direction and emphasis of the anthropology of Guatemala produced by North American and Guatemalan ethnographers. A pioneer of anthropological research in the country, Tax influenced the analytical and empirical frame of contemporary anthropological engagements as much as those to follow. Méndez-Domínguez points out that anthropologists looked to establish "(i) definition, delimitation and characterisation of the people under study; (ii) delimitation of social units; (iii) processes of change" (Méndez-Domínguez 1975, 542). Thus, it may be contended that the work of Tax and that of the Instituto Indigenista Nacional during the Arévalo and Árbenz administrations and beyond were centered on the interrelated problematics of taxonomy, mapping, and teleology of ethnicity in Guatemala.

A primary example of the process of forging a taxonomic order is the publication *Distribución de las Lenguas Indígenas Actuales de Guatemala* (Goubaud Carrera 1946, 12). With reference to the Q'eqchi', for instance, the text marks the presence of *Quekchí* in Alta Verapaz *and* in Petén and Izabal. In Petén, *Quekchí* figures in San Luis and Sayaxché and it is interesting to note that these markers of ethnicity in the southern and western regions of the *departamento* substantively disappear in later analyses (Schwartz 1990).[16] As for Petén, Goubaud Carrera also lists *Lacandón* in the area of San José, a category to be later transformed into *Itzá* by Schwartz (1990) and *Itzaj* by the Maya Indigenous Movement (COPMAGUA 1995). The taxonomic order of the *Distribución de las Lenguas Indígenas Actuales de Guatemala* did not exclusively produce linguistic/cultural categories of indigeneity. Crucially, it tied linguistic and related cultural taxonomic orders to place. This is obvious in the way the taxonomic order established a link between ethnic markers and *municipios*, or administrative centers. To a significant extent, this was an effect of Sol Tax's preoccupation with "social units," and more specifically with the *municipio* as social unit (Tax 1937; 1942).[17] Méndez-Domínguez summarizes this point sharply:

> An oversimplified statement of Tax's views could take the following form: there are Indian populations that can be defined and understood in relation to other terms, such as municipio; they can be delimited by self-identification and observable features; and they can be

> characterized by surface as well as covert aspects of culture. In this statement, social-relational aspects are seriously considered neither at the definitional level nor at the delimitational level, but only at the level of characterization . . . Goubaud Carrera . . . set himself the task of finding characteristics that make a person Indian. He surveyed the criteria people of various communities used to classify *them*. Hence his conception is descriptive and necessarily based on *surface* features, but instead of using the third person's (a nonparticipant's) criteria or those of the first person (self-identification), he used those of the second person, *the community*. Goubaud's work therefore holds up to criticism the notion that "Indian" exists as an entity in itself, objectively determinable, social-relationally free, and potentially definable by a single synthetic structure of meaning. Rosales used to say that if you had a town without Indians, people would invent them (Méndez-Domínguez 1975, 542; my emphasis).

During the 1940s and 1950s, both Tax (1942; [1953] 1963) and his senior colleague Robert Redfield (1956) sought to provide cultural rather than racial understandings of ethnicity. They sought to identify a number of sociological categorizations by which ethnicity might be articulated in a specific locale (Smith 1990, 26, footnote 1), and so did their Guatemalan colleagues. "Big and little traditions" in Guatemalan anthropology (Méndez-Domínguez 1975; 1980) produced taxonomic and teleological orders that were culturalist, constructionist, and to some extent relational, but also invariably socio-structuralist and nativist. Furthermore, Wade (1997, 43) points out that pluralism and harmony connoted Tax's understanding of ethnic relations.

The products of the collaboration between Tax, Redfield, Goubaud, and Rosales were to become extremely influential for future anthropologists and other social scientists, as well as for readers of anthropological texts. Conversely, the issue of influence of individual practitioners on intellectual genealogies and traditions remains a vexed one (see also Adams 2011). Taxonomic orders and related analytical imaginings were produced through complex personal and intellectual exchanges and collaborations. Sol Tax had received his doctorate from the University of Chicago under Radcliffe-Brown's supervision (Rubinstein 1991; Sanjek 1994). He then joined the Carnegie Institution's Maya Indians research project on which Robert Redfield also worked. At Chicago, Redfield had been a student of Radcliffe-Brown and Malinowski, who had taught in the anthropology department between 1931 and 1937. Since then, Redfield had been very responsive to a Malinowskian approach to fieldwork, a direction that was strengthened by the relationships established during his research in Yucatán with his collaborator Villa Rojas:

> Preferring "objective" observation and survey work, Tax felt comfortable questioning key informants, but Redfield repeatedly pushed him to settle in one location where he could improve his Quiché language skills and attend more to the pulse of ongoing interaction. This Malinowskian use of the unpaid informant (or actor) and focus on speech-in-action, Redfield reveals [in his letters], was one impressed upon him by his Mexican collaborator Alfonso Villa Rojas in their work in Yucatan, where Villa Rojas, but not Redfield, understood the local language. Villa Rojas, a schoolteacher when Redfield met him, had gone on to conduct fieldwork and write ethnography on his own, and he visited Tax in Guatemala in 1937. A similar trajectory for Antonio Goubaud Carrera, a Guatemalan with some college education and an enthusiasm for anthropology, was urged on Redfield by Tax after meeting Goubaud in 1934 (Sanjek 1994, 930).

The genealogical line of early efforts in the anthropology of Guatemala bifurcated: one led back to Malinowski and Radcliffe-Brown, the other to Villa Rojas. As anthropologists carved out a space for the discipline in academic and government institutions,[18] the labor of "identity differentiation" stretched to their experiences of fieldwork. In epistolary exchanges with Redfield, Tax noted the remarkable hostility to North Americans he was encountering in Guatemala during his fieldwork (Rubinstein 1991, 54, 69), a reaction he attributed to the influx of tourists, to landowners, and to the unauthorized presence of a film crew shooting a Tarzan movie (Rubinstein 1991, 69; Sanjek 1994, 931). Thus, it seems that the cultural-typical and relational quality of identity was not just the ethnically marked Guatemalan subjects', but also the anthropologists'.

Of Essences and Classes

During the 1960s and 1970s much social and cultural analysis of Guatemala was still preoccupied with the study of ethnicity, although analyses were increasingly focused on ethnicity understood as the product of group or class relations. Those influenced by the work of Frederick Barth (1969) dismissed ideas concerning the relevance of cultural traits and resorted instead to an analytical focus on group boundaries. As pointed out by Wade (1997, 60), Barth-inspired analyses rendered ethnicity situational. In this view, ethnicity was profoundly relational and not biologically nor culturally essentialist. In Guatemala, the work of Colby and van den Berghe (1969) in the Ixil-speaking area of the department of Quiché was influential in this respect.

Those undertaking Marxian-inspired analyses, on the other hand, stressed the mutual constitution of ethnic, class, and colonial relations. While social and economic change may determine a shift from colonial to class relations, ethnic distinctions endured across systems of exploitation and domination (Stavenhagen 1975). Smith (1990, 4) added that racialization should also be included in the analysis, insofar as local theories of heritage and descent had produced different systems of racialized hierarchy at different times (Casaús Arzú 1995; Nelson 1999; Smith 1990, 4) and may thus be mobilized in historically specific systems of inequality. Nevertheless, Marxian approaches did not conceive of class relations as being more salient than ethnic relations. Rather, an interest in inequality and exploitation highlighted two key institutions seen as the site of articulation of both ethnicity and class, namely the community and the state (Smith 1990, 12). An interest in the community as a social unit was not new, having been pioneered by Tax and Redfield in the 1930s and 1940s, but the addition of the notion of class produced different forms of cultural and historical contextualization:

> (1) There was little or no "class" difference between Indians and ladinos until the plantation period [early plantation period 1870–1944]; only Indians were subject to tribute, but both Indians and ladinos were mostly self-employed, producing small surpluses for trade, rather than tenants on large estates. . . . (2) With the development of coffee plantations, many Indians were reduced to the position of a "semi" or seasonal proletariat, while ladinos became either tenant farmers in eastern Guatemala or a full-fledged proletariat on the plantations; while most urban production remained artisanal, most "managerial" or "middle" positions in production (both rural and urban) were monopolised by ladinos. (3) The coffee oligarchy, only some of whom existed as important families in the colonial period, was mostly "white" and "capitalist" (rather than seigniorial) in their economic intentions and means. (4) A major element in the maintenance of Indian cultural identity has been Indian resistance to full proletarianization and

to capitalist relations of production within the community. And (5) in this respect, Indians feel little class identity with ladinos (Smith 1990, 25–6).

Interestingly, in this account ethnicity is viewed as salient in the colonial (1540–1800) and independence (1800–1870) periods, but class is not. During the plantation period (1870–1944), processes of production of "ethnicity" and "class" are understood to give rise to an indigenous semi-proletariat, a fully proletarian ladino constituency, and a "white" oligarchy. Further, the permanence of indigenous identity is explained in terms of indigenous refusal to undergo the full proletarianization that exclusive engagement in the plantation economy would entail. Indigeneity thus depends both on refusal and on practices that—by sustaining forms of community organization other than those of capitalist relations of production—ultimately stave off assimilation and ensure cultural survival. This may give a sense of Marxian-inspired contributions to an understanding of cultural dynamics as coterminous with ethnicity, vis-à-vis the dynamics of political economy viewed in terms of class relations. The common ground among different analyses actually rested on the production of knowledge as preeminently local, and the relevance of analytical constructs such as ethnicity and class in terms of historically specific and geographically delimited communities. Marxian analysis (Smith 1990) was thus marked by an acute awareness of the local character of these processes and the problematic status of any generalization: "Class relations in Guatemala have almost always been mediated by the state, rather than existing as stark relations between oppressed and oppressor. In addition, relations of exploitation have varied widely by region, and in each region class relations have been mediated by culture (ethnicity) and community in different ways" (Smith 1990, 26).

Boundary- and class-based orientations had rather different analytical implications. The former implied that social change would entail possible dissolution of indigeneity through processes of acculturation and ladinoization, while the latter stressed the relation between the permanence of indigeneity and the perpetuation of systems of exploitation. An intermediate position between the content-free boundary approach and the Marxian focus on relations of production, underscored by the common theme of exploitation, is that of Guatemalan historian Martínez Peláez, whose work I have already discussed. In his book *La Patria del Criollo* Martínez Peláez (1970) contended that indigeneity was fully a product of the colonial encounter and thus fundamentally inauthentic in its postcolonial manifestations. *La Patria del Criollo* represents a foundational text for debates over the status of indigeneity in Guatemala, and for histories of insurgency. During the course of my ethnographic fieldwork, Martínez's text was the oft-cited basis for analyses of the "Indigenous Question" and critiques of *indigenista* positions and arguments. Critiques of Pan-Maya cultural activism viewed as overwhelmingly concerned with pressing state institutions to recognize matters of "*cosmovisión*" (cosmovision, cosmology, worldview) set out in the "Agreement on Identity and Rights of Indigenous People" (Guatemalan Peace Accords 1996), rather than focused on pursuing the claims outlined in the "Agreement on the Social and Economic Aspects and Agrarian Situation" (Guatemalan Peace Accords 1996) and specifically on the land question, were underpinned by references to *La Patria del Criollo*. While sociological, anthropological, and historical texts were mobilized to bolster different positions along the political spectrum, local contextualizations of the analytical categories of "class" and "ethnicity" troubled the narratives concerning their status and relations found in social and cultural analysis.

Symbol, Discourse, and Practice

From the 1980s to the 1990s, more critiques of essentialism emerged alongside a number of more or less nuanced social constructionist positions. A complexity and multiplicity of local discourses and practices were documented, as social scientists strove to represent ethnographic subjects' historical agency and responses to social change (Nelson 1999; Watanabe 1992; Wilson 1995). While the shift from socio-structural and structural concerns to discourse, representation, and practice was preceded by forays in symbolic analysis (Warren 1978), important ethnographic community-based studies moved beyond essentialism and ahistoricism. Watanabe's (1992) ethnography of the Mam-speaking town of Santiago Chimaltenango and Wilson's (1995) work with Q'eqchi' communities in Alta Verapaz are cases in point.

In his ethnography of Q'eqchi' ethnic revivalism, Wilson (1995) adopted a radical social constructionist position when he gave an account of Q'eqchi' religious practices related to *tzuul taq'as*, or spirits of the mountains, in Alta Verapaz. Wilson showed how beliefs and practices related to *tzuul taq'as* were not some essential cultural trait, residues of a precolonial past, or postcolonial inventions. Rather, they were self-consciously revivalist practices, which took into account historical events such as the violence that was sweeping the region. In other words, they were linked to Q'eqchi' subjects' responses to the historical conditions they inhabited. It is Hervik's (2001) contention, that despite their propensity for contextualizing and historicizing the experiences of subjects and communities in their respective geographical areas, both Wilson (1995) and Watanabe (1992) deployed essentialist and ahistorical analytical strategies, in that they called upon materials from the regions of Chiapas and Yucatán, "sometimes centuries apart," to produce their contexts, thus making "uncritical use of cross-regional, cross-temporal sources. At this level of ethnicity, Mayan-ness becomes essentialized across time and space and against all warnings" (Hervik 2001, 345).

Hervik's (2001) rebuke is interesting in several respects. For one, it shows context-making efforts and strategies develop in the direction of ever more localized analyses, to the point that the purpose of any cross-regional, cross-temporal, and, one suspects, cross-cultural comparison seems to be invalidated. Not all analysis may be willing to forego comparison (Castree 2005; Gingrich and Fox 2002) in an attempt to defend forms of contextualization envisaged as ever more local and myopic in scope. In point of fact, anti-essentialism need not be predicated on the dimension of the local alone, and certainly not on visions of the local imagined as narrow parochialism. Interdiction on movements across time and space, be they experiential and/or textual, works against attempts to make sense of complex local configurations. Thus, what is foregrounded in Hervik's (2001) rebuke is a pernicious form of essentialism and a denial of the ways subjects, here including the researcher and her interlocutors, in fact do move across time and space, albeit in ways that are thoroughly local.

La Cadena del Anuncio: Knowledge Practices and the Conflict

From the late 1980s to the present, a new genre of enquiry in Guatemala developed in response to the violence that was sweeping the country, and in some instances engulfing social scientists alongside their interlocutors.[19] Foundational in this respect was the publication of the work of anthropologist and Jesuit priest Ricardo Falla. *Quiché Rebelde*, an account of responses to Acción Católica (Catholic Action) in San Antonio Ilotenango, *departamento* of Quiché, was first published in Guatemala in 1978. In *Masacres de la Selva*, Falla (1992) provided an account of the massacres that took place in Ixcán in the early 1980s. He views the labor of social and cultural analysis to be participant observation once removed, and his role to be to tell what others have seen, in *la cadena del anuncio*, or a "chain of annunciation":

> Why write a book about massacres? It seems a negative and denigrating effort. Why remember those crudities and cruelties without narration (*sin cuento*)? The witness offers us the key. The testimony

> that emerged from the bottom of his emotive memory—"I will never forget"—announces a reality that is existentially positive for him: I am alive. His testimony is good news. While ever more terrible/horrific is the narration of what he witnessed (*presenciar*), more marvellous is the reality that he announces: I am alive. This book [*Masacres de la Selva*] assumes the finality of this and hundreds more of these witnesses, who want to tell the people of Guatemala and the nations of the world: we are alive, incredibly, we are alive. . . . We [writers, anthropologists, social scientists?] are only intermediaries of the announcement. We are not immediate witnesses of what we are going to narrate. But we have been entrusted with the task by fate or history, whatever we may want to call it, of transmitting what the immediate witnesses have seen, smelled, touched, heard, felt, interpreted, thought, fought . . . We cannot silence it, because they have narrated it as a marvellous story/history (*historia maravillosa*). . . . In this chain of announcement, faith (*fe*) is an indispensable element that transverses all the testimonies, because the good news cannot but be accepted voluntarily. In the first instance, it is to believe the witness himself, because he believes that it is worthwhile to narrate his testimony. But there is a further important aspect of his faith. It is not so much that he may believe in what he is seeing, in the fire and the slaughterhouses (*destazadores*). What he sees and hears, he experiences directly. But on narrating it, he realizes that for many, it will be difficult to believe that human beings (*hombres*) may be capable of dehumanization so gruesome as the one they have witnessed, because to himself and to many of the victims it has been laborious to believe that the Army would commit such crimes, and, as we shall see in many testimonies, that absence of faith cost them their lives (Falla 1992, ii–iii; my translation).

As a result of Falla's work, exhortations for an *antropología comprometida* (Manz 1995), that is, a theoretical and methodological practice of social and cultural analysis that refuses the "luxury of indifference,"[20] were widely taken up (Carmack 1988; Grandin 2004; Manz 1988; 2004; Thompson 2001). The analyses of the violence thus produced represent the inception of a new mode of doing anthropology and one that is "on the move," as it accompanies the displacements forced upon communities by the violence inflicted by the Guatemalan Army during the late 1970s and early 1980s. The notion of a "committed" form of social and cultural research also establishes a new complicity between and among subjects, as researchers and their interlocutors become linked in "chains of annunciation" (Falla 1992, iii). Ethnically marked subjects feature in these analyses as the designed victim of genocidal state violence. Social scientists have labored to develop frames for an understanding of experiences of *La Violencia* in local contexts (Carlsen 1997; Carmack 1988; Wilson 1995), accounting for the conflict from the perspective of a community or a region. Others have engaged with the violence after the fact, and dealt with fear, terror, and their effects on memory for gendered constituencies of widows (Green 1999; Zur 1998), for example, and in Guatemalan society more generally (Little and Smith 2009). The urban perspective proposed by Nelson (1999), who focuses on violence and body politics in the national imagination, as well as contemporary analyses of postwar violence and insecurity (Little and Smith 2009; O'Neill and Thomas 2011) complement these subtle ethnographic and historical analyses of the violence in rural areas. Nelson's most recent work, moreover, confronts the problem of "reckoning" the conflict head on and deals with the complex tasks of offering accounts of it, but also establishing accountability for it, in the conflict's open-ended aftermath (Nelson 2009). O'Neill and Thomas (2011), on the other hand, argue that the postwar period is characterized by structural violence that requires a systemic understanding of the connections between past and present, a point lucidly developed by Smith and Offit (2010).

Movement, displacement, and deterritorialization have become ever more relevant to practices of contextualization (Thompson 2001), as analyses increasingly deal with the movements engendered in, and through, the conflict.[21] Anthropological context-making has become increasingly multi-sited in its analytical practices, as it strives to represent the violence and invoke a sense of complicity and solidarity among ethnographic subjects. Furthermore, some important anthropological perspectives on Guatemala are increasingly concerned with the study of the relations between ambivalence, ambiguity (for example, Hale 2006), and, following Nelson (2009), "duplicity," as central to a multiplicity of context-making efforts. Concept-metaphors that emphasize ambiguity therefore emerge as central to the ways histories of violence and conflict and related socialities of secrecy are grappled with locally, as it will be extensively demonstrated in the chapters that follow.

Conclusion: Incommensurability and Out-contextualization

During the course of my fieldwork, the analyses produced by a range of social scientists were in the process of becoming important interlocutors of the Pan-Maya movement and other constituencies, often representing a record against which to validate cultural practices. Richard Wilson's (1995) elegant ethnography of Q'eqchi' knowledge and ritual practice related to maize and *tzuul taq'a* (beings of the mountains) was published in Spanish in 1999, and the influence of this text was felt beyond the boundaries of Alta Verapaz. In 2000, on a visit to the Q'eqchi' school and cultural center Aj Awinel in El Estor, Izabal, I was asked whether a copy of Wilson's recently translated book could be made available. The text was perceived by the Q'eqchi' teachers and activists as an important tool in the work of "recuperation" of Q'eqchi' culture, work to which the school was committed.

Consumption and circulation of texts on the social and cultural analysis of Guatemala (and of their authors) followed disparate routes. Between 1999 and 2000, anthropological and historical research carried out by Norman B. Schwartz (1990) was the primary reference for the operations of local and international non-governmental organizations and multilateral agencies in Petén, Guatemala. This point is also noted by Sundberg (1998), who highlights the normative character that some anthropological writings have acquired in the region: "[f]or cultural and historical data, NGOs tend to rely on anthropologist Norman Schwartz's (1990) work, *Forest Society*, which seems to have acquired prescriptive status in Petén" (Sundberg 1998, 89). *Forest Society* had thus become a repository of "truths" about regional ethnic identities and relations and a record against which ethnic conflict and ethnically marked disputes over land were understood. Through explicit assignation of authenticity and environmental knowledge to the "autochthonous" populations, and implicit attribution of foreignness, environmental "ignorance," and hence "destructiveness" to migrants who have most recently come into the region, *Forest Society* directly informed the validation of demands of those groups who had come to be considered rightful residents, at the expense of those who were increasingly deemed to be "invaders" (Sundberg 2003). Interestingly, *Forest Society* (Schwartz 1990) and the region that is its subject, namely Petén, both have been consistently out-contextualized in much social and cultural analysis. They have been placed out of context, demoted from, or recuperated in reviews of the history of different disciplinary engagements in the country.[22]

Social and cultural research is thus deeply implicated in the production of essentialist taxonomies of ethnicity and related topographies—in their gendered dimensions. When "the local" is spatially and conceptually qualified in terms of indigenous ethnicity (see also Nelson 1999, 121), situated contrapuntal histories are made to encroach upon and redefine imperial and national logics. Mostly centered on and around *cabeceras* (administrative towns) of *departamentos* (administrative regions), representations of the local in question often belie a certain nativism.[23] Social and cultural analysis and Pan-Maya narratives thus occasionally converge to stress the importance of diversity, plurality, and indigeneity as records of Guatemalan counterhegemonic histories. Opposing historical determinism and a sense of dispossession as destiny, they illuminate plural narratives and experiences, aim to counteract epistemic violence, and, in the case of Maya intellectuals and activists, claim their rightful space in the consciousness and apparatus of the nation.[24] However culturalist, both sets of discourses also participate in the solidification, normalization, and prescription of (ethnic) difference in contemporary Guatemala.

Social and cultural research is also intimately implicated in the delineation of these dynamics. Through disciplinary propensity for all indigeneity, however marked, social and cultural research has made important contributions to debates concerning the ethnicized and racialized political economy of imperial agency. An analytical concern with the definition of the status of indigeneity vis-à-vis imperial dynamics has produced numerous accounts. These include a sustained engagement with analysis and representation of multiple experiences of the conflict. Different approaches to the contextualization of indigeneity nonetheless share a set of pre-theoretical commitments (Moore 2004). Through such analytical attention to the status of indigeneity, ethnically marked and unmarked subjects have been envisaged as products of and incited into existence by colonial and imperial agency. Alternatively, ethnicity has been viewed as a marker of that which empire has routinely failed to annihilate.

As noted by Strathern (1995a), culture as an item of knowledge is part of local native discourse as much as social scientific discourse. Since the pioneering work of Ricardo Falla, researchers and their interlocutors have developed complicit relations through which denunciations of violence and terror have been possible. With these accounts, a complex field of experiences and interpretations has emerged, itself the subject of local reappropriations.[25] An effect of this has been the out-contextualization of the researcher (Strathern 1995a) and the exposure of the researcher's culture as somewhat different from anyone else's (Strathern 1995a, 11).

Out-contextualization works on a further register in that it produces incommensurability. In the case of the social and cultural analysis of Guatemala I have reviewed, I noted how critiques of essentialism at times resulted in denials of the analytical viability of comparison, thus making local experiences mutually incommensurable. The contextualization of local experiences marked by tropes of indigeneity has also produced the simultaneous out-contextualization of experience in local contexts that are connoted as nonindigenous. This might go some way toward explaining the absence from my review of analyses dealing with the region of Petén. The northern *departamento* has been regularly out-contextualized by different traditions of social scientific research, partly through claims to its perceived nonindigenous and sparsely populated character. I have surreptitiously introduced Petén into my discussion of local appropriations of texts dealing with social and cultural analysis of Guatemala. In turn, analyses of the conflict have out-contextualized the historical experiences of guerrilla militancy. In the chapter that follows, I strive to contextualize what has been out-contextualized, that is, what has been placed out of view or deemed unworthy of attention, that is, in Dilley's terms (Dilley 1999, 37), I consider connections that have been made, and where discontinuities might begin.[26] I am aware that my context-making practices may produce incommensurability,[27] but it is interlocutors and readers themselves who will ultimately make connections and contextualize or out-contextualize social and cultural analysis, including the present account.

2
Violence, Sovereignty, Governmentality

They make slaughter and they call it peace.
—Tacitus, in Hardt and Negri, *Empire*, 2000, 3

Introduction

This chapter explores the "contexts" of the present research further, and specifically the ways in which different cultural texts may illuminate contrasting and often contradictory aspects and interpretations of social life in Guatemala. Through juxtaposition, partiality and what is or has been "out of context" are brought into the descriptive frame (Fardon 1990; Strathern 1987). In my analysis I aim to delineate "plurality in context," through reflections on the contextual and located character of selected accounts and the systems of representation that may be said to underpin them. Accounts and fragments of social reality relationally contextualize each other while also pointing to what has been out-contextualized and kept out of view. Furthermore, the juxtaposition of heterogeneous cultural texts—as much as their mutual out-contextualization—gives a form to the multi-sitedness of my fieldwork.[1] In other words, the complex social reality of Petén is here contrived to reveal itself in the pieces and parts of the itinerant and multi-sited research practices, through which Petén contextualizes and contextualized itself in that elusive and open-ended interval that was and is the temporality of the field/fieldwork (Hastrup 1990; 1995).

In this chapter, I take issue with the systemic models of analysis and representation of the social and cultural realm, and the exclusions they engendered. I note that social and cultural analysis of Guatemala has deemed Petén to be "out of context" in the sense of being tangential to national, regional, and international dynamics. Conversely, I explore how Petén, rather than being peripheral vis-à-vis national, regional, and international contexts, has in fact been enmeshed in complex relations with the nation-state and regional and transnational geopolitical realities. To reflect on the relation between Petén and the nation-state, I discuss the administrations of

Juan José Arévalo and Jacobo Árbenz and note how these impacted configurations of social life in the *departamento*, notably through policies of colonization. Further, I note how the forest of Petén was the training ground for the counterrevolutionary forces that staged the invasion of Cuba in 1961, thus challenging accounts that have represented Petén as peripheral vis-à-vis national and international events. In point of fact, the region of Petén was a site of early militarization and counterinsurgency. I proceed to document the establishment and operations of the government agency in charge of the development of the region between 1960 and 1989, namely the Empresa Nacional de Fomento y Desarrollo de Petén (National Enterprise of Fomentation and Development of Petén; FYDEP) and argue that since its inception, FYDEP amounted to an organism of oligarchic self-governance, which was under direct control of the Guatemalan Army. As such, a focus on FYDEP allows for the delineation of processes of relentless and progressive militarization of the *departamento* in the second half of the twentieth century. Further, I consider the operations of FYDEP and specifically FYDEP's role in overseeing the colonization of Petén as a project of governmentality, through the accounts of FYDEP personnel.[2] I argue that through a consideration of different orders of connections that have produced Petén historically as a site of governmentality, histories of insurgency begin to contextualize themselves. Defying linear periodizations of the conflict, I conclude by noting contemporary forms of violent governmentality in the guise of conservationist agendas and document the displacements they generated during the course of my fieldwork.

El Petén

The *departamento* of El Petén is the northern region of Guatemala, which has consistently occupied a relatively peripheral location in both a capital-centered national imagination and the highlands-oriented gaze of social and cultural analysis. Contemporary Petén amounts to roughly 36,000 square kilometers enclosed by the Guatemalan highlands of Alta Verapaz to the south, the *departamento* of Izabal to the southeast, and the periodically disputed borders with Mexico to the northwest and Belize to the northeast.

Envisaged as a vast, remote, and sparsely populated rainforest punctuated by innumerable ancient Maya archaeological sites,[3] Petén was said to be for most of the twentieth century a relatively distant outpost (Samayoa Rivera n.d.; Schwartz 1990; Soza 1970).[4] "To the untrained eye, that is, to most of us, as late as 1970 Petén looked like a tropical rainforest—much of it still does," wrote Norman Schwartz in 1990, adding that in order to

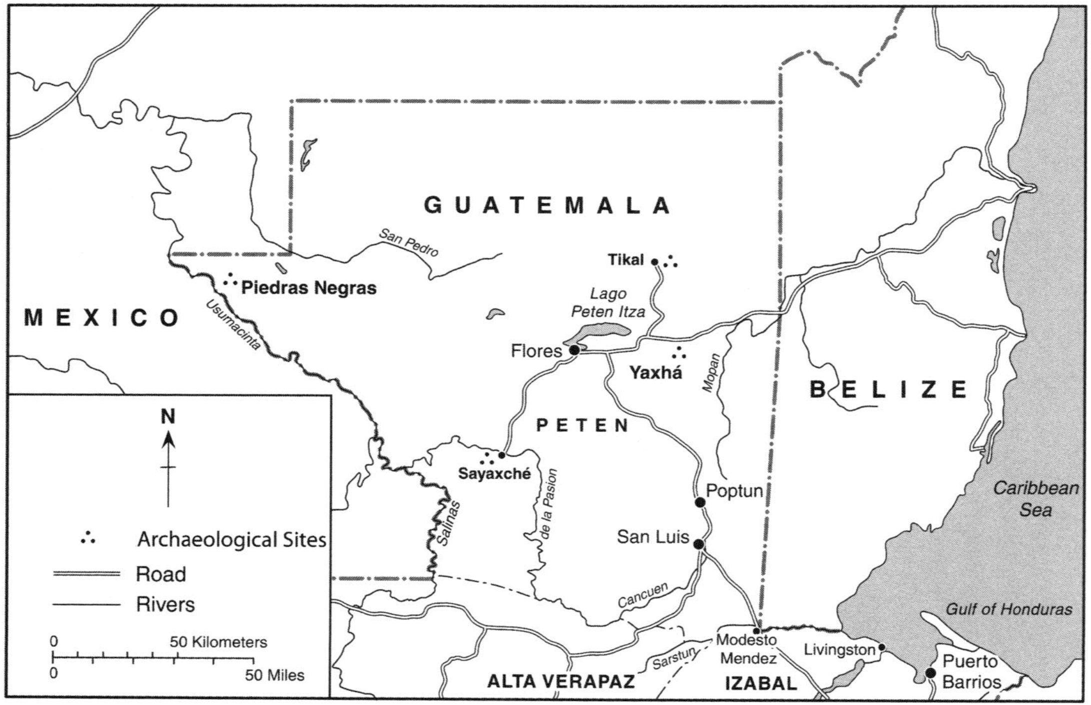

Map 2.1. Map of Petén.

envisage the Petenero landscape, one would best "keep in the mind's eye an image of a tropical lowland frontier" (Schwartz 1990, 10). To many Guatemalans, Petén was an inhospitable and inaccessible place, of which some thought "las tierras no sirven," that is, even the land, the most disputed of resources in the country, was "no good" (Samayoa Rivera n.d., 11).

The sense of the singularity of Petén, seemingly apparent in its distinctive landscape, was substantiated by further notable Petenero differences vis-à-vis the national context. In the first instance, the region had hosted specific histories of resistance to the Conquest and localized postconquest colonial arrangements. Between 1700 and 1821, colonial administration and control of this "frontier military district and penal colony" (Schwartz 1990, 42) were in the hands of criollo families that took residence in the town of Remedios. The colonial center of Remedios was built on the site of Tayasal, which, in turn, had been the preconquest Itzá capital.[5] Tayasal, vividly remembered by Peteneros for the fierce and prolonged resistance organized by the Itzá against the Spaniards,[6] was the last city to capitulate to the Conquistadores in 1697.[7] In the postconquest aftermath, criollo families settled on the shores of the lake Petén Itzá in the new colonial town of Remedios ruled over this remote "hinterland within hinterlands" (Schwartz 1990, 39). Distance from the metropolitan colonial centers throughout the colonial period made it possible for Petén to enjoy relative independence from the Bourbon administration. Petén's difference, however, is represented as reaching far back to preconquest times. Schwartz, for instance, notes that preconquest and postconquest indigenous populations living in Petén had affinities with the Yucatán region, rather than with the Guatemalan highlands or the Pacific Coast (Reina 1964; 1967a; 1967b; Reina and Schwartz 1974; Schwartz 1990, 31–76).[8] In historical and anthropological accounts (Schwartz 1990; Soza 1970), Petén has consistently been represented as sui generis and peripheral vis-à-vis the colonial and postcolonial national contexts.

Between the 1870s and the 1970s, Schwartz (1990, 202) argues, the development of the chicle industry, namely the extractive economy of the sap of the chico zapote tree, proved a remarkably lucrative activity for the prominent descendants of colonial criollos in Petén, and for the nation's coffers alike. Formally tied to the nation through the office of the *Gobernación* and the figure of the *Gobernador*, and substantially connected through fiscal ties, Petén paid tributes to the national government. Fiscal contributions, however, failed to secure any notable dedicated investment in the region. As noted by Schwartz (1990, 203), "[o]ver the years, very little of the revenue from chicle was used to invest in productive activities. Fiscal linkages were as limited as production linkages." Relative isolation and general disengagement from national political developments, according to Schwartz, continued virtually unaltered in the twentieth century, and during the progressive decades of the Arévalo and Árbenz administrations. Schwartz argues that "Árbenz's land reforms, important as they were elsewhere in Guatemala, had *no effect* on underpopulated Petén. There, until the 1970s, there was no pressure on the land, and few highlanders rich or poor had any interest in the distant northern lowlands. For example, between 1945 and 1954, there were 1,497 local agrarian committees set up in Guatemala, but not a single one in Petén" (Schwartz 1990, 191; my emphasis). With the exception of the establishment of SUCHILMA (Sindicato Único de Chicleros y Laborantes de Madera), the *chicleros* (rubber tappers) and woodcutters union that operated fairly independently for about a decade and successfully ended debt peonage in the chicle industry (Schwartz 1990, 191–2), in this account, Petén is said to have maintained its peripheral position vis-à-vis national affairs. Schwartz (1990) consistently maintains that Petén's marginality vis-à-vis the national political context often worked in the interests of the local population, as this meant that the population in Petén was spared some of the violence and strife that befell the rest of the country at times of national and civil unrest. However, this analysis does not address and account for the manner in which violence, surveillance, and control may have functioned in Petén in ways that were thoroughly Petenero, and indeed thoroughly local, yet no less brutally productive and capillary (Foucault 1980, 38–9).

Schwartz's own texts contain the traces of these local histories as well as pointers to the complex configurations of power in the *departamento*, and their effects. By way of example, the historical realities of unionization of rubber tappers and woodcutters in SUCHILMA may be considered. Schwartz (1990, 191) identifies that the unionization effort was fully a product of the progressive reforms that were being implemented in the country as a whole during the Arévalo and Árbenz administrations (1945–1954). Nevertheless, Schwartz swiftly forecloses any productive evaluation of the historical experience of union organizing, noting that SUCHILMA was from its inception viewed by many *chicleros* themselves as a corrupt organization that had detrimental effects on the overall demand for chicle.

The ambivalence that seems to have characterized the relation between *chicleros* and the union is extremely interesting, and a number of factors are highlighted by Schwartz (1990, 192) as having played a part in the relative failure to establish class consciousness and solidarity among *chicleros*. First, chicle extraction was often an individualized and isolated activity ill-suited to collective action in the sense of cooperation in productive activities and union organizing efforts. Second, the combination of subcontracting relations and kinship ties often determined individuals' ability to endorse the union free from pressures from kin and/or managers. Third, hierarchical relations based on subcontracting were interchangeable, and as individuals were not entirely in consistent and univocal hierarchical relations to one another, unionization based on specific and stable subordinate status was unlikely (Schwartz 1990, 192–4). Fourth, the overwhelming majority of SUCHILMA leaders, as "direct descendants of the old colonial Creole and Creole-Ladino families" (Schwartz 1990, 332, note 43), were securely tied to the local system of racialized oligarchic power. Fifth, in the period following 1954, and mirroring national patterns of anti-union violence and repression, reprisals from contractors against union supporters became more overt (Schwartz 1990, 192). Schwartz goes on to say that "[f]inally, in recent years, Suchilma has been *partly subsidized by FYDEP*, so even aside from *the anti-union stance of the government*, Suchilma has not been free to press hard for worker interests" (Schwartz 1990, 192; my emphasis).

The above excerpt is no minor detail and the nature of Schwartz's "aside" no small matter. What emerges so vividly is, first, the important sense in which Petén was in fact linked to developments in the nation as a whole, notably during the progressive decade of the Arévalo and Árbenz administrations (1945–1954) and its violent, counterrevolutionary aftermath.[9] Second, noting the eventual subordination of SUCHILMA to FYDEP, Schwartz points to the violent system of local governmentality established in Petén in 1960 through the creation of FYDEP.[10] Understanding the operations of FYDEP seems therefore critical to an analysis of social life in the *departamento*, and key to any attempt at tracing local histories of violence, surveillance, repression, and control. In turn, however, the creation of FYDEP and its violent operations in the three decades that followed require that the peculiarity of relations between the national government and Petén in the period prior to 1960 be considered.

With reference to the mid-twentieth century, it is important to note that in the aftermath of the Revolución de Octubre and during the administration of Juan José Arévalo (1944–1951), Petén became of increasing importance to the proposed national program of land reform.[11] As noted by Bell (1993) in his comprehensive and insightful analysis of the place of Petén in the progressive reforms of President Arévalo, the region was seen as the ideal receptacle for landless indigenous populations from the highlands. Under the aegis of the national program of land reform and redistribution, the project of colonization of Petén seemed "acceptable to *finqueros* (landowners), that is, the landowning elite, as this did not affect their *fincas* (properties) directly but did respond to the national interest, meeting both military and Guatemalan international political objectives" (Bell 1993, 23; my translation). The movement of indigenous populations to the lowlands of Petén aimed to contribute to national economic development and increase agricultural productivity through the opening of new agricultural areas. Romeo O. Samayoa Rivera, Army major, agro-engineer, and FYDEP employee, describes Arévalo's contribution thus:

> During the government of Dr. Juan José Arévalo, man of travel, of great administrative ability, and with a clear mind focused on bestowing on his country progress, well-being, and prosperity, [Arévalo] met with his staff (*asesores*) with the objective of promoting the incorporation of such Petenero territory into Guatemala, given that it [Petén] lay completely forgotten . . . [T]hat is how overnight the Colonia Agrícola de Poptún [Agricultural Colony of Poptún] was born . . . The colony was created as a political measure and with the objective of realizing that the Peteneros could feel [themselves] to be Guatemalans, a labor of approximation (*acercamiento*) and productivity, as for hundreds of years [Petén] lay forgotten, lost, ignored, sad, and relegated to a second position, and what is worse, with no means of transport but the plane, and with only God the Almighty living with and in the hearts of its [Petenero] people (Samayoa Rivera n.d., 24; my translation).

Arévalo's "labor of approximation" and the task of creation of a feeling of belonging to the nation-state amounted to projects that ultimately sought to promote "social progress," but as Bell (1993) points out, because of failure to achieve any discernible degree of success by the end of Arévalo's presidential term, the project of colonization was largely halted, and indeed inverted, during Árbenz's presidency. Petén did figure in Árbenz's government program as a possible site of development (Bell 1993, 24). The Revista Agrícola published by the Minister of Agriculture in 1953 notes how, "[i]n the context of the plan of cattle farming rehabilitation (*plan de rehabilitación ganadera*) proposed/promulgated by the Government, the magnificent opportunities offered by the northern region of the country have not been neglected, notably some areas of the vast Petén. On these grounds, since 22 January of the present year, and following relevant studies, free export and trade of live cattle, refrigerated meat, and subproducts of the same industry have been granted for the forthcoming ten years in the *departamento* of Petén" (Villegas Rodas 1953, 52; my translation). Government policy in support of the budding cattle farming industry in Petén was supported by a visit of the Agriculture Minister and a team of professionals and officials, to inspect cattle farming activities around La Libertad. For most of the Technical Commission, this was their first encounter with Petén.

> At half past nine the bird of steel (*pájaro de acero*) rises and directs its course northwards. The Major of the aviation pilots (*pilotos aviadores*) Arturo Guirola flies it with magisterial ability. We revel in the splendid luminous morning. It has been some time since we desired to know the fabulous territory of Petén. And it was when we least thought of and expected it, that such welcome privilege was presented to us. We had read and heard much about this area (*jirón*) of the nation (*patria*), so much so that our appreciation at a distance was entangled in most instances in the brambles (*marañas*) of the florid jungle (*de nutridas selvas*) populated by wild beasts (*fieras*) and tribes of anthropoids (*tribús de antropoides*), such is the myth/legend of the Lacandones (Villegas Rodas 1953, 53; my translation).

The account of the ministerial visit combines emphasis on the modernity of the present ("the bird of steel," numerous mentions of "jeeps") with the optimism of a modernity to come. However, it was the strategic military role of Petén in the dispute over the territory of Belize that came to the fore during Árbenz's term. Guatemalan claims to sovereignty over Belize were tinged with anticolonial zeal during Árbenz's presidency. According to Bell (1993), the territorial dispute over Belize did not impinge directly on the interests of the military, the landowners, or the Church and was therefore a rather uncontroversial policy (Bell 1993, 25). With the exception of nationalist arguments that it was in the national interest to regain the territory of Belize, and that such policy could only be pursued from Petén, the region largely languished at the periphery of the nation-state during the 1950s (Bell 1993).

With its mixed results, the Arévalo administration and its program of colonization of Petén is significant in two respects. First, the colonization effort represents the antecedent to successive programs of the 1960s. More generally, the Arévalo administration marked the inception of visions of development and modernity in Petén, endeavors also pursued during Árbenz's term through the construction of the road between Flores and the newly established Colonia of Poptún (Samayoa Rivera n.d., 27). Second, and most importantly, through the emphasis on the strategic and military importance of the *departamento* vis-à-vis territorial disputes with Mexico and

Belize, the Arévalo administration created the conditions for the installation of the Army in Petén. The prominent role of the Guatemalan Army in the social, cultural, political, and economic life of the *departamento* was to continue through the years of *La Violencia*, past the Peace Accords of 1996, and in post–Peace Accords times. In 1960, the *departamento* managed to secure de facto administrative independence through the creation of the Empresa Nacional de Fomento y Desarrollo Económico de Petén (FYDEP), the National Enterprise for the Economic Development of Petén. An institution nominally created to promote and oversee the economic development of the region, FYDEP in fact, between 1960 and 1989, amounted to an organism of oligarchic self-governance with considerable direct ties to the military. Although Arévalo had heralded plans for the colonization of Petén in the 1940s, it was left to FYDEP to spearhead the venture in earnest.

FYDEP, Governmentality, and the Military

In the second part of the twentieth century, Petén exercised a remarkable degree of administrative autonomy from the nation-state. As (physically) remote, (symbolically) peripheral, and (administratively) disconnected as Petén may have been (see Schwartz 1990), the salient historical link between its local institutions and the Guatemalan Army would suggest that Petén was tied to the nation, albeit in peculiar ways.[12] For one, it should be noted that FYDEP was established by General Ydígoras Fuentes in 1959 (Samayoa Rivera n.d., 27) in a highly poignant political climate. Ydígoras Fuentes rose to power following the murder of Colonel Carlos Castillo Armas. Castillo Armas nominally headed the infamous overthrow of the Árbenz government organized by the United States Central Intelligence Agency in 1954 (Ball et al. 1999; CEH 1999, Chapter I, Item 78; Landau 1993; Schirmer 1998). Subsequent to the coup d'état in 1954, the program of social reform and land redistribution proposed by the Árbenz government was violently quashed and repression ensued under Castillo Armas. The Partido Guatemalteco del Trabajo (Guatemalan Workers' Party; PGT) was banned. All political opposition was brutally suppressed and the country entered a protracted period of military dictatorship and weak civilian rule. Castillo Armas proceeded with the program of reforms initiated by the Arévalo and Árbenz administrations, with the exception of the program of land redistribution. The rules of both Castillo Armas and Ydígoras Fuentes were marked by a fervently embraced and violently enforced anticommunist stance. During the late 1950s and early 1960s, Guatemala assumed a preeminently strategic role for US foreign policy and became instrumental to

US plans to circumscribe the perceived communist threat gaining ground in Central America and the Caribbean Basin. The successful ousting of Cuban dictator Batista and the related rise to power of Fidel Castro in 1959 were a cause of serious concern for the US government. Under Ydígoras Fuentes, Guatemala, and Petén in particular, became a training outpost for those CIA-supported Cuban exiles who were to stage the 1961 invasion of Cuba (Landau 1993; Vinegrad 1998): "Following the triumph of the Cuban revolution the CIA secured the support of the [Guatemalan] government presided by Miguel Ydígoras, installing a military base in the proximity of San Juan Acul, Sayaxché, to train the Cuban exiles who were to invade the Bay of Pigs in 1961. The lagoon that goes by the same name served as landing place for the hydroplane PBYs, which were used as means of transport. Before international disquiet and the discontent of important sectors of the country, Ydígoras indicated that the rationale for North American military presence was to train the Guatemalan Army in counterinsurgency tactics, due to a supposed Cuban intention to invade the country" (FEDECOAG 1993, 11; my translation). Petén was therefore an early site of counterinsurgency and the training ground for the counterrevolutionary Cuban exiles and the Guatemalan Army. Having landed at the Bay of Pigs, the Cuban exiles were swiftly defeated by Castro, and Cuba became a crucial point of reference for those militant Guatemalans with communist, Arbenzista, and socialist orientation (CEH 1999, Chapter I, Item 104; Landau 1993; Vinegrad 1998). Despite the success of the Cuban revolution, in Guatemala the repressive climate of the late 1950s and early 1960s produced the Empresa Nacional de Fomento y Desarrollo Económico de Petén (FYDEP), the institution appointed with the task of bringing modernity to the region. As noted by Schwartz,

> [w]hen it was organized, FYDEP was charged with responsibility (1) to build an infrastructure to foment agricultural, industrial, and touristic development in Petén; (2) to administer and exploit Petén's resources, except oil, for domestic and overseas markets; (3) to sponsor colonization and to provide landless peasants with land and thereby increase production of food staples; (4) to settle farmers along the Usumacinta River in an effort to bar a proposed Mexican hydroelectric project from flooding Guatemalan soil and to prevent Mexican colonists from encroaching on Guatemalan land; and (5) to promote medium-scale capitalized cattle ranching in south-central and central Petén. The area north of parallel 17°10' (roughly 33 percent of Petén), several small forest reserves in the south, a thin strip of land running

> along Petén's southern border, a military zone in the southwest, and a number of archaeological parks—a total of roughly about 1,517,023 hectares—were exempted from colonization (Schwartz 1990, 252–3).

This point is confirmed by government documents published in the decade that followed:

> In June 1959 the Decree 1286, Law of Creation of FYDEP (Empresa Nacional de Fomento y Desarrollo Económico de Petén) was passed. This has as its goal fomenting and developing in adequate form the natural riches of that northern *departamento* in order to achieve its effective integration in the national economy by means of the use and scientific preservation of its forests and other natural reserves; its improvement (*saneamiento*), colonization (*colonización*), industrialization (*industrialización*), and other policies and activities that may contribute to such aims. FYDEP, in accordance with the above law, depends directly from the Presidency of the Republic (Secretaría General del Consejo Nacional de Planificación Económica 1965, 14; my translation).

However, it has been argued (FEDECOAG 1993, 12) that along with the forward-looking emphasis on "*fomento*" (fomentation, improvement) and "*desarrollo*" (development), the creation of FYDEP was born out of the perceived necessity of ordering the migratory flows directed to the *departamento*, as landless *campesinos* trickled in from the southern and eastern coasts, and to a lesser extent, from the highlands of Alta Verapaz, in search of land. Thus, FYDEP was from its inception a reactive initiative that sought both to induce (FEDECOAG 1993, 12) and to regulate/control the movement of land-thirsty populations displaced from other regions of the country. As it "depends directly" from the presidency, FYDEP amounts to a quintessential project of governmentality.[13]

In Michel Foucault's definition, governmentality refers to "[t]he ensemble formed by the institutions, procedures, analyses, and reflections, the calculations and tactics that allow the exercise of this very specific albeit very complex form of power, which has as its target population, as its principal form of knowledge political economy, and as its essential technical means apparatuses of security" (Foucault [1978] 2004, 219–20). According to Foucault, governmentality developed in the West during the course of a transition from the "state of justice" of the Middle Ages to the "administrative state" in the fifteenth and sixteenth centuries (Foucault [1978] 2004). This resulted in the rise to prominence of governmentality's peculiar exercise of power in the form of sovereignty and discipline. Thus, "government" depends on "the formation of a whole series of government apparatuses [and] the development of a whole complex of knowledges (*savoirs*)" (Foucault [1978] 2004, 219–20).

Foucault's interest in governmentality and its analytical focus on the "how-to-govern" problem (Burchell et al. 1991, 7) suggests that any analysis of the establishment of FYDEP should explore not only the processes through which institutions of government were established but also the practices, discourses, and knowledges in and through which institutions and subjects were created. What is at stake in such a Foucauldian-inspired analysis is the range of practices through which FYDEP exerted control over the population, and, in turn, how the population was constituted as the subject of governmentality, and how specific subject positions may be forged as a result. Poblete, following Foucault, has noted that "[p]ower and its exercises manifest as objects of study within a continuity of macro- and microphysical domains" (Poblete 2001, 138). When considering the creation of FYDEP in the context of the political climate in the country in the mid-twentieth century, it is unambiguous that FYDEP embodied peripheral governmentality. FYDEP set out to provide a vision of a planned future of development and to sponsor, regulate, and supervise the extractive economy that would strengthen the links of the region to the capitalist world system and, to a lesser extent, to the nation. Likewise, the task of FYDEP was, literally and metaphorically, to "evitar la anarquía en el territorio más grande que Guatemala posee," that is, "avoid anarchy in the largest territory of Guatemala" (Samayoa Rivera n.d., 2). That FYDEP's mission was to stave off real or imagined "anarchy" is particularly significant when one considers that FYDEP's operations were, from their very inception, undertaken under the aegis of the Army. The relationship between FYDEP and the Army is most transparent when one considers the figure of the "*Promotor*," that is, the head of FYDEP, a subject position that came into being with the establishment of the organization and that from its creation was the prerogative of military personnel who took up the role for the duration of the national legislature. The first *Promotor* of FYDEP, Colonel Oliverio Casasola y Casasola, headed the institution until 1969, while in 1978, with the election of President Lucas García, the office of *Promotor* was assigned to Colonel Jorge Mario Reyes Porra. Remarkably, given the prominence and visibility of the relation between the governance of FYDEP and the Guatemalan Army, Schwartz's (1990) social history of Petén leaves the question of the relation between FYDEP and the Guatemalan Army, and hence of the longstanding militarization of institutions of government in Petén, largely unexplored.[14] The task here is to place the creation of FYDEP within the histories of militarization in Petén.[15] Histories of insurgency and counterinsurgency that marked the region from the early 1960s to 1996, and the interlocked experiences of migration and displacement, remain to be fully documented and accounted for (see Stølen 2007; van der Vaeren 2000). Nevertheless, the intimate relation between FYDEP and the Guatemalan Army presented itself rather unambiguously during my fieldwork. As Don Alfonso, a high-ranking ex-FYDEP employee, recalled during our conversation,

> [FYDEP] was a government, the law bestowed upon it the faculty of a government here at the local level, as if it were a nation-state (*como si fuera un estado*), though it was a *departamento.* It was a government within/inside another (*era un gobierno dentro de otro*), according to the law. A government that administered all resources, land, and woodlands of Petén. So the interesting aspect was that the funds (*recursos*) that Petén generated would remain here as works/infrastructure (*aquí se quedaban en obras*). They built hospitals, roads, schools, health centers; [gave] support to municipalities and leaders, administer[ed] woodlands; logging concessions (*concesiones madereras*) were properly overseen (*controlar*). In the end, the only shortcoming/defect (*defecto*) was that it forever depended on the military government of Guatemala (*gobierno militar de Guatemala*), hence they would appoint Army personnel (militares) to work here as promoters of development (*promotores de desarrollo*) . . . The creation of FYDEP was necessary, starting FYDEP was very necessary because of the state of abandonment (*abandono*) in which [Petén] was, hence one had to have a manager here (*entonces había que tener un administrador aquí*), [a manager] of this huge *finca*, to be able to look after it and develop it. That is how the government created the law in 1956 [*sic*], I recall.

Don Alfonso added that:

> The interesting aspect is that it [FYDEP] did accelerate development. Because of the abandonment in which Petén was, the central government did not have the capacity to attend to Petén, and Petén ran the risk to be kept marginalized and suddenly perhaps to annex itself to Mexico (*anexarse a Méjico*), such was the rumor (*rumor*). With

> that new law they nominated a person to direct/oversee the complete development of the whole of Petén and started the process to bring Petén closer to the country/nation (*acercarlo al país*)—to incorporate it into the development of the country (*al resto del país para incorporarlo al desarrollo del país*). What's interesting is that this was actually achieved. The only point still pending was this road that was covered with asphalt, but a great deal was done for Petén and that's how entry to migrants began to be granted, the majority of them *campesinos* to work the land. For the [situation with] maize was unusual/curious (*curioso*), this was part of the country and the maize used to be brought over from [other parts of] Guatemala by plane when there was famine (*carestía*), and beans came from Chiquimula. So much land and there was no one who could devote themselves to agriculture, so few of them, because the main activity was chicle and wood logging. So there were many needs here.

Modernity, the Human Wall, and *Paralelo 17*

According to Romeo O. Samayoa Rivera,[16] Army major and agro-engineer who worked for FYDEP for seven years in the capacity of head of the Department of Colonization,

> On 8 June 1965, the Cabinet (*Jefatura de Gobierno*) at the order of Colonel Enrique Peralta Azurdia issued the decree with the force of law (*decreto ley*) 354 through which all institutions then dedicated to Colonization and Agrarian Reform were ordered to give utmost priority to the formation of a Human Wall (*Muro Humano*) to defend our border shared with Mexico, by means of settlements of people from the whole of the republic who voluntarily wished to go and settle, organized in cooperatives, on the banks of the rivers Pasión and Usumacinta, thus halting the construction of the famous plants [hydroelectric plants] Boca del Cerro and Agua Azul, which would have flooded a third of Petén, thus destroying the land (*suelo*), the forest of five-thousand-year-old woods, and the archaeological riches that are so plentiful in the region. Such nationalist mandate was thus undertaken and the construction of the project nocuous for Guatemala was halted (Samayoa Rivera n.d., 3; my translation).

The period of colonization inaugurated in 1965 amounted to a "nationalist directive," that is, a political strategy aimed at defending national territory from the perceived threat of plans for technical development projects proposed by the Mexican government. With its dependence on the creation of a "human wall," the colonization of Petén constitutes a quintessential project of governmentality, in that a subject population had to be first amassed, and then fashioned into appropriate subjects of development and modernity. The subjects of governmentality that might allow for the construction of the human barrier needed first to be drafted from other areas of the country. The process of fashioning of these subjects of colonization was underpinned by a discourse that implied processes of reification through which subjects were turned into objects,[17] in an initial move that turned people into tools at the service of the national strategy of defense. In turn, the constitution of the "human wall" depended upon the establishment of a discourse and ethos of colonization. FYDEP official Samayoa Rivera envisioned the project of modernity that colonization entailed as follows:

> Colonization of a territory means progress and entails: communications, interchange, schools, markets, hospitals or health centers, terror, horror, death, life, violence, changes to the *modus vivendi* of the populations . . . [Colonization] makes of the territory something large, mighty, powerful (*pujante*), though with great sacrifices and the miracles of the Creator . . . Colonization is change, innovation, life, progress, new faces, new peoples, agriculturists, craftsmen, traders, usurers, speculators, petty thieves, dealers, loose women (*mujeres de la dulce vida*), murderers (*matones*), thieves (*ladrones*), all of them living together, some for good (*bien*), some for ill (*mal*), villages rise that were never seen before, with names that were never heard before, signs appear overnight and villages disappear through the art of magic (*por arte de magia*) (Samayoa Rivera, n.d., 5; my translation).

In Samayoa's vision, colonization amounts to the constitution of material infrastructure (schools, markets, hospitals and health centers), and a social ontology (communications, interchange, change, innovation, progress) to which correspond specific states of being (terror, horror, death, life, violence, change). The image of colonization is connoted by dynamism, difference, and pious moral relativism. While it is clear that the project of colonization is firmly the product of human agency (peoples, agriculturists, craftsmen, traders, usurers, speculators, petty thieves, dealers, loose women, murderers, and thieves), aided by peripheral divine miracles, settlements are established overnight, and, disturbingly, may disappear just as swiftly.[18] The phenomenology of colonization, with its embodied, social, and moral ontologies, is underpinned by the production of multiple subjects, chief among them the colonist: "The colonist is an individual who is willing to gamble it all (*el todo por todo*), lose what he's got, abandon it, trade it, give it with the only aim to better his life and the life of his family, without caring for what he leaves behind. Men willing to bake under the sun, to leave one's life behind for an ideal of conquest and freedom, but who always will be . . . colonist[s], no matter what race (*raza*), color, creed or religion, language, all that matters is the courage for seeking new horizons and [to] risk one's life to better his family which is all to him, that's how the colonists of Petén reached those inhospitable lands" (Samayoa Rivera n.d., 5–6). The colonist, firmly gendered in the masculine, is marked by a moral disposition that makes him mobile across space and moral universes. Premised on courageous risk-taking alone, the subject position of the colonist is, in principle, open to anyone. The colonist thus seems to move across and beyond the complex systems of production of difference and subordination, which Samayoa himself identifies as implicating "race," ethnicity, religion, and language. This is a rather radical vision that defies local and national raciological orders and is said to be the genesis of the sociality of colonization. In the biblical imagery that characterizes Samayoa's narrative, the sociality of colonization comprises people, domestic animals, and goods. However, it is through the prescription issued by the government and executed through the figure of the FYDEP *Promotor* that colonization is initiated, the first settlements established, and families counted.

> The coup d'état (*golpe de Estado*) came, and the man who took power, Colonel Enrique Peralta Azurdia, [was a] businessman (*emprendedor*) aware that that territory [of Petén] could accommodate many landless Guatemalans (*Guatemaltecos carentes de tierras*) across the Republic; it was intolerable for *campesinos* to resist the pressure and temptation to migrate to that territory unknown to Guatemalans, full of surprises, magnitudes and miseries, the rumor (*voz*) spread to the cry: "Colonization," tuned to a celestial clarion and [it] started the migration: pilgrimage (*romería*), caravans of people who arrived on foot from the mountains of Cobán, others from the Southern Coast and their lorries, vehicles, carts, the swarms/crowds (*enjambres*) of *campesinos* even arrived by plane, with their whole families and animals: dogs, cats, pigs, chickens, sometimes cows and donkeys loaded with useful goods, to start a new life, people who walked hundreds of kilometers, for weeks, to reach the promised land . . . the Government ordered the *Promotor* [head of FYDEP] that colonization [be]

> started with sixty-four families, who arrived and settled in the village of Colpetén, on the road to Poptún (Samayoa Rivera n.d., 29–30; my translation).[19]

With regard to this account, it is important to consider the ways in which the colonist materializes in Samayoa's narrative as a subject of colonization in general, and as the product of governmentality practices in particular. Vision was often clouded; subjects responsive to the incitement of colonization were soon so numerous they required governmentality's forceful intervention.

> The pressure from colonists was so great, that if we did not take immediate action, people could occupy in disorderly and anarchic fashion any land that they wished and it would have turned into a battlefield, they would perch where they liked, as if they'd been a swarm of butterflies on the sides of rivers or roads . . . The Department of Colonization worked intensely day and night, with a group of agronomists, topographers, drivers, tracing the perimeters of *fincas*, collecting groups of people—the agronomists and their secretaries drew up acts (*levantar actas*), filling in forms to request land (*formularios de solicitud de tierras*) and at the same time giving placement to the families in orderly fashion and giving them instruction (*pláticas*) as to how they should behave (*comportamiento*), their duties, their obligations to their neighbors and to their new home . . . That is how the planning and execution of projects was born, to be able to have order (*ordenamiento*) and settlement (*alojar*) of families in specific sectors, looking to group them in homogeneous, ordered, and disciplined form where they would live for ever and ever, amen (Samayoa Rivera n.d., 31, 33; my translation).

A team of professionals was thus fashioned and enlisted to manage the influx of population and a number of practices were instituted to order and discipline the process of colonization. Practices included administrative procedures through which subjects were made into applicants for land concessions (*títulos*). Aiming at perpetual homogeneity, governmentality would instruct the colonists in the kind of sociality they would have to uphold. This process of mastering movement and difference was not without its problems: what was presented was the refractory quality of difference, marked, in Samayoa's narrative, by indigeneity and religious affiliation: "The problems of colonization were multiple and complex, each family represented a responsibility for our Department[.] I recall that we founded a village of Catholic Apostolic indígenas and *Cobaneros* [i.e., Q'eqchi'], and the village would not make any progress; an injection (*inyección*) of more indigenous people (*gente indígena*) became necessary, but from other *departamentos* where they really did work, unlike the aforementioned. . . . [T]he village grew, and is now prosperous" (Samayoa Rivera n.d., 41). Paternalism, and an ethic of responsibility, are held with a prescription to achieve tangible progress. Failure to do so required prompt intervention and the "injection" of ad hoc population. In the above passage, stasis and failure and their antinomies, progress and prosperity, are marked—both ethnically and in terms of religious affiliation. Despite Catholic Apostolic *Cobaneros*, who are said to be lagging behind due to their slack work ethic, governmentality's intervention—through the addition of indigenous population of unspecified provenance and Evangelical religious affiliation—turns the fate of the community on the prescribed track.[20] Governmentality's social engineering causes strife and unrest:

> I recall that in the Municipio of San Luis lived 150 indigenous families (*familias indígenas*) who thought they were the owners and masters of the place, occupying land that they wanted without the assent of the law, and without respecting anybody. That municipality is rich in resources such as cocoa, chicle, hule, chico zapote, fruit, cattle farming, pig farming (*ganado vacuno y porcino*), birds of all types, wild animals (*animales de monte*), game (*cacería*), good rivers and it is nothing less than the golden door to enter Petén[.] On a daily basis pilgrimages (*romerías*) and swarms (*enjambres*) of families would arrive carrying sick, tired and hungry children full of worms (*lombrices*). . . . That is how San Luis begun to be populated with hardworking people (*gente trabajadora*) who really were willing to gamble their lives (*jugarse el pellejo*), while the mayor of the place and the indigenous people (*los indígenas*) who wanted to rule the place started to mistreat (*tratar mal*) and quarrel (*pelear*) with the newcomers whom they called foreigners (*extranjeros*), wanting to remove them forcefully from the land they had been assigned by [FYDEP's Department of] Colonization[.] [T]hese misnamed (*mal llamados*) San Luiseños, goddamned indigenous people (*indígenas rejodidos*) and their mayor, another old indio (*indio viejo samarro*)[,] met in the *salón social*,[21] which was a large insalubrious shed (*ranchón de mala muerte*) with rough and dilapidated furniture, and in that very place they were making plans for the slaughter (*matanza*) of the intruders (*intrusos*) at blows of machete

(*filo de machete*), not caring whether it was children, women, or elderly people (*ancianos*)[.] [T]hey wanted to despoil them of their properties and make [the properties] their own, together with the mayor who was one like them (*que era otro igual a él*). They hated to death (*odiaban a muerte*) white people (*la gente blanca*) who did not speak their dialect (*el dialecto*), and for that reason they would call them foreign intruders (*extranjeros intrusos*). My intelligence service (*servicio de inteligencia*) informed me of what those dangerous people were plotting (*tramar*), in view of the seriousness of the matter, they called me via radio from San Luis to the capital and the Delegate of Colonization informed me of how dangerous (*peligroso*) the municipio was becoming and that my presence was urgently needed. Given the seriousness of the problem I requested a special flight from the Fuerza Aerea [Military Air Force] giving them all sorts of explanations on how delicate the matter was and they offered to take me to Poptún[.] [I] immediately made the connections via radio with the delegate in Machaquilá, who immediately offered to meet me on landing in the company of another employee who spoke their dialect (*el dialecto*), and the delegate in San Luis was informed and told to be ready for my arrival[.] [T]he trip lasted about two hours, it was in the precise moment when the *indial* [mass of indigenous people, derogatory] was listening to their leader (*líder*)[,] cacique and mayor (*cacique y alcalde*), that we plunged upon them (*habiendolos sorprendido*)[.] On arrival, I noticed that many people were armed with sharp machetes, some sitting on benches, others on the floor and some in the proximity of the door. My accolade (*comitiva*) entered [the *ranchón*] like a whirlwind and we sat at the table (*mesa directiva*), pushing to one side numerous *indios shucos* ["dirty Indians," strongly derogatory] who were talking like mad (*hablaban como locos*). I asked to speak and asked the mayor to be my translator unaware of the "*pava que era*" [the sort he was][.] I gave them a complete explanation of the work/program of colonization in the whole of Petén and specifically there with them, what our plans and programs of work were and that the authoctonous people (*oriundos*) or residents (*vivientes*) of the place had no more right (*más derecho*) than any of the new colonists (*nuevos colonizadores*), but that all had to be done in orderly fashion (*ordenadamente*), that we invited them to fill in their documents (*documentos*) and we would give them in ownership (*propriedad*) the sites where they were currently living or had cultivated plots (*cultivos*)[.]

The mayor translated at his whim (*a su antojo*), lamenting my words (*malogrando mis palabras*) and setting me against them (*poniéndome en contra de ellos*), [and] the FYDEP employee who knew the dialect told me: "Ingeniero, this character (*individuo*) is fooling you (*lo está fregando*), he is telling them everything differently (*les está diciendo todo cambiado*)"[.] The natives (*nativos*) were very angry and brandished their machetes signaling strife (*a son de pelea*). Seeing that attitude I pulled out my revolver[, a] 38 short, I placed it on the table, removed the mayor from the table and imposed a new translator who told them that everything that the former translator [had] said [was] all lies (*mentiras*) and that I had six shots in the barrel (*séis tiros en la recámara*), that the first person to cause any problems was a dead man (*hombre muerto*)[.] The natives (*nativos*) started to understand what I had said clearly (*mi exposición clara*), without false pretext (*tapujo*) and they calmed down their rage (*se calmaron los ánimos*), and in that instant two girls came in to sell pieces of *zapote*,[22] [and] I indicated that they should be distributed to everybody and met the cost myself and this saved/rescued the situation. If it had been otherwise, we would have faced a violent breach of public order (*zafarrancho*) with many casualties (*muchos muertos*). People understood the tragedy (*tragedia*) that might have ensued and how malicious the mayor was, so much so that he was filling their heads with lies (*llenandoles la cabeza de mentiras*)[.] Hence, they gave their consent (*anuencia*) and assurance (*seguridad*) that they accepted colonization with enthusiasm (*de buena gana*), and that in the event of any problem arising, they would come to speak in person with the Delegate in the area, and that they would not count in any way on that character (*individuo*) who was placing them in a bad position (*que lo estaba poniendo en mal*). Thanks [to] God and since that day everything proceeded well, there was harmony (*armonía*) and we would see the locals (*los oriundos*) regularly in the offices of the agronomist, as they would call on the expert (*perito*) so that he would give them land (*tierras*) with its respective contract and they were no longer nomads (*dejar de ser nomadas*). In the end they entered the loop (*el aro*) and the consolidation (*consolidación*) of all the problems of San Luis was achieved with no regard for (*sin tomar en cuenta*) creed, color, size, religion, language, and ideology, as assistance (*asesoría*) was the same for one and for all (*parejo para uno y uno para todos*) . . . and the best thing was the injection of people from the eastern regions (*gente oriental*) that the

> town received, new people (*gente nueva*) with different ideas, different and more developed customs (*otras costumbres más avanzadas*), hardworking people (*trabajadores de pelo en pecho*), peoples (*gentes*) who would occupy mountainous lands full of infestations (*plagas*), snakes (*culebras*), tigers (*tigres*) and where there was only mud (*lodo*) [to start with] (Samayoa Rivera n.d., 44; my translation).

Samayoa's account is remarkable in the way it gives a sense of the violence inherent in the process of colonization of Petén, FYDEP's encounter with the residents of San Luis, and the process through which governmentality's order was established. During the course of my fieldwork, conversations with ex-FYDEP employees confirmed Samayoa's narrative. Don Militón, for instance, pointed out that migrants came looking for land (*buscando tierra*): "*Esa era la ilusión de todos*," that is, land was everyone's illusion. Don Militón differed from Samayoa in some respects, however. Moved by a similar ambition to document his experience of work in Petén, and aware of the historical weight of his role in the FYDEP Department of Colonization, Don Militón harbored anthropological/ethnographic concerns. Based in the *municipio* of Dolores, he had taken an interest in the migrants who had settled there. In the course of our conversation, Don Militón argued that in Dolores, people had come mainly from Jocotán, Camotán, and Chiquimula and added: "Here, they are pure Chortí (*puros Chortís*). They don't speak their language (*idioma*), nor do they practice/speak of their religious ceremonies (*ceremonias religiosas*). These people don't tell you anything (*soltar*). They don't want anyone to know (*querer dar a conocer*), not so much out of fear (*miedo*), but rather out of selfishness (*egoismo*), I think. Many are nomads, they do not settle down (*nomadas, no se asientan*)." The colonization programs pursued by FYDEP in Petén brought migrant populations from other regions of the country within the rationalities of decentralized rule linked to the entrenchment of the Army in the *departamento*. A techno-scientific lexicon of expertise on agricultural matters was combined with hierarchical Army structure in the pursuit of modernity and progress. These operations of governmentality were linked to the emergence of new subjects, whose conduct became the object of interventions drawing distinctions between the deserving and underserving through discourses of gender, ethnic, and religious difference. The racism and violence inherent in FYDEP's operations are illustrated very clearly in the published chronicles provided by FYDEP employees (Samayoa Rivera n.d.) and the interview materials noted above.

Cooperatives, Catholics, and *Comuneros*

In the mid-1970s, the cooperatives that had been created as a "human wall"—to stave off the perceived threat of Mexican annexation—were organizing as *Comunidades Católicas* (for example, CEH 1999, Annex I, Volume I, Case I). The impetus for this new form of community association was given by Catholic priests based in Petén, whose religious practice was informed by Liberation Theology.[23] In an interview, a *catequista* (catechist) and later *guerrillero* remembered his religious and political concientization thus:

> There was a group of priests here in Petén, the majority of them were from Spain and some from the United States. They stayed with the people (*con el pueblo*), giving them orientations (*orientandoles*) toward . . . well, they would say that they raise up in arms (*que se levantaran en armas*), but in the courses (*cursos*) they would administer to us they would say that one had to fight because the kingdom of God was here on earth and we should not wait for anything beyond, on the contrary, that [it] is here that we have to construct the kingdom of God (*reino de Dios*). Let's try to better our condition (*vivir mejor*), to live well, to live in peace, God is just and God gave the world for everybody, not for one individual alone. So that is how we progressively raised our consciousness (*conscientizandose*) [acquired class consciousness].

Cooperatives, however, were soon the target of Army intimidation to the extent that many who lived in them resolved to flee over the border and into Mexico. A resident in one of the cooperatives remembered events during our conversation.

> Of those who lived here, many left. They said, we don't like the cooperative, so we will leave, and they left and the conflict started among those who stayed behind, there were those who wanted/supported the [idea of the] cooperative, and those who did not want cooperatives. Many left, others resisted, and others still went to live on the other side of the stream. And in the meantime, the issue of the conflict, of the war, was already there more or less, there were the questions of politics (*asuntos políticos*), not so much the Army, but rather the guerrilla, well one would hear, I heard it very often, as one would hear that people were gathering on behalf of the guerrilla. And that at

> the same time, it was said that there were ears (*orejas*) and that there was a group that was working cooperatively [as a cooperative], and that the Army was controlling that group the most, and that there was a list (*listado*) they had of a group already, and more than anything else, we started realizing that it was us.

Surveillance and intimidation were soon replaced by violent Army incursions into villages. As the resident of a cooperative on the Usumacinta River recalled,

> The time came when I had my *trabajadero* [cultivated plot of land] and I was working and I had my *milpa* [maize crop] this high, around the month of June, when I went back [to the village] at about ten in the morning, everyone had left for the other side, for Mexico, because in Arbolito [cooperative] they had already massacred, and as they were saying that there was a list here, that the Army had a list and that most of all was the group of, because they would not call us "*cooperativistas*," they would call us "*comuneros*," "*comuneros*" they would say, they would not say the word "*comunista*" directly, and rather "*comuneros*," they would say. I, seeing that people had left, we also left for the other side, to Mexico. June 1981 is when we had to leave for the first time. On the other side, a person arrived who had been wounded in Arbolito, he arrived there with us, they had fired a shot here and it had exited here, but he didn't die, but he had to spend eight days in the jungle, wounded, and when they managed to locate him, he had worms already, it was very difficult to cure him. Well, there the Mexican authorities got us out, because when we returned here [they were sent back to Guatemala], there was nobody left there [in Mexico], the people who got there got there by plane, we were thrown back here.[24]

Despite the violence suffered at the hands of the Army, community leaders recalled that at the time, they had no knowledge of *la guerrilla*. As they put it, "para nosotros la guerrilla todavían no existían directamente," that is, "for us, the guerrilla did not exist yet." Three months later, however, they were forced to flee their communities again under the threat of Army violence. The Army had mistaken a man for a *guerrillero* and had ordered him to lead them to the *campamento guerrillero*, the guerrilla base camp. As the community leader remembered, seeing a neighbor approach in Army uniform, it was clear to him they would have to leave everything behind and move fast. As they ran into the forest, fellow villagers gathered (*concentrar en la selva*) and eventually came across the guerrilla. The guerrilla, however, said they could not protect them. It was September 1981.

Routes in the Ethnographic Present

In contemporary Petén, most people come from somewhere else. For some Peteneros, this "elsewhere" may be a few kilometers around the lake. They may live in San Benito, the urbanized conglomerate that extends up to the northwestern shores of Lake Petén Itzá, and yet have come from El Remate, a village on the northeastern shore. They may say that once upon a time they were able to live off the land. The fertile soil for the *milpa* (maize crop) produced two *cosechas* (harvests) a year and other crops such as *frijol* (beans) and *ayote* (pumpkin) could be cultivated in the *rancho* and sold to the wealthy families of Flores, or in the market in Santa Elena. On the site of their *gran platanal* (area for plantain cultivation, approximately thirty trees) is now the incongruous meadow, looking like a cricket ground, of the Hotel Camino Real International. Years before, pressure to sell the land to the local developers and subsequent explicit threats (*amenazas*) resulted in a meager one-off payment that supported the move to San Benito. Manual wage work thus replaced subsistence agriculture, and yet from a *canoa* (canoe), one can still see some of the plantain trees on the lakeshore.

The distance people have traveled to come and settle in Petén may have been a much longer journey that extended beyond the administrative boundaries of the *departamento*. For *Sureños* (Southerners), those "*de Oriente*" (from the eastern regions), or Q'eqchi' from the highlands of Alta Verapaz, the journey may have been undertaken long ago, and people may care to mention a *departamento* and the *municipio* (municipality), rather than the town or *aldea* (village/hamlet) of "origin." People in Petén may also have come from Europe or the United States. The long-standing presence of itinerant tourists has most recently acquired a new type of fellow foreign migrant. Post-1996, personnel of multilateral and non-governmental agencies have also come to settle more or less permanently and in relative comfort. Tourists, however, stick to their own routes, to and from ancient Maya archaeological sites and to and from Mexico and *los cayos* (quays) of Belize, while *gringo* personnel roam around in four-wheel drives and reach the most remote *aldeas* on "serious business." Like colonial officials, they take great pride in illustrating the extent and purpose of their worthwhile activities, aided by sinister maps tracking their "coverage" and influence. What *gringos* share is access to privileged forms of travel.

Petén is and has been a site of more or less permanent residence, of struggles over land and resources, of legal and illegal trades, and, crucially, of travel. In and through Petén, people move willingly or unwillingly, voluntarily or forced, for different reasons and to different effects. Goods are bartered, traded, and smuggled. There are routes of commerce to and from *aldeas*, the *cabecera* of Flores (administrative capital of the region), and the *municipios* and market towns of Santa Elena, San Benito, Santa Ana, Dolores, Poptún, San Luis, San Francisco, Sayaxché, and La Libertad. People venture farther afield, beyond the boundaries of the *departamento* to Izabal, Alta Verapaz, and Guatemala City, and to Mexico and Belize. In 1999–2000, three transport companies managed the human traffic from Petén to the capital, exposing en route social stratification based on the class of travel one is able to afford. One may travel on buses of La Pinita or purchase a ticket for any of the differently priced buses of La Fuente del Norte. Wealth affords you a trip on La Línea Dorada. The fast, colossal, and air-conditioned Golden Line buses with uniformed attendants are deemed to guarantee *gringo* tourists what is culturally acknowledged to constitute adequate comfort and security. Were there *asaltantes* (assailants) or *ladrones* (thieves) along the road, one cannot see how they would dare come in the way of the Golden Line.[25] On La Pinita, one can travel through La Libertad, chasing oil pipelines to Betel. In the direction of Frontera Corozal, and Mexico, one is likely to move in the company of *mojados*, the illegal migrants (literally, "wet ones") led through Petén by *coyotes*, the ringmasters leading the way to the ultimate trial, the United States/Mexican border.

Whatever the vehicle, many are and have been on the move. Migration in Petén consists of numerous displacements out of which people fashion a sense of permanence, subjectivity, and sociality. To localize these multi-sited constituencies and trace histories, subjectivities, and socialities, I also traveled. As noted by a Roman Catholic priest during our conversation,

> The reality of Petén is extremely complex. We should not reduce reality to the single factor of the war. There are a number of other factors that mark the contemporary reality of Petén. Perhaps, the overwhelming factor is not war, but rather "displacement" (*desarraigo*), that is, the configuration of a society, of some social collectives here in the *departamento*, an arrangement where social groups from the whole country are being joined, social groups that have come here due to different factors and for different reasons. Some came here searching for land, others have arrived fleeing from violence from *Oriente* or other parts of the country, they have come from Alta Verapaz to

> seek refuge from violence, others are *fugitivos de la justicia* (fleeing from the justice system), this is a refuge for people who have crimes on their shoulders. I think these are the important factors.

Tropes of indigeneity and settledness are antinomies of the ethnographic context I encountered. When these tropes surfaced, they did so independently of each other. In fact, *desarraigo*, or "displacement," was the trope most commonly deployed by my interlocutors, across the peripheral and transverse region of migrants who make up Petén. Indigenous and ladino ethnicities on the move constantly redraw the bounds of *ethnos* and of place (see Barth 1969). In July 2000 an ex-*comandante* of the Fuerzas Armadas Rebeldes drew an image of the country for me (Map 2.2) while discussing the history of the guerrilla organization and his own involvement in the insurgency. In trying to make sense of the movement and fluidity of the *comandante*'s narrative, I added my own notes on the edges of the drawing after the interview, conscious of the fact that any attempt to fix what had been said and what the drawing represented was an inept ethnographic stratagem.

In Petén I set out to follow a displacement within displacements. In 1999–2000, that is, four years after the signing of the Peace Accords and about eighteen months after the dismantling of the temporary residence camps set up and overseen by the Misión de Verificación Naciones Unidadas Guatemala (United Nations Verification Mission in Guatemala; MINUGUA), ex-*guerrilla* combatants were on the move. Many of those who for some time in their lives held association with the Fuerzas Armadas Rebeldes (FAR) settled in Petén. Most of these, while lacking a definite locus of belonging, were "coming home" to the *selva* (jungle) that had housed them during the war years. Others had not attended the *concentración* and never left Petén. Others still were traveling through the region having come from homes across national borders. A small number of those who had been active in the urban fronts or in the ranks ensconced in the Universidad San Carlos (San Carlos University) were visiting, for the first time, the land where their *compañeros y compañeras* had fought for years *en la montaña* (clandestinely). Others still, having spent the years of *La Insurgencia* (The Insurgency) attending to matters other than *la lucha armada* (armed struggle), were reunited with militant relatives and were contextually and privately acquiring quasi-ex-guerrilla status. Ex-*combatientes* of the Fuerzas Armadas Rebeldes appeared as a quintessentially displaced, itinerant, porous, and opaque constituency in a migratory region with old and new disputed external and internal borders,[26] the latter being the reminder that while sub-

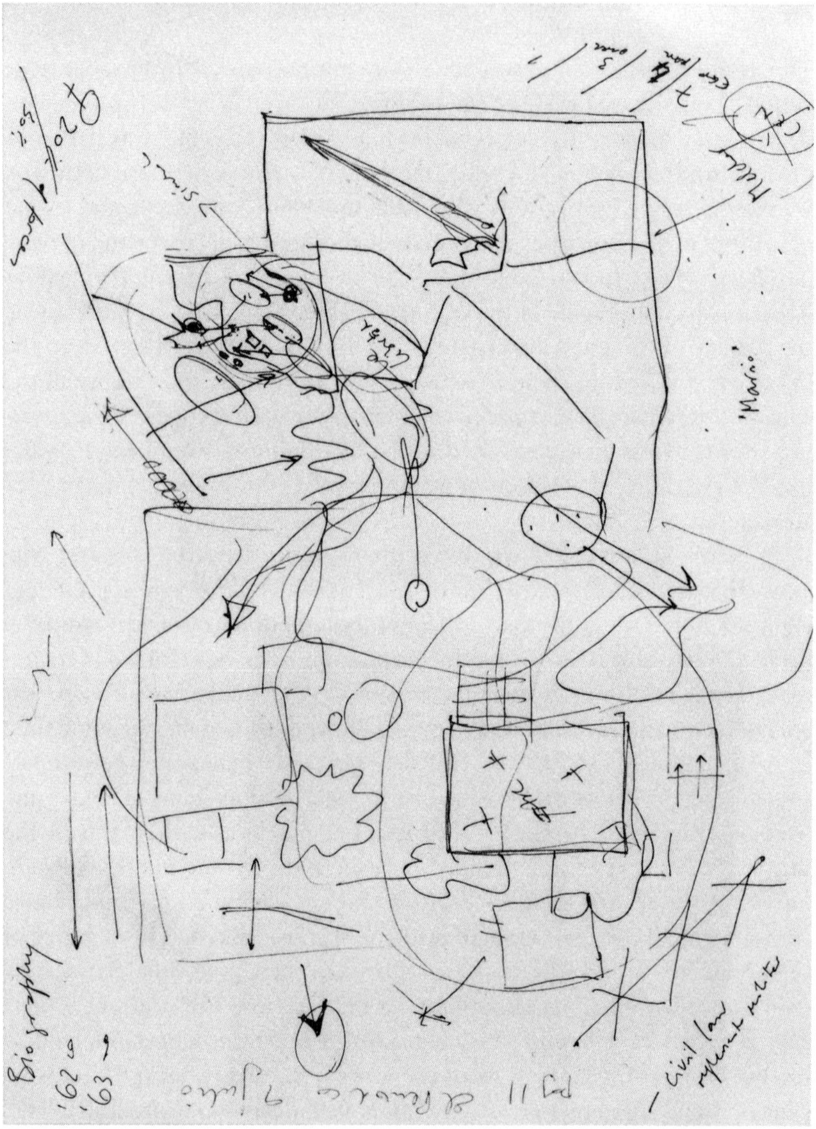

Map 2.2. Map of Guatemala drawn by an ex-*comandante* of the Fuerzas Armadas Rebeldes, Guatemala City, 2000.

jectivities may be in transit and socialities may be secretive and partial, the mark of empire had not disappeared: "porque los enemigos estaban latentes, como están ahora en lo que es la vida política, ellos nunca han descansado ni van a descansar," "as the enemies were latent/lurking then as they are now in political life, they have never rested and never rest," as a dispersed ex-combatant poignantly said. In these contexts, multi-sitedness stands for a reflexive awareness of the specific ethnographic and theoretical strategies through which anthropological knowledge comes into being (Marcus 1998). Multi-sitedness calls for a reconfiguration of the concept-metaphor of the "field" in and through which ethnographic practice is undertaken, in spatial, temporal, methodological, and epistemological terms. The delineation of what may constitute the "field" of fieldwork as much as the "field" of anthropology is a complex undertaking that relies on specific analytical and representational strategies to conjure up the object, subject, space, and time of study (Clifford 1988, Chapter 1; 1997; Fabian 1983; Fardon 1990; Gupta and Ferguson 1997; Hastrup 1990; 1995; Moore 1997a). Multi-sitedness, as theory and practice (Marcus 1998), must however necessarily confront the fact that the task of providing a context for the intelligibility of ethnographic subjects is already marked, if not overdetermined, by numerous teleologies and eschatologies. Thus, I take multi-sitedness here to refer to both an itinerant form of fieldwork that follows a fundamentally displaced constituency, that is, a research practice that "followed the people" (Marcus 1998), and a theoretical practice that traces routes through subjectivities and socialities marked by plural histories of conflict and cultures of secrecy, thus "following metaphors" (Marcus 1998). I traveled through Petén following *el desarraigo*, the traces of insurgency and guerrilla secrecy.

Widows, *Lavado*, and Death

Ethnography is a fragment of social reality (Clifford 1997), a shred of lived experience that, through specific representational practices, acquires a certain uncomfortable degree of permanence. One of the notable questions that arise out of the crystallization of the "field" is confronting previous processes of sedimentation with related silences and disavowals. In the case of women who, following the Peace Accords and in the context of an increasingly visible and hence easily surveilled civil society participation, identified themselves collectively as "widows," the conflict features prominently in their narratives of displacement.[27] In the 1980s, at the height of the counterinsurgency campaign waged by the Guatemalan government and Army against insurgents and civilians, migrants who had come from the east of the country in search of land, or who were fleeing earlier waves of Army violence, were making a living out of agricultural and/or commercial activities (*milpa* and *tiendas*) in Petén. However, their lives soon became embroiled in *La Violencia*. Personal rivalries or disagreements sometimes triggered episodes of violence, as personal disputes came to be settled by denouncing opponents to the Army as *guerrilleros*, and Army repression followed. Often, the suffering, intimidation, and murder inflicted by the Army on these settlers were seemingly random. Women remembered their experiences in conversations with me.

> In the beginning, we dreaded everything, with that fear, that apprehension, that trembling. Before, in the time when they would kill people, we didn't sleep. Before, they would haul up dead people into trucks, they would go and wash the trucks on the shore of the *aguada* around here,[28] they would kill many people. In those times, on the Naranjo route, they would kill many people, they would even destroy their animals, it was a great pity to see people in this predicament.
>
> We suffered greatly before, when there were those slaughters of people (*matazones*), we lived down below in a cooperative, we left and emerged in Sayaxché, and on and on and we came over here, but after that, they killed my two sons, so we stayed. They got it wrong, they were looking for somebody else, but they said it was them [my sons]. We were afraid before, the soldiers had us, if only you had seen it, we could not even talk or anything.
>
> We suffered greatly in those times, we used to go from one place to the next fleeing the shootings (*tirazones*), we were in a *finca* and then came here, always in Petén, we were in a *finca* far away, as one, being poor, has to work hard, so we were working there and had to come in this direction, leaving everything behind . . . Was that the Army? Well, one could not work it out (*atinar*), what we really feared were the shootings, we were not sure. Now my work is to look for laundry, and when I have no laundry, I prepare food, *tamales* to sell.
>
> It happened to me in 1981, I was living in the *parcela* of one of my sons-in-law. My son-in-law had an enemy (*enemigo*) to whom he owed 200 quetzales, so it was that man who started the trouble (*fregada*) . . . so the man who charged my son-in-law 200 quetzales said, he went to accuse [L's son-in-law] of being a *guerrillero* and in the night they came for him, but they did not find him, they found my son, because we were living in the same *parcela*. So it was him [L's son] whom they killed, they came at two in the morning, that was in 1981, at two in

> the morning, they dragged him out of the house, they dragged him out of bed, they killed him in the *patio* [courtyard] just like that, as they did not find my son-in-law, they killed him [L's son] unjustly. And from this it went on, because they told us that if we did not leave, they were going to kill us all. This happened around La Nueva Libertad. And the one who betrayed us, it was him who came to hand him over. Imagine, I recognized him, that man [on the night of the murder], that it was him, the enemy of my son-in-law. "So, he is not here? Then kill that boy." Well then, the Army therefore killed my son. What they said was that they were going to come back for us, so what we did was that we left, we left all that we had there to waste, the house and everything else, and they took much of what was there, as my daughter had a *tienda* (shop), they took all the money off her, they took everything there was in the *tienda*, they put everything in *costales* (sacks) and they took everything with them and they left us with nothing, utter thieves, and they killed my son, and four more from La Nueva Libertad, there in front of the house they killed them too, together with my son. Imagine how hard (*duro*) was that year, 1981. So we fled, we went to Mexico for two years, and when Ríos Montt came to power, we were told that one could draw near (*arrimar*), so we came back, after about two years.

Q'eqchi' *Revuelto* and *Tzuul Taq'as* in the Lowlands

Through apparent ethnographic serendipity and along the routes of ex-guerrilla secret socialities, I once met Oscarito, a Q'eqchi' FAR ex-combatant. He recalled a visit to Alta Verapaz, while in the FAR ranks, and gave an account of the ethnic configurations taking place in Petén.

> One day, during the war, I got to Alta Verapaz [from Petén]. Everything looked different (*diferente*) there. So I said to a man [in Q'eqchi'], may I have two chilies, and the man gave me four. I can't speak Q'eqchi' very well, I said, I come from Petén. That's okay, the man said, to say "two," you say *wiib*. Ah, so I said to him, I have almost lost/forgot (*perder*), as I can't speak Q'eqchi' anymore. And how is Petén, the man asked me. Ah, it's very pretty (*bonito*), just like the area around Panzós [in Alta Verapaz]. We have to recognized we cannot speak properly anymore . . . they are pure Q'eqchi' (*puro Q'eqchi'*) in Alta Verapaz, we speak scrambled Q'eqchi' (*Q'eqchi' revuelto*[29]). We are all scrambled up (*revueltos*) in Petén.

According to Oscarito, Petén was a site of scrambled ethnicities and scrambled Q'eqchi' indigeneity. On my way to visit an acquaintance, I sat on the *camioneta* (bus) and followed the unraveling of oil pipelines on the side of the road, to my destination. Once in the village, I looked for the person I had come to see and eventually ended up talking to one of the elders. Don Luis told me there were five *tzuul taq'as* (beings of the mountains) in the vicinity. Four were located within a two-kilometer radius, the closest at five hundred meters from the settlement. A fifth *tzuul taq'a*, Doña Rosa, was known to exist but the location had not yet been revealed. Don Luis told me the names of the *tzuul taq'as* and said he would take me to the *cueva* (cave) Don Andrés. On the way, we picked up Eulalio, who also wanted to go. The three of us walked in a southwesterly direction for about half an hour across slightly hilly terrain, extricating ourselves from *milpa* and *monte*. We reached a small hill, and Don Luis pointed to an opening on the slope, paused, and took off his shoes. Out of his bag he drew candles and a bundle of *pom* (incense). He gave a candle to me and one to Eulalio. He held one himself, did the sign of the cross, and said he would recite a *Padre Nuestro, Ave María*, and *Gloria*. He prayed very quietly, did the sign of the cross again, and entered the cave. Don Luis lit our candles, knelt down, and started to pray. While Don Luis prayed, he lit the *pom* and the cave was slowly filled with scent and smoke. He prayed for about ten minutes, then stood up and showed us the spots where they lay the candles when they "did *mayejak*."[30] He said he started using colored candles after having attended a *cursillo* (course, workshop) in La Libertad. Before then, the candles he used were the color of untreated wax. He showed us the spots for the candles and said they were located at the four cardinal points, *entrada y salida del sol, entrada y salida del aire*, entrance and exit of the sun, and entrance and exit of the air/wind. We walked around the cave and inspected the stalactites. Don Luis showed us a trap for *tepezcuintles* (large wild rodents). He said people discovered the cave while hunting. Don Luis told me that only the *cheekel winq* (male elders) visited Don Andrés Cave, while *las señoras no conocen hasta allá*, the ladies don't know the site. I wondered about my status, *ixq* (woman), *winq* (man), young or old, or just foreign. Perhaps *gringa* overrides gender and age in some instances.[31] Don Luis was seventy-two and had lived in the village for eleven years. During the war, he said, the *mayejak* had been banned. However, when he moved to the village, he knew the *tzuul taq'as* were alive (*vivos*). He had known through a dream. The identities and locations of the *tzuul taq'as* were revealed to the *chekel winq* and *chekel ixq* in dreams. Don Luis told me that

Figure 2.1. *Tzuul taq'as* in the lowlands, photograph by the author, Petén 2000.

despite the *cursillo* he attended in La Libertad, he did not like the idea of using candles of different colors. The *sacerdote Maya* (Maya priest) said there is no God (*Dios*), only *tzuul taq'a*, and that they should only be concerned with the *tzuul taq'a*. This we did not like, said Don Luis. To find out more about the dream, I should speak to Don Colax.[32]

While Oscarito had pointed to the "scrambled" character of Q'eqchi' identity in Petén and the loss of linguistic proficiency, Don Luis had dreamt the location and names of the *tzuul taq'as* soon after settling in the community in Petén. Don Luis worried about Q'eqchi' culture, but did not strictly fear a progressive ladinoization and related loss of Q'eqchi' cultural and linguistic proficiency. Rather, his unequivocal dissent focused on formulations of Pan-Mayanism with its newly fashioned religious orthodoxies and homogenized Pan-Maya religious practices. He objected to the suggestion that candles used in religious practice should be of different colors, when he had always used plain wax candles. Similarly, he did not see why practices related to the *tzuul taq'as* should be at odds with his belief in God, as the Maya priest had argued.

Histories of insurgency, counterinsurgency, and multiple *desarraigos* (displacements) in and through Petén haunt the records. With opacity and transience in mind, social and cultural analysis must address the multiple histories of violence and the related cultures of secrecy that have unraveled from the second half of the twentieth century to the present day in Petén. It is through multi-sitedness, as a methodological and analytical strategy, that contingency and partiality emerge to qualify the ethnographic subjects, including the researcher. Multi-sitedness also requires that ad hoc epistemological and representational strategies be devised to counteract ontologies of presence and make space for partial, scrambled, complex, and unelucidable ethnographic subjects.

Contemporary *Desarraigos*: The Maya Biosphere Reserve

Histories of governmentality in Petén and their links to violence, conflict, and displacement did not end with the dismantlement of FYDEP in 1989. In 1990, the Guatemalan government with the support of international donors, notably USAID (United States Agency for International Development), created the Reserva de la Biósfera Maya (RBM; Maya Biosphere Reserve) with the objective of preserving the tropical humid forest and the important archaeological remains scattered across it. A government institution was also established, namely the Consejo Nacional de Áreas Protegidas (National Council of Protected Areas; CONAP) to oversee the complex administration, management, and surveillance of the newly "protected" territories. The Maya Biosphere includes eight core areas known as *zonas núcleo*, where no human settlement is permitted. Among these are the archaeological site of Tikal, the Laguna del Tigre National Park, and the Sierra del Lacandón National Park. A buffer zone known as *zona de amortigüamiento* and a multiple-uses zone, known as *zona de usos multiples*, where human activity is permitted, are also part of the Biosphere and fall under CONAP's aegis (see Posocco 2008).[33] CONAP's operations are complemented by the operations of local and international non-governmental organizations (Sundberg 1998). Overall, the Maya Biosphere covers 21,000 square kilometers, equivalent to 68 percent of the overall surface of Petén (Grünberg 2001, 99; see also Perera 1993). Analyses concerning the rationale and management of the Maya Biosphere are often predicated on discourses about the "advancement of the agricultural frontier" (Effatin and Elías 2002; Grünberg 2001; Hayes et al. 2002), and the "population explosion" that has seemingly characterized demographic patterns in Petén in the past thirty years. In fact, population estimates for the region of Petén are highly contested and profoundly politicized. In current debates, they are underpinned by discourses concerning the progressive disappearance of a "forest society" (Schwartz 1990) of sparse native populations engaged in shifting agriculture and forest extraction activities such as rubber tapping, and concerning the relentless expansion of the agricultural frontier at the hands of land-thirsty migrants construed as responsible for deforestation, soil erosion, and dented biodiversity (Sundberg 2003). Despite acute critique of this position (Sundberg 2003), neo-Malthusian sentiments can be found in analyses that point to the exponential growth of the population of Petén and construe such growth as a problem in need of governmental intervention, quantification, and management (see, for example, Grandia 2000).[34] Citing government statistics, Carr (2001, 365) states that "[s]ince the 1960s, the population of Petén has grown explosively from a few *chicleros* (rubber tappers) to approximately 600,000 people." Most demographic growth is imputed to migration of landless *campesinos* to Petén from other areas of the country in search of land.

In 2000, I was told that three *comunidades* (settlements) had been evicted from one of the *zonas núcleo* of the Maya Biosphere and moved to a "temporary" site. The municipal authorities had promised that sufficient water would be supplied to the community by means of a water truck, until an agreement was reached as to a satisfactory resettlement. When I visited them, the representatives of the communities explained that they had been evicted from core areas, where no human activity was permitted under the law that governs human settlement in and around the Maya Biosphere. I was told the three communities had been settled there for four years. They had first fled their villages following a massacre and since then they had moved across the land, looking for a place where they could plant and harvest maize. For a time, they had settled in a *finca*, but Army repression was still raging, and many of their relatives had died there. As one representative said, "We have suffered greatly, as if we were a pregnant person desiring things that we don't have within our reach, when I think of that it gives me *tristeza* (sadness, anguish). The Army took us out and we went to the *monte*, they persecuted us as if we were animals."

As we talked, it emerged that many of the men had been guerrilla combatants. One of them asked whether I wanted to see his *carnet de desmovilización* (demobilization card), and I replied that of course it was not necessary. We spoke of acquaintances we had in common and I was asked to give their regards to some of the ex-combatants I was due to see. The news of communities being evicted from the Maya Biosphere was not unusual during the course of my fieldwork, although the sight of the population of

Figure 2.2. Drying *chile* and *pepitoria* in a Q'eqchi' village in the Maya Biosphere Reserve, photograph by the author, Petén 2000.

three entire villages being made new refugees was new to me. Rolando, ex-FAR combatant, had spoken of how communities had been made into "invaders" and were evicted from their homes. We were discussing how difficult the resettlement had been for communities of returnees from Mexico, when he said:

> This was the first problem with the communities of returnees, the quality of food [aid] was terrible (*terrible*), the maize that would arrive was not good to eat (*llegaba el maíz que no era bueno para comer*). And, now, imagine, there is a group who is currently being moved, and without any support/aid (*apoyo*). Well, there is support of sorts, from the Fondo de Tierra and CONAP, who are interested that they move (*salir*) from where they are because they are in a protected area (*área protegida*). They [Fondo de Tierra and CONAP] say that they will support the move (*translado*), and perhaps some aid enough for how many families there are. There are between forty-two and forty-four families. They were settled within the buffer zone (*zona de amortigüa-*

> *miento*). They had to leave their village, as they were accused of being invaders (*los acusaron de invasores*). They wanted to evict them (*desalojar*), but they were fighting not to have to leave (*estaban luchando de no salir de allí*). And despite the fact that they [Fondo de Tierra and CONAP] would evict them, they [the community] would return to the site. They cultivate maize and earn a living with the logging trade (*venta de leña*). They are wood loggers (*cortan la madera*). So that when one visits, one sees all the trunks (*leña*) there, on the side of the road, that's how they make a living.[35]

In 2000, Petén was the site of new displacements brought on by the regime of governmentality that had replaced the FYDEP era. There appeared to be new systems of governmentality and new practices of surveillance. For instance, an international non-governmental organization held a database of profiles of 196 settlements located within the Maya Biosphere, detailing name and type of settlement, ethnicity, language, provenance, community organization, date of foundation, access to water, health, education, economic activities, land tenure, accessibility, population, and so forth. The *Base de Datos Sobre Población, Tierra y Medio Ambiente en la Reserva de la Biósfera Maya: Petén, Guatemala* (Grünberg and Ramos 1999) was published with the aims of "documenting the great diversity of *sociedad campesina* in the north of Petén, which is part of the ecosystems of the region and which is transforming them in their new habitat; promoting a realistic vision of the agricultural and cattle-farming frontier of Petén to realize an agrarian policy that is consistently directed toward the socio-environmental consolidation of Petén; divulging knowledge about *comunidades campesinas* who migrated to Petén in search of a permanent space for life and peace" (Grünberg and Ramos 1999, Introduction). It cannot have occurred to the authors that their seemingly benevolent aims were in fact the mark of the role increasingly assumed by non-governmental organizations in surveillance of the population, and that the database itself may amount to most elegant intelligence.

New technologies of surveillance were also emerging as increasingly relevant, notably NASA technology of remote sensing increasingly deployed to monitor human activity in the territories of the Maya Biosphere Reserve and related environmental change and deforestation (see Hayes et al. 2002). Everyone's activities in Petén were being surveilled from space through new technoscientific instruments and regimes of visuality and detection (Haraway 1991).

Figure 2.3. Petén and Star Wars Imaginaries. Illustration of the "Time-series Forest Change, Land Cover/Land Use Conversion, and the Socio-economic Driving Forces in the Petén District, Guatemala," carried out within the Land-Cover Land-Usage Change (LCLUC) interdisciplinary scientific theme of the Earth Science Enterprise (ESE) of the United States National Aeronautics and Space Administration (NASA). The satellite is shown hovering over the archaeological site of Tikal. Reproduced by kind permission of Professor Steven Sader.

Conclusion: Complexity and Plurality in Context

The tasks of social and cultural analysis have been, historically, understanding and representing the partiality, complexity, and disruptions of regions like Petén. In some traditions, social, cultural, and historical processes—like those that characterized social life in Petén—have been figured through coherent wholes and entities, strong narrative histories, and discrete geographical locations. In my figuring of the social reality of Petén, I have opted for a different analytical strategy and one that seeks to represent the overlapping complexities that produced the region of Petén. However, histories of colonization, militarization, violence, and displacement have not been equated with any notion of social breakdown. Rather than relying on meta-narratives that presuppose continuity and that posit permanence and stability as necessary conditions for the functioning of the social realm and for its representation, I have stressed complexity and "plurality in context." The emphasis on multiple, rather than singular, trajectories of social change—their multifaceted interactions and effects—is still underpinned by theoretical models. Social and cultural analysis has imagined plurality in different perspectives and scales. Theories have often been systemic, that is, they have figured the social and cultural realm to be made up of coherent units such as the "community," the "ethnic group," and the "*municipio.*" Systemic models are being progressively supplanted by theoretical models that emphasize fragmentation within and between units—with the effect that units increasingly appear to be porous entities that contain plurality within, and produce plurality without, in complex ways (Moore 2004). In the next chapter I consider the limits of claims of plurality further and explore the condition of possibility for thinking in post-plural scales, testing the potential of post-plural models of the social and cultural realm for the analysis of secrecy in post–Peace Accords Petén.

3
Secrecy, Relation, Connection

¡Identifíquese compañera!
Identify yourself, comrade!

Introduction

This chapter opens with a discussion of an ethnographic moment of partial disclosure, when I first realized that ex-combatants deployed different names for themselves and others and that names qualified different, multiple, and complex relationalities. I discuss naming practices and argue that whatever the scale, through names, pseudonyms, and nicknames partial relations and connections were established. Connections may have been articulated positively through disclosure, or occurred through negation and foreclosure, but led to connections nonetheless. I also consider names and naming practices in relation to secrecy, and the implications of secrecy for guerrilla hermeneutics of the Other, and for knowledge practices more broadly. I argue that while guerrilla naming practices may be thought of as holographic, guerrilla secrecy engendered forms of connective relativization. The guerrilla secret subjectivities and socialities, and related partialities and connectivities, require relinquishing appeals to a plurality of discrete cultural/social entities and subjects to envision instead post-plural scales. The scales of post-plurality exhibit specific temporal qualities and ever-shifting horizons that may be imagined as a performative operation through which the conditions of possibility for resignification and a break with context are enabled.

Positionality and Difference, Partiality and Connection

In the early stages of fieldwork in a community of Fuerzas Armadas Rebeldes (FAR) ex-combatants and their families, I learned about community life, having been granted permission to visit the settlement regularly by the Junta Directiva, that is, the group of community members randomly selected (*sortear*) out of a pool of candidates. Members of the Junta Directiva were appointed on a fixed-term basis and took on legal responsibility for the running of the settlement. To ensure continuity and to limit the loss of experienced members, only about half of the Junta Directiva was replaced by new appointments every year. In accordance with Guatemalan national law, the structure of the Junta Directiva reflected the legal requirements that applied to cooperatives and any other association or group that wished to manage funds and that therefore must seek legal recognition. A president, vice-president, secretary, treasurer, and two administrators (*vocales*) made up the Junta Directiva. *Alcaldes auxiliares* (auxiliary mayors) also worked closely with the Directiva. In this community, where the population was made up of mainly FAR ex-*guerrilleros/as* and their families, there were a number of additional committees. The Comité de Trabajo (Work Committee) for instance, was dedicated to the organization of collective daily labor. Although labor (*actividades productivas*, productive activities) was organized collectively, the Comité de Trabajo allocated time for individuals to undertake household-based work and subsistence agriculture. Other committees were the Comité de Jovenes (Youth Committee), coordinating activities for and by the youngsters, and the Comité pro-Mejoramiento (Committee for Improvement) in charge of planning the economic and social development of the community. The Comité de Seguridad (Security Committee) had responsibility for security matters but also dealt with unforeseen crises such as forest fires encroaching on community land during the dry season. The Comité de Mujeres (Women's Committee) successfully lobbied the Work Committee to take into account women's triple burden of domestic, collective, and political work. As a result, women who were full members and *beneficiarias*, that is, who had formal and legal status as members of the cooperative, were granted shorter collective labor shifts. Temporary committees such as the Comité pro-Feria were instituted to coordinate activities for the celebration of the first anniversary of the community.

When the community was founded, subsistence agriculture had also been collectively managed. Agricultural collectivization was, however, short-lived, as agricultural techniques were taken to be a key signifier of (cultural) difference. There was general agreement that agricultural work was culturally specific and that the plurality of views on how to best approach "agricultural" tasks such as planting and harvesting was ultimately too difficult to manage collectively, notably in a multicultural community such as the one at hand. As a result of the perceived unmanageable quality of "agri-cultural" difference, it was decided that plots of land be given to *beneficiarios/as*, and that households be responsible for their own subsistence. Some ex-*guerrilleros/as* argued that individualization of "agri-culture" amounted to positive engagement on the part of the ladino majority and an example of ladino acknowledgment of the "agri-cultural" difference among them, and the difference of the indigenous minority—notably of the Q'eqchi' presence. In short, the ladino majority had allowed for Q'eqchi' cultural practices related to the *milpa* (maize crop) to take place and had resisted implementation of policies of assimilation. During the planting season, Q'eqchi' families followed the patterns of labor recruitment noted by Wilson (1995). Q'eqchi' men went to the fields together and all took part in planting each other's plots. Women worked collectively to prepare the food for the celebration that followed the planting. To my knowledge, no *yo'lek* (vigil for the maize seeds; see Wilson 1995) was held. However, having regularly visited the Q'eqchi' households and asked numerous questions about Q'eqchi' culture and language, the families kindly invited me to attend the celebration and I followed events with the women. No one else from outside the Q'eqchi' community was present at the celebration. When I subsequently asked whether anyone knew that the day was of great importance to the Q'eqchi' families in the village, no non-Q'eqchi' person seemed to know about it. In the light of this, I would argue that the decision to overturn collective running of "agri-cultural" activities and opt for atomized "agri-cultural" practices may in fact amount to an extremely partial form of ladino engagement with indigenous difference.

In the early stages of fieldwork in this community of FAR ex-*guerrilleros/as* and their families, I became aware of ex-*guerrilleros/as* addressing one another by means of pseudonyms (*pseudónimos*) and nicknames (*apodos*). Pseudonyms and nicknames became of increasing relevance as I tried to arrange and schedule interviews. Abiding by the initial agreement I had entered into with the Junta Directiva of the settlement in question,[1] community leaders would arrange for interviewees to be relieved from the responsibilities of collectively organized daily labor so that they would have the time to converse with me. I would be told that on a given day, say, Pedrito would be available. I would thus look for Pedrito only to find, in the preliminary stages of the exchange, that the person I was conversing with was *not* "Pedrito." He did not introduce himself by this name, despite the fact that everyone in the community addressed him as such. On this particular occasion, Pedrito introduced himself by a first name, second name, paternal surname, and maternal surname. He did concede that he had several pseudonyms, but he chose not to elaborate on these or answer to the nickname by which he was known in the community. While it seemed that in-

Figure 3.1. Ex-combatant inspecting crop failure, photograph by the author, Petén, 2000.

dividuals were *and* were not their names, there were reasons for Pedrito *not* to be Pedrito in the course of the interview.

Gringa Positionalities, *Gringa* Differences

In the first set of interviews in this community, I had the distinct impression that the relations between my interlocutors and myself were characterized by a formality that went beyond mutual lack of acquaintance. Interlocutors would answer questions with the deferent attitude and rhetoric that in Guatemala is often reserved for those perceived to occupy a superior position in the multifarious hierarchies (Casaús Arzú 1995; Grandin 2000; Schwartz 1990) relative to one's subordinate gendered, ethnicized, classed, and racialized positionality. I seemed to be eliciting formal responses to the effect that I attributed the ensuing relational distance to that hierarchical (mis-)placement on the part of subjects thoughtfully noted by Nelson (1999, Chapter 2) in her discussion of "gringa positioning" in the context of her own fieldwork in urban Guatemala. Specifically, Nelson's analysis of "how being a *gringa* anthropologist is both power-filled and a wounded body politic, and how that identity is formed in relation with multiple others" (Nelson 1999, 41) seemed very much to the point.[2]

Drawing on the work of Abigail Adams (1997), Nelson notes that *gringo* "is generally a negative term, and few Guatemalans would be so churlish as to call you a gringo to your face . . . *Gringo* is defined as 'disparaging' in the dictionary and carries a burden of hatred. A possibly apocryphal origin story attributes Mexican coinage during the U.S. invasion, as a way to tell the green-uniformed yanquis to go away ('green-go!')" (Nelson 1999, 63).

"*Gringo*" thus evokes questions of positionality, difference, and power in that, as Adams (1997) points out, the term is articulated on the relational grounds between the United States and Latin America: "a North American is not a gringo until she crosses a border" (Adams 1997, quoted in Nelson 1999, 41). "'Gringo' is a category produced through interactions, and as such, it works on a variety of borders including but not limited to national frontiers, stereotypes of phenotypic difference, sartorial codes and—as 'gringa' (marked by the Spanish feminine)—gender boundaries" (Nelson 1999, 41).

The instantiation of gringo subjectivity and locatedness is therefore enmeshed in the geopolitical hegemonic historicities that link Latin America to the United States (Mirandé 1987), a power-laden relationality that also impinges on transnational relations of solidarity between North American activists and Guatemalans in struggle (Nelson 1999). More specifically, the derogatory inflection and related ambivalence inherent in the term *gringo* produce, according to Adams, a certain "failure of rapport" (Adams 1997, quoted in Nelson 1999, 63), to the effect that for *gringa* anthropologists in the field and activists alike, "open-armed welcome may be more pragmatic than personal, more tied to historically specific tactical needs than one's 'niceness.' We often *fail* in attempts to identify with the Guatemalan people and to differentiate ourselves from our government, from tourists . . . Quincentennial Guatemala offers special challenges for gringa self-fashioning" (Nelson 1999, 62–3; my emphasis).

The issues at stake in the deployment of the term *gringo/a* may partly be those of identification, location, and negative relationality, if not relational "failure" as such. So, although one may not share the identificatory labor of having to differentiate oneself from "one's" United States government, one may nevertheless have to reckon with a range of homogenizing assumptions about one's sense of "ownership," "belonging," and "location." Given the centrality of reflexivity as a set of knowledge practices tied to offering an account of oneself, and despite—or perhaps because of—the seemingly inescapable multiple overdeterminations of the self, one may feel compelled to forcefully and yet quixotically oppose a discursive framing that makes wounds into simulacra (Baudrillard 1988) to be attributed to hyper-real *gringa* bodies,[3] as the sites of hyper-real privilege and narcissistic solipsism. Ultimately, at the heart of the question, and at the center of such a seemingly antagonistic work of (self-)differentiation, however, is the refractory quality of the anthropologist's location, subjectivity, and positionality in contemporary anthropological analysis (Moore 1997a), and in related fashion, the unelucidable quality of *gringa* as a category of difference and catachresis.

Thus, while at one level the elaboration of "*gringa* positioning" signals a sensitivity to questions of subjectivity and location, this may easily become tied to a new set of homogenizing assumptions concerning, for instance, the assumed link between *gringa* identity and the United States. In turn, the terms of the discussion on *gringa* identity incite a specific order of objections, the most immediate being that of having to appeal to the multiplicity of understandings and usages of the term *gringa* in one's experience in the field. Thus, one may wish to note that in contemporary Guatemala the epithet *gringo* marks European as much as North American bodies and selves and it does so contextually, often with ironic purpose rather than affront. *Gringa* therefore marks bodies and selves who are perceived as foreign *and* geopolitically privileged, as well as female. To further dislodge the link between *gringa-ness* and the United States, and to point to the ways in which one may have strategically tested the discursive and relational boundaries of the term, attempted to "set the record straight," and/or hoped to deserve any epithet but the relentless *gringa*-calling, I would often say, naively, "La verdad es, yo soy de Europa," "The truth is, I am from Europe."

On occasions, I tried to substantiate this fundamentally brittle and thoroughly unsatisfactory statement by tracing on the ground unsteady contours of selected continents imagined through dubious unearthly perspectives. The improbable quality of those shapes and the relations between them forced me to dig myself into even deeper trenches: "Soy de Italia y de Inglaterra," "I am from Italy and England."

So, it turned out, I was from Italy and England, singular European-ness instantly splitting into two genealogies of affect and belonging and still not exhaustive of the complexity I wished to convey in my refutation of *gringa* homogenization. So strong is the desire to convey the complexities of one's sense of affinity, belonging, and location, that one catches oneself in the act of mobilizing essential categories of identity (Braidotti 1994; Spivak 1988; 1999) to at once resist all manner of homogenization, including the quality of *gringa-ness* imputed by one's interlocutors in the field. In so doing, however, one runs the risk of upholding the fallacious terms on which the debate over the status of *gringa* positionality is predicated, and once again bringing up the question of whether, beyond differences between "anthropologists and their informants, or perhaps between anthropologists," what may need addressing are the differences "within each anthropologist" (Moore 1997a, 131).

Some of my youngest interlocutors in the field were already marking differences between, as much as differences within, as to them I was not just *any gringa*. I was, rather aptly, "*la gringa pelona*," or I was the *gringa* with no hair.[4] There was possibly no need on my part to try and set any record straight to begin with, as at least my *gringa* credentials were already queer, plural, between, and within. In the chapter "Situated Knowledges: The Science Question in Feminism and the Privilege of Partial Perspective," Donna Haraway has argued for an ontology of the subject that focuses on "splitting" rather than "being," adding that "[t]he topography of subjectivity is multidimensional . . . The knowing self is partial in all its guises, never finished, whole, simply there and original; it is always constructed and stitched together imperfectly, and *therefore* able to join with another" (Haraway 1991, 193).

The multidimensional and multilayered qualities of difference are therefore not just the ground for ever-increasing and ever-deepening differentiation. Beyond enumeration of the plurality inherent in *gringa* positionality, the task seems to lie in analyses of the ways in which difference and partiality are *not* markers of relational failures and relational foreclosures. The task at hand is, then, that of tracing the ways in which difference and partiality may be markers of connection, in whatever manner relationality may come to be articulated. In what follows, I aim to show that connection may be variously articulated, and that with reference to secrecy, connection may occur through relational partiality and connective relativization.

Scales of Secrecy

In the light of this, it seems important to further dwell on the aspect of Nelson's argument that focuses on the relational instantiation of the anthropologist's locatedness in the field.[5] In convergence with Nelson, I felt constrained by the way I was being hierarchically (re-)positioned/(mis-)placed, and bestowed with status that I thought I did not command. I was therefore concerned to find a more or less direct way through those asymmetrical orderings and distant privileged relationalities seemingly set up in my favor by the ever-more agentic subjects of interlocution. In a context characterized by plural histories of conflict and cultures of secrecy, no degree or amount of "self-fashioning," even of the relational kind, is to any avail, when confronted with the agentic subject (Other).[6] The realization that in the initial interview settings those who agreed to be interviewed were not actually interviewees came only retrospectively. In those exchanges, it is very likely that *I* was the interviewee—a perspective/prospective *compañera*?—and hence the one actually and actively being questioned. The first interviews were the last of a series of more or less subtle procedures that I retrospectively think I was made to undergo, as in this specific instance the community, and indeed Pedrito, considered what degree of concealment and disclosure would characterize our relations.

When actually straying on that assumed quintessential terrain of closure that Nelson herself noted and elegantly marked with parenthetic occlusion in her statement that "in Guatemala we encountered . . . almost shocking openness (except, of course, as regarded guerrilla affiliation)" (Nelson 1999, 43), "the pragmatics of open-armed welcome" seems to require further analysis, premising that there may be more to "openness" and "open-armed welcomes" than historically specific "tactical needs" (Nelson 1999, 62–3; see also Nelson 2009). A glimpse of the proliferation of names and the ambiguous hierarchical strictures of the initial ethnographic relationality that I experienced testify to the presence of more or less rigidly "guarded secrets" (Simmel 1906) among the seemingly bounded constituency at hand.

In his essay on secrecy and secret societies, Simmel (1906) discusses the relative merits of discretion as the "respect for the secret of the other" that is exercised through a restraining from knowing what the other does not positively reveal (Simmel 1906, 452). Simmel notes, however, that "[v]ery often it is impossible for us to restrain our interpretation of another" (Simmel 1906, 456). Relations may be based on a discreet relationality, and yet be marked by an overriding and compelling hermeneutics of the other. According to Simmel, even between subjects whose relation to one another is grounded on a shared interest, discretion amounts to "[an] attachment of secrecy, in which not the attitude of the person keeping the secret, but that of a third party, is in question, in which in view of the mixture of reciprocal knowledge *or* lack of knowledge, the emphasis is on the *amount* of the former rather than on that of the latter" (Simmel 1906, 456–7; my emphasis). For Simmel, then, reciprocally entertained knowledge *or* lack of knowledge affects our interpretative approaches to the other. The way we know or do not know the other affects our attempts at knowing the other, where knowledge of the other is a question of how much we do or do not know and how much we would want to know or wish we knew. The hermeneutics of the Other is therefore quantifiable.

Quantification and related proportionality of knowledge entertained are an effect of *scale* (Strathern 1991). Strathern points out that social scientific knowledge is characterized by complexity: "the more closely you look, the more detailed things are bound to become. Increase in one dimension (focus) increases the other (detail of the data)" (Strathern 1991, xv). Complexity of phenomena and the notion of potentially "*increasable* complication—that there are always 'more' things to take into account"—are the product of changes in the scale of observation, scaling and scale switching being intellectual practices grounded in Western pluralism (Strathern 1991, xiv). Similarly, it could be argued that quantification and proportionality of the hermeneutics of the Other, and the related assumption that there are potentially "more" things to be known, are effects of socially, historically, and culturally specific practices of deductive scale switching: "[T]he interesting feature about switching scale is not that one can forever classify into greater or lesser groupings but that at every level complexity replicates itself in scale of detail. 'The same' order of information is repeated, eliciting equivalently complex conceptualisation . . . The amount of information remains . . . despite an increase in the magnitude of detail" (Strathern 1991, xvi). Scale—in its epistemological dimensions—and the related practices of scale switching are crucial to an understanding of secrecy in a context such as the one at hand.[7] A focus on practices of naming in the insurgency, and on the routes of guerrilla scaling and scale switching, allows for a consideration of how complexity and relationality are replicated in the scale of nominal detail.

Nominal Holographics, Complex Relationality

"Pedrito" had a different name prior to joining the struggle (*la lucha*). In Guatemala, at birth, a child acquires a first name, often a second name, and the surname of the father and the mother. Newborns are registered in birth registers of the *cabecera* (administrative town) whenever possible. Accordingly, Pedrito had first, second, and family names that had characterized his life prior to joining the insurgency. These were set aside when he joined the guerrilla ranks. Throughout his years of militancy up to the time of our exchange, he was known as "Pedrito." "Pedro," his pseudonym proper, was bestowed and adopted in an attempt to make his former first, second, and family names redundant. In a context marked by low-intensity conflict (Schirmer 1998),[8] periods of brutal state-sponsored counterinsurgency campaigns, and permanent social surveillance, those joining the insurgency often—but not always[9]—strove to erase the connection between themselves and the apparatus of conference, management, and surveillance of identity by the nation state, and, crucially, the regional government.[10] Pseudonyms were devised to allow the persons to operate, physically move, and negotiate their way through multiple systems of surveillance and repression. Long-term and seasonal labor migration, compounded by the ever-increasing displacement caused by the recrudescence of the conflict in the early 1980s, made absences from one's place of residence not uncommon. Early on in life, Pedrito had also been a labor migrant. With his family he had traveled from *Oriente* (the eastern region of Guatemala) to the *Costa Sur* (southern coast) looking for work in the cotton plantations, where labor conditions were said to be promising. His family had settled in one of the *aldeas* (villages/hamlets) at the periphery of a cotton plantation (*finca algodonera*), on the proximity of the seashore, as only the less fertile soil was left for the laborers to settle in. Pedrito's father had wanted nothing to do with either the Army or the guerrilla: "The guerrilla used to speak to him [Pedrito said about his father], and would say that if he did not want to join their ranks (*incorporarse*), all that they would ask of him was that the matter be kept secret (*que fuera secreto*) because the *guerrilleros* were the very same neighbors. So, of course, they had to keep the secret, one could not divulge (*divulgando*) that the *guerrillero* was so-and-so, for the very situation, because here in Guatemala anyone who got caught would be killed straightaway. At least in El Salvador there were prisons for political prisoners, while here in Guatemala there was no such thing." Although his father had not given signs of any specific political propensity, Pedrito left his community in 1980 to attend a course (*curso*) organized by the guerrilla. The understanding was that all participants would return to their communities on completion of the course. At the end of the six-month period, however, the situation had deteriorated and safety could no longer be guaranteed. Those who had returned to their villages early had been killed and Pedrito decided to stay on, thus becoming a guerrilla migrant and moving from *Oriente* to Petén as a *guerrillero*, no longer a labor migrant and never as a displaced victim of state violence. The latter was the fate of his immediate family, who, following the abduction and murder of Pedrito's father in 1980, moved back to the *Oriente*. Pedrito progressively lost his connection to his former name and only visited his town of origin and his family after the demobilization process was formally completed in 1997. During the war years, a number of pseudonyms made it possible for Pedrito to seek refuge in Mexico when seriously wounded, and later to travel to *Sandinista* Nicaragua and to El Salvador to receive political and military training.[11]

Among the *compañeros/as*, however, he was known by his *apodo*, that is, the nickname Pedrito, meaning "small/young Pedro." As the diminutive form of "Pedro," "Pedrito" is a possibly ironic and definitely endearing reference to some perceived qualities of the person, in this case the person's age, demeanor, and physical presence on joining the guerrilla ranks. *Apodos* are of great interest, for they give an insight into guerrilla practices of name bestowal, as they evoke the multiple relationalities in which guerrilla names and subjectivities came into being. In the way they move across scales, they constitute guerrilla nominal holographics: "The concept of relation can be applied to any order of connection. It is *holographic* in the sense of being an example of the field it occupies, every part containing information about the whole and information about the whole being enfolded in each part. . . . [The relation] requires other elements to complete it. . . . This makes the connecting functions *complex*, for the relation always summons entities other than itself" (Strathern 1995d, 17–8).

A prominent ex-guerrilla combatant who for years had held a position of great responsibility in FAR once suggested that if I wanted to speak to women ex-combatants, I should interview "Alma." As he was due to visit Alma's community on a business-related trip, he offered to personally introduce me to her. I returned to the community on my own at a later date to carry out the interview with great discretion, as only Alma's closest family relations knew about her past in the guerrilla.

> I ask what her pseudonym (*pseudónimo*) was and she replies Alma. I then ask whether she had a nickname (*apodo*) and she says that yes, she had one. But the guys (*los muchachos*) did not say it to my face, they used it among themselves. I ask what the nickname was. They called me Hombrote. I ask why they called her so. Well, they gave me that name because from the very beginning, I showed physical prowess (*capacidad física*) inasmuch as combat was concerned, I had considerable physical prowess, as much as any man, so the guys were really surprised (*se admiraban*) by it, as men, well, the *machismo* that was at times deployed (*se manejaba*) was about being macho and all that, so that is where it all came from. . . . I ask whether they really never called her Hombrote directly. Well, I heard it but never directly

> as such, they would never call me that, I mean, they gave me that nickname but always with great respect (*respeto*) because they knew that I could get tough (*actuar muy recio*) with them (*contra ellos*).

Alma was one of a relatively small number of women and an even smaller number of indigenous women combatants in the FAR ranks in the early 1980s. Alma's nickname, "Hombrote," literally means being manly and a "macho." As she pointed out, "Hombrote," with its associations to the term "macho," refers to the culture of "machismo" that she identified as significant during her time in the guerrilla. In Latin American societies "machismo" is usually taken to refer to "a way of orientation which can most succinctly be described as the cult of virility. The chief characteristics of this cult are exaggerated aggressiveness and intransigence in male-to-male interpersonal relationships and arrogance and sexual aggression in male-to-female relationships" (Stevens 1973, 90).

Interestingly, Alma noted that the nickname "Hombrote" was intended as a sign of respect (*respeto*) to the extent that the *compañeros* never called her "Hombrote" directly. If that had happened, Alma was sure everyone was aware that she would have retorted like a "proper" rowdy macho. With reference to Mexico, it has been noted that, unlike Stevens' (1973) envisaging, the term "macho" encompasses negative and positive conceptions of masculinity. While being a term that refers to notions of hegemonic masculinity, "macho" often stands for qualities such as courage and integrity (Gutmann 1996; Lancaster 1992; Mirandé 1997). Further, it can be used to refer to both men and women (Chant with Craske 2003; Mirandé 1997). In view of this, it could be argued that Alma's nickname "Hombrote" is a sign of female masculinity.[12] As noted by Halberstam (1998), analyses of female masculinity unhinge the link between masculinity and men. Thus, the image of the macho *compañeros* acknowledging Alma's masculinity among themselves, but not daring to refer to Alma's macho qualities in her presence, instantiated her contingently hegemonic and their contextually subordinate masculinities. The scale of detail of the *apodo* "Hombrote" produces the holographic effects of female masculinity and macho guerrilla relationalities. Crucially, however, the gender relationality that Alma discussed on the day of the interview was a fact of memory, as none of her neighbors or fellow villagers knew of her past as Hombrote.

The gender relationality inherent in Alma's *apodo* is here taken as an example of the nominal holographics characteristic of guerrilla practices of naming. Gender relationality is but one scale of detail that defines the whole and through which complex relations are established. Guerrilla nominal holographics summon further elements: "I ask Sandra whether she had a nickname in the insurgence (*en la montaña*). 'Well, that is what I have, a general one (*uno general*) with which they call me everywhere (*que me dicen dondequiera*), only "La Blanca" they call me.'"[13] Sandra's nickname conjured up relationalities of gender and racialization. Disclosure of guerrilla secret nominal holographics was on occasions unexpected. I met Romualdo in his capacity of community leader. Our first meeting was uneventful, but on subsequent occasions Romualdo spoke eloquently about the history of his community and I asked him whether I could interview him on matters pertaining to histories of Q'eqchi' migration to Petén and ritual practices. He finally agreed to a date and a time for the interview, kindly finding time for me in his busy schedule as community leader. It was not until the tape recorder was switched on that I heard Romualdo's personal history. I was utterly unprepared for the intensity of the account that followed.

> I was with my cousin in Santa Lucia, Fray Bartolomé de las Casas [Alta Verapaz], he took me to work, he told me there was a job of *tapisca* around Cantabal, Ixcán [Quiché].[14] We left in a car that gave us a lift from Raxujá [Alta Verapaz], it was a *carro juletero* we boarded,[15] we got to the crossing (*cruce*) in Chisec, where Cobán and Petén meet, and what, I think the Army had already had a clash (*enfrentamiento*) before going through Chisec or before getting to the crossroad (*cruce*), as I then was a rude youngster (*patojo maleducado*), I had much longer hair (*yo andaba muy peludo*) than what I have now, so the car had a flat tire, and they were fixing the tire when the Army arrives and they get us to show our documents and all (*nos ponen a registrar y todo*[16]), [and] I did not have ID as I was still a child (*era patojo todavía*), I was about fourteen and a half, that's where they caught me (*me agarraron*), they caught me from here and they threw me in their truck, and from there they blindfolded me (*taparon el ojo*) and they took me away, and they left my cousin there, they only took me away and they hit (*golpearon*) the people who were there. From there they took me to the military zone (*zona militar*) number twenty, I think, which is in Ixcán, which is in Playa Grande, that's where they took me and that's where they went on hitting me (*me estuvieron golpeando*) and they tied me to a pole that was there, [they said] this is the *guerrillero* that has to go and show us where the *compañeros* of this son of a bitch are (*hijo de la gran chingada*). They were talking about me (*me mencionaban allí*) but they were keeping my face covered (*me tenían tapada la cara*), I only had two small holes from which to breathe/

sigh (*suspirar*), so from there, after like three days they got me out of there (*me sacaron*) and they took me in a helicopter up to falling (*caer*; "to fall," rather than "to land") in Cuarto Pueblo, so they say, as I did not even know where that was, we went down there where they used to have a church before but it was already all *amantado*,[17] and that's where they told me, now you are going to be useful as a guide (*servir vos de guía*), I was *hombre punta*,[18] they told me and they dressed me up as the Army, as I was rather small (*chaparrito*), I was a rather sickly man (*hombre enfermito*) in those days, so they put a cap on me, with a shirt and some trousers, and with the same shoes I had on, they told me, go now, we will follow you, go now then, we will follow you and I did not even know what that was/what it was all about (*que era eso*), so for all [the] blows (*golpe*) I was receiving I decided to go, like that, like at the northeast of the field (*campo*) of the church of Cuarto Pueblo, and from there I went, we walked no more than two kilometers and a few meters when I hear a shot in front of me, I was thinking that those who had shot me were the *compañeros* who were in the vegetation (*monte*) [i.e., the guerrilla], they shot the soldiers who were walking behind me, and as I was carrying no weapon, they only gave me a knife and nothing else, I was carrying no weapon, nothing, so perhaps they saw I was not carrying anything, the two soldiers who were walking behind me, they [the guerrilla] killed them, and as from that point I kept standing up/still (*yo me quedé parado*) and they carried on *hechando verga*,[19] so I threw myself, there was a little furrow (*sanjita*), so that's where I stayed, I threw myself right in there (*cabal me aventé*), they went on for about three hours firing there, so that's where I stayed. As the noise (*la bulla*) stopped, I pretended I was dead (*yo hice el muerto*), I pretended I was dead and I just stayed there with my mouth down (*hice el muerto y me quedé allí de boca abajo*), it went on for something like three hours that mess (*cuentazo*), then they came to touch me (*me vinieron a tocar*), they were poking me with the barrel there (*me puñaban con el cañon allí*), luckily the soldiers did not shoot me, "throw soil on this son of a bitch" (*héchale tierra a este hijo de la chingada*), the officer said. Then, they threw soil over me, sticks and branches and all, in the small cave that was there, I fit perfectly there (*cabal cupía yo allí*), when they shot, when they threw granades, them, what are they called? Those who are now the ex-combatants, they were landing on the soldiers, and the great quantities of blood (*los pocones de sangre*) and the bodies that were blowing up (*y los cuerpos que le estallaban a ellos*), were falling on top of me/on my back, and from there they threw soil over me and they left me there. They left and from there, as they said I was dead, I stayed there, but how/where would one have got out of there, how? Who knows! (*¡saber!*). As they took me there by helicopter, and from there, I stayed there, the night fell, and the next day I woke up (*amanecer*) crying, crying, crying, I was there for fifteen days, in the midst of that bad smell that was there, as they had taken with them the bodies of the soldiers, even if in pieces but they took them with them, but I pretended I was dead there, and they buried me there, as I did not even have relatives who were going to account for me (*responder a mi*), so I stayed there and after about fifteen days of having stayed there, plus three days of having been in the [military] zone, it is eighteen days, after fifteen days of having stayed sitting there in the vegetation (*monte*), I was crying loud (*llorando fuerte*), I lowered my forehead, my god, what am I doing here, why are they doing this to me, I said, when all of a sudden a girl and a boy come out in front of me and they talked to me, and I was shaking there out of fear, that perhaps they were those of the Army, and they said to me, "we join you in your sadness (*te acompañamos en tu tristeza*)," "let's go," they said, "accompany us," and I went. Another girl arrived, a fat girl (*gordona*) and she held me, as I was weak and malnourished (*desnutrido*), she grabbed me and she sat me on her rucksack, and off I went, I felt we did not walk very far when we got to the camp, as I was going piggyback (*cucucha*) and I was not feeling anything, I was already about to die (*ya estaba por morirme yo*), so they gave me medicines, they treated me right and I don't know what they gave me/put on me (*me hecharon*) but I got better. A girl looked after me there, but I don't know what her pseudonym (*pseudónimo*) was, what she was called, but as I survived in such a place full of mosquitos (*como me salvé dentro de tanto zancudero*), for that reason they named me Mosquito there, as there they don't ask somebody's name, they just make one up (*solo allí le inventan a uno*),[20] ah ah, so it's from there [that his nickname originates], and I, while I was there *en la montaña*, I would tell myself where I was from (*y como yo estando allí en la montaña me decía, que donde venía yo*), I would say I was from Petén, as I was born here in Petén, but my relatives were in Cobán [Alta Verapaz]. I ask Mosquito where in Petén he was born.[21] Here in Petén. I tell Mosquito that I seem to remember him telling me his mother spoke Mopan. Yes, but she was *Cobanera*.[22] So from there I would spend my time crying and crying (*de tanto llorar y llorar me*

> *mantenía yo allí*), but they would treat me very well and all, they were even giving me [military] training (*entrenamientos*), it was a girl who would look after me (*solo una muchacha que me mantenía allí*), she would give me my training (*me enseñaba mis entrenamientos*), there she would give me a little weapon (*me daba un armita allí*), for me to move and all that, for any eventuality, if anything should happen (*cualquier cosa si ocurriera algo*).

The conversation with Mosquito revealed the embodied states of violence and the prosthetics of suffering and survival. Romualdo had wanted to tell me about how, having survived the torture and violence at the hands of the Army, he had been rescued by *guerrilleros/as*, had acquired a nickname, and later joined the guerrilla ranks in Petén. The revelation of Romualdo's experiences was as swift and sudden as Romualdo's subsequent withdrawal into silence regarding the topic. Romualdo and I never spoke of Mosquito again.

Scales of pseudonyms and nicknames, inherently relational in their bestowal, acceptance, and signification, produce holographic effects and necessitate other information for completeness. Guerrilla nominal holographics contain information about the relevance of complex relationalities of gender (Hombrote), ethnicity and racialization (La Blanca, El Moreno), and solidarity and survival in a hostile environment (Mosquito). Other relational scales refer to internationalist affinity, as in the case of "Moscú,"[23] and anti-imperialist continentalism, in the case of "América." Many referred to qualities of the person (La Chaparra, the Short One; El Chino, the Chinese One), while others referenced the animals and insects found in the forest (e.g., Mosquito, Loro).

Guerrilleros switched nominal scales and thus reproduced the relational effect of complexity. In *apodo* relationalities, the whole seems to splinter through the complex partiality of relational signification. Indeed, Mosquito noted that in the guerrilla "*solo allí le inventan a uno*," which could be taken to mean that "they" made someone up through nominal and relational practices of fabrication of subjectivity. The complex and relational nominal holographics in fact constantly illuminate other routes and summon other entities on the terrain of guerrilla secrecy.

Relational Partiality, Connective Relativization

In addition to complexity, scale switching instantiates a plurality and partiality of perspectives. Plurality, partiality, and complexity in turn lead to relativization (Strathern 1991). Guerrilla secrecy relied on specific relational partialities, the first of which I define in terms of a negative relationality of nondisclosure.

Jorge had been active in the insurgency since the 1960s. I had asked him to elaborate on aspects of guerrilla training when he said: "The primordial basis of man is that he be secret—to die shattered in a thousand pieces, but never say who he is, neither his name, nor where he was born, or where he lives . . . if they kill us, let them kill us, but they will never know who we are." Jorge's statement is an example of the role of secrecy in the guerrilla organization of which he was a long-standing, active member. Secrecy here seems to amount to a survival strategy and a way of staving off annihilation. In Jorge's own words, secrecy is "*la base primordial del hombre*," the primordial basis on which the existence of "man" is predicated on a terrain marked by constant impending disembodied danger. The relationality of secrecy is articulated in the negative here, as one is instructed to never reveal who one is. The markers of identity negatively mobilized by Jorge—that is, those that should not be disclosed—are one's name, one's place of birth, and one's place of residence. All three are indeed primary identity markers in Guatemala. Since the work of Goubaud Carrera, Sol Tax, and Robert Redfield, which I reviewed in Chapter 1, through to the more recent contributions made by Norman Schwartz (1990) with regard to Petén specifically that were reviewed in Chapter 2, it has been argued that identity in Guatemala, notably ethnic identity, is not explicitly articulated—that is, in Guatemala people have not, until the rise of Pan-Maya activism (Fischer 2001; Fischer and McKenna Brown 1996; Gálvez Borrell 1997; Hendrickson 1995; Montejo 2005; Warren 1998), objectified ethnicity as an ontological property of the self (see, for example, Hale 2006). This is the case for indigenous ethnicity in the sense that people do not deploy objectifying idioms of statements such as "I am Q'eqchi'." Rather, indigenous Guatemalans tend to articulate notions of identity in relation to a provenance—they stress, for instance, the town or administrative region (*departamento*) where they are from.[24] The latter is also the case for ladino ethnicity, although ladino ethnic identity may be more commonly objectified in statements such as "*soy ladino*." Articulations of ethnic identity that highlight provenance, far from essentialist or inherently nativist accounts of identity, are indeed shared by Maya and ladino Guatemalans and are often part of broader diasporic accounts of flight, migration, and movement.

I take Jorge's statement and its disavowals to be examples of that negative relationality of secrecy through which relations of nondisclosure are established.[25] That is, I argue that nondisclosure, based as it is on negation, still engenders relationalities of secrecy.

"The primordial basis of man is that he be secret," Jorge said and yet, as

Jorge articulated secrecy in terms of a founding principle to stave off annihilation, the injunction not to tell was problematized by my hesitation, in that pause in our conversation when I was left to wonder whether the "man" whose primordial basis was being discussed was a figure gendered in the neutral to mean a masculinist version of "humankind" or whether this primordial basis might in fact already harbor the very seeds of its undoing—in that conspicuous absence of a subject gendered in the feminine whose existence this same primordial basis seemed to foreclose. This was Jorge's own qualification of his statement: "Many men have fallen into the arms of death or into the hands of the enemy for loving a woman . . . So, when a man . . . has a [sexual] relationship with a woman, he must not disclose his mission, neither tell her his secrets, if he conquers her, well, that is an individual matter/his prerogative, but he should never tell her, I am, I have, or talk about his work." The negative relationality of secrecy was qualified by Jorge in terms of a further injunction, namely one that was gendered and sexualized. There appeared to be threats to secrecy, and these were, at least in the context of this interview, gendered in the feminine and marked by heteronormativity. It is here possible to discern the kind of partiality secrecy entails for subjectivities and social relations. Subjectivities and social relations in a terrain marked by secrecy are inherently partial, based as they may be on a negation, on nondisclosure, or on the threat of exposure.[26] As noted by Simmel (1906, 465), however, the relationality of secrecy is not always rendered through prohibition or foreclosure. Conversely, relational secrecy is often based on disclosure. Jorge explained,

> What we would do was that a *compañero* would come from afar (*venía un compañero de lejos*), and we would have another one with us, but we would be already in agreement with the former, and we would meet him there, we would meet him on our way, and we would greet as if we were strangers (*desconocidos*), but then, as I knew already, I would say to the one accompanying me, I am going to be back shortly, I have some errands to attend to, you two can talk. While I was gone, the *compañero* would talk to the one who was accompanying me, but this person would not know that I knew what he was going to tell him, so that one would not say one day that I knew too. We would use a strategy (*política*). Later, the person who had been accompanying me would tell me himself, he would say to me, look, that one we met the other day, didn't he say anything to you? He told me such and such a thing, and I am telling you now in confidence and trust (*en confianza*), and so we would carry on with the relationship (*relación*), until later, when I had complete trust in him (*yo confiaba directamente en él*), I

> would say to him, look, the struggle (*lucha*) is exactly so and so, our duty is to cover ourselves (*cubrirnos*), and it is good that you work in it. When I may be in a position to help you with something, I will help you, don't worry. I may even work in it myself at some point in the future. Some of them kept on thinking that I did not know anything, but they trusted me because I was a person who was not involved in disagreements (*pleitos*), in theft, just in my work, with real honesty. That is how we worked training (*formando*) people.

Although one's allegiance to the organization should be kept secret, recruitment of new members involved a telling. Seemingly fortuitous encounters were arranged and prospective new members told about the organization. The remarkable aspect of this specific relational moment of disclosure was that, at least in the intention of those willing the relation, the new member would not suspect who the person ordering the relation was. Although Jorge disclosed his sympathies for the insurgents, he did not expose the nature of his role in the organization. In this case, then, disclosure involved at once telling and misleading the prospective member. In the case of selective disclosure, relationalities of secrecy were again marked by partiality.

Negative relationalities of secrecy and relationalities of selective disclosure occurred concurrently with positive relationality of secrecy based on relations of disclosure: "Since the beginning, the *compañero* union organizers who would give us *doctrina* (political training) in the Southern Coast would tell us, the time will come when we will be persecuted . . . they will persecute us in the homes, in the schools, in the towns, in the hamlets, in the workplace. Hence, they would tell us, we have to be secretive, talk quietly, know signs." The scene where the importance of secrecy was first spelled out to Jorge was already a social context, namely one in which union organizers raised political awareness among *campesinos*, that is, agricultural workers toiling on the foreign-owned plantations of the Southern Coast. Jorge remembered the conversation with union organizers as a moment of initiation into a culture of secrecy of which he was a participant for over thirty years. His first recollection was unambiguously that of a social context, and the fact that one would have to proceed by "talking quietly" and "knowing signs" implied that one would have an interlocutor, an audience, and would be enmeshed in a set of relations. Secrecy, therefore, may have been about concealment and misdirection, but as a predicament, activity, or endeavor, it inherently implied partial relationalities and a sociality of possible selective disclosure.

Guerrilla secrecy thus seemed to have positively engendered certain kinds of social relations, some of which rested on a commonality of secret semiotics, as well as relations engendered in the negative, and grounded on nondisclosure. Secrecy may be founded on injunctions not to tell, as much as on certain ways of telling (Simmel 1906). In all instances, guerrilla positively and/or negatively inscribed relationalities of secrecy. Relational guerrilla secrecy did produce contingent secrets and it would be inaccurate to say that guerrilla secrets amounted to a formalistic device, behind which no secret actually lay (Taussig 1999). That *guerrilleros/as* harbored selective and contingent secrets becomes apparent retrospectively when one considers guerrilla secret relationalities vis-à-vis other relationalities. As a guerrilla sympathizer explained: "Because they are very humanitarian (*humanitarios*), and even if it was just a tortilla, in those days they would offer it to you without asking anything in return (*te la ofrecían y no te pedían nada a cambio*), and for that [one] has to be grateful to them, and one would feel much safer (*y se sentía mucho más seguro*) with an indigenous person (*indígena*), for they would cover your secrets (*que te cubrieran los secretos*) much more than a ladino." Positive and negative relationalities engendered by guerrilla secrecy were articulated on a terrain already saturated by other relations. Gender and sexual relations of nondisclosure, for instance, were contingently said to pose a threat to secrecy, while ladino/indigenous relations of disclosure did not, as stated in the interview abstract noted above. Guerrilla secret relationalities, however, seemed to operate parallel and/or antagonistically to relations based on kinship: "What I would do was, when I would talk to someone, I would see what his/her opinion was (*le tomaba la opinión*), and I would say to him/her, look, I have a friend who wants to talk to you, but you have to be careful (*cuídate*), don't go and tell anyone (*no lo vayas a contar*), don't tell your brothers [or siblings], or your father, until we may get to know your family very well, if it is convenient that they know, otherwise it is best they don't know." As one was told not to let family members know about one's association with the guerrilla, one could never be sure that one's kin were not also in some way associated with the insurgency—or, indeed, with the Army. Ramón's case is an example of this predicament. Ramón told me how he ran into the guerrilla while in his teens. He started making purchases for the insurgents and delivering goods at secret locations. Ramón never told his father about his activities, as Ramón's father was a local *comisionado militar*—that is, he was the civilian representative of the Army in Ramón's *aldea* (hamlet). It has been documented, and widely acknowledged, that the establishment of *comisionados militares* was a counterinsurgency tool aimed at a progressive militarization of the countryside, and an extension of surveillance that was initiated by the Army in the 1980s (CEH 1999, Chapter I, Item 216-20; Manz 1988; Wilson 1995). One day, Ramón's father found Ramón in the fields talking to the *guerrilleros*. Ramón explained the situation and Ramón's father and the guerrilla commander were left to talk in private—to exchange secrets. Ramón told me that to this day, he does not know what was said in that exchange. However, it later transpired that Ramón's father, the local *comisionado militar*, had been secretly passing information to the insurgents for some time prior to that encounter in the fields. Unbeknown to Ramón, his sister had already joined the guerrilla ranks and was a combatant in hiding. Positive and negative relationalities of secrecy engendered guerrilla subjectivities marked by partiality, as one would be enmeshed in relations, albeit partial ones.

Positive and negative socialities of secrecy did not belong to the past—they persisted in the context of my exchanges with the ex-*guerrilleros/as*. By way of an example of the manner in which the relational partiality of secrecy shaped my relations with the ex-guerrilla, in the course of our conversation, Ramón urged me to reflect on the procedure that I followed in order to get to meet him: "You looked for me, a *compañero* told you to look for Ramón or Pablo, I don't know what name they gave you, and today you were on your way, you had established contact with a *compañera* who was going to come to meet you, and you knew we were going to meet—that is how we used to operate." At the time, it seemed that I was also a part of a nonorganic whole and in some peripheral position in the scale of guerrilla relationalities of secrecy. In the case of my exchange with Ramón, for instance, he was articulating a positive relationality of selective disclosure, and letting me in on some of his secrets. Conversely, there were many instances in which my interlocutors articulated secrecy in the negative. In view of this and recalling the initial exchange with Pedrito, it remains unclear exactly what secret Pedrito disclosed by ceasing to be Pedrito and where the secret actually lay, for I may have been the one harboring it, not him. Relational partialities imply connective relativization, but connectivity nonetheless (Strathern 1991).

Conclusion: Post-plurality and Post-perspectivism

> The realisation of the multiplier effect produced by innumerable perspectives extends to the substitutive effect of apprehending that no one perspective offers the totalising vista it presupposes. It ceases to be perspectival.
>
> —Marilyn Strathern, *Partial Connections*, 1991, vxi

Guerrilla scale and scale switching created nominal and relational complexities marked by partiality. Following Strathern (1988; 1991; 1995d), I argue that the partiality of subjects and relations implies connections, albeit connections between subjectivities and socialities that are inherently partial. The partiality at issue is not strictly a product of the researcher's deductive hermeneutic scale. Rather, the partiality at stake is the partiality of guerrilla secrecy, which is a social, cultural, and historically specific partiality that is the product of a social, cultural, and historical context marked by histories of conflict and cultures of secrecy. This relational knowledge marks a point of diffusion, engendering secrecy as a partial form of knowledge always in tension between acts of withholding and exposure. This is not an index of an ontological state, but rather this is a culturally and historically specific position and form of knowledge/non-knowledge. This seemingly universal fact is an ethnographically specific point of juncture: the reciprocity of the secret is the reciprocity of a concealed object and an object of partial knowledge, namely the pseudonym. Pseudonyms mark relations among subjects marked as partial, so that partiality itself is not an ontological state, but, rather, it is a gift that carries with it a history of relationality marked by violence and necessity. Pseudonyms, and the knowledge practices of secrecy that underpin them, conjure rather than locate relations, so that the partial knowledge of the secret is generative of connections, rather than descriptive or even expressive. While these processes can be framed through the theoretical idioms of performativity, the secret is not only explicitly performed through acts of selective disclosure and revelation. A refusal to perform is also a constituent part of its performativity, not as a limit to what will, in this instance, be known or knowable, but as the inaccessible other to performativity itself.[27]

In view of this, it is of interest to transpose and reinscribe Simmel's statement in the Strathernian terms that have characterized my analysis here. Secrets no longer refer to "the mixture of reciprocal knowledge *or* lack of knowledge" of the other (Simmel 1906, 452; my emphasis). Rather, they refer to "the mixture of reciprocal knowledge [*and*] lack of knowledge" characteristic of the partial relationalities of secrecy that marked the ethnographic encounters discussed here. Hermeneutic awareness of scale allows for the apprehension of, and related switch to, a specifically post-plural scale. Fractal graphics,[28] holography, partial connections, and connective relativization allow for both reciprocal knowledge *and* lack of knowledge to exist simultaneously, and to go beyond principles of noncontradiction in the multiple hermeneutics of the ethnographic exchange—in this context marked by positive, negative, and partial relationalities of secrecy. For Simmel, relations in which parties are being discreet are characterized by reciprocal acts of discretion. I take discreet relations in the post-plural scale of guerrilla secret relationalities to refer to discrete relations between subjects marked by partiality, and these discrete relations give ground to partial socialities. These partial subjectivities and socialities of secrecy were instantiated through connectedness and intermittence, and my attempt at finding the appropriate hermeneutic scale is intended as an exercise in post-plural and post-perspectival knowledge practices.

4
Secrecy, Sociality, Merographic Analogy

Introduction

In the previous chapter I discussed naming practices among guerrilla combatants and associates and their role in the articulation of secretive and complex relationalities, grounded in selective forms of disclosure and foreclosure. I argued that secrecy challenges knowledge practices and related understandings of sociality in terms of pluralities of discrete entities. I argued for the relevance of knowledge practices in post-plural scales for describing and understanding the partial subjectivities and socialities engendered in guerrilla secrecy. In this chapter I provide a different order of post-plural contextualization, and consider the ways in which violence and ambivalence, and their effects, figured in the narratives of ex-combatants of the Fuerzas Armadas Rebeldes (FAR). Through the accounts of ex-combatants, I focus on representations of the conflict offered by the guerrilla, highlighting how entities were rarely viewed as monolithic, coherent, and opposed wholes. Rather, violence and secrecy, imbricating each other, produced ambivalence and indeterminacy in guerrilla subjectivities and socialities.

The Secrets of the Maya: The Theft of Stones, Knowledge, and People

On one of my usual visits, I passed by Luis, an ex-combatant who had been involved in political organizing efforts and in the guerrilla organization for almost four decades. Luis, originally from *Oriente* but displaced to the *Costa Sur* from the age of five,[1] had been a member of the very first FAR units that were active in the early 1960s. In 1966, following violent curbing of political activity among plantation workers in the *Costa Sur*, Luis migrated to Petén with his immediate family. Luis told me that while his family came to Petén in search of land, the main reason for the move was to escape the repression that was being targeted at *campesinos* like himself who had links with the unions.[2] I was asking Luis to comment on the indigenous question in Guatemala when he told me this story.

> Between 1977 and 1978, Luis had met an elderly man about eighty-eight years old. The elderly man was Q'eqchi' and Petenero, in the sense that he was Q'eqchi' and had been living in Petén for a long time. Luis and the old man started talking about the destruction of indigenous people in Guatemala (*la destrucción de los indígenas*). The elderly man said that he did not approve (*no le parecía*) of the murder and destruction of those people who knew the things of the Maya (*sabían las cosas de los Mayas*), as this knowledge was useful (*útil*) for the future. The man told Luis that a stone had been robbed (*se habían robado*) from Tikal, that the indigenous people in Cobán (*los indígenas in Cobán*) were still a Maya race (*era raza todavía de los Mayas*),[3] and that proof (*prueba*) of this was in that stone where the name of a Maya person who was living in the highlands of Cobán appeared. The elderly man said to Luis that this was the definite proof that the Maya were not extinct/finished (*terminado*) and it was a coincidence (*casualidad*) that on that engraved stone (*piedra escrita*) that was stolen from Tikal by the Americans (*americanos*) there appeared the name of that man and of his daughter, or rather [Luis said] the man's granddaughter. In any case, there was the name, and the granddaughter could read/understand what was written on the stone. Six to eight months following the theft of the stone, the FBI arrived in Cobán to take the *indita* with them (*para llevarse la indita*).[4] They told her father that they were going to pay for her education, so that she could get better schooling (*para que se preparara major*), and so that they could educate her. These were all lies (*mentiras*). At the time, people were really afraid (*temorizada*) and the Army accompanied those Americans and seeing an Army soldier (*un militar*) was like seeing the devil (*diablo*), as one was only waiting to be killed by them, as that was the only thing they were doing/did.[5] So, there is no doubt (*no cabe duda*) that this eighty-and-over indigenous man (*este indígena*), no [said Luis], he was in fact one hundred and fifteen years old, [and] at this age he knew for sure that if he was not to give up his daughter, the Army (*militares*) would have killed him. Facing this threat the man handed over (*dio*) his daughter and they took her away (*se la llevaron*). So the man went to approach the Army (*ejército*) and said

that those men (*esos hombres*) had visited and they had agreed (*quedaron*) to bring the man's daughter back and the date had come and they had not returned her. He had not heard from her and wanted to know what had happened to her, trusting (*confiando*) that there were soldiers (*soldados*) with the FBI. Well, he had come to let them know (*avisar*), as one says, surely you must know (*ha de saber*), because there were soldiers (*soldados*) present when they took her away on that certain date, and when the date came they did not bring her back. It turns out that what they told him was that he should not go round claiming/demanding/insinuating (*reclamar*) anything, because what could happen to him was that he could be killed (*matarlo*). So without any doubt (*no cabe duda*), they either have the girl (*muchacha*) alive or they killed her. I interrupt Luis at this point and ask whether they may have killed the girl after she revealed to them what was written on the *estela*. That may have been the case [said Luis]; they may have killed her after she had deciphered (*decifrado*) the Maya inscription/tradition (*leyenda*). To the present day, it is not known whether they hold her alive or whether they killed her. But what we think is that they must have killed her, as the *indios* in Guatemala have never really had any defense/protection (*defensa*), or support from the law (*apoyo por las leyes*), they have been mistreated (*tratados mal*). And that is where we, the *mestizos* come in, to receive the same punishment (*castigo*), the same suffering (*sufrimiento*) of the Maya, because some of us, the *mestizos*, do not agree (*no nos parece*) with the way in which indigenous people (*los indígenas*) are treated, what they do with them, with all the scorn/contempt (*mensoprecios*). So, the way we saw the matter when we spoke to that man who told me this story, I said to him/I say to you (*le digo yo*) why did not the Guatemalan government allow (*permitido*) that she studied here, that they did not take her away, because she would have been very useful to the very same Guatemalan government, the indigenous girl (*muchacha indígena*) as much as the elderly man (*viejito*), because in them were the Maya secrets (*secretos Mayas*) that people don't know anymore, in him there were important Maya stories (*historias Mayas*) for today's generation (*generación*), so rather than supporting them, they destroyed them (*los destryueron*). I say to Luis that they seem to have stolen the *estela* and the people (*gente*) too. That is exactly the case [Luis said]. The indigenous peoples (*pueblos indígena*) in Guatemala have lost the confidence/trust (*confianza*) in the law (*leyes*), in those who execute the law, because they are not fair (*justos*), because it's an injustice, so it is in this way that in Guatemala very important things (*cosas*) have been/are being lost (*se ha ido perdiendo*). There are people who know (*lo saben*) but people are afraid (*tienen temor*).

In my analysis, the story told by Luis is a ladino narrative on the predicament of Guatemala, as a multicultural country marked by the arbitrary exercise of authority and violence, perpetrated by the Guatemalan Army in its acquiescence to, and collusion with, United States imperialism. Set in Guatemala in the late 1970s, the narrative recounts how antiquities, knowledge, and people are stolen through violence and deception by foreign powers, and how a woman, who is identified as the bearer of knowledge, is commodified, exchanged, and appropriated in the process. In this respect, the story is as much about ladino representations of indigeneity and gender as it is about the theft of knowledge and secrets. The story opens with the theft of a "Maya stone" seen as the repository of ancient Maya knowledge, but a form of knowledge that is understood to be directly related to the present. Indeed, the names of living individuals are inscribed on the stone. The individuals whose names appear on the stone can read the inscription and thus can decipher the secrets of the Maya,[6] which are the targets of the FBI's interest.[7] When faced by the FBI and the Guatemalan Army, the elderly Q'eqchi' man decides to give up his (grand-)daughter in order to save his life. Interestingly, at this point the figure of the Q'eqchi' girl is commodified and becomes the object entangled in a system of exchange (Rubin 1975) between the masculinist neo-imperial powers of the FBI, the Guatemalan Army, and the girl's father/grandfather. The arrangement is a temporary one, aimed at providing the girl with better schooling, and the elderly Q'eqchi' man approaches the Army when the girl is not returned on the agreed date, as it is within his right to have his (grand-)daughter/property returned. The response of the Army is dismissal. The Q'eqchi' man is ultimately betrayed in his trust. Up to the moment of revelation of the deceit, he had viewed the Guatemalan Army as guarantor to the transaction. The fact that there were Guatemalan Army soldiers with the FBI on the day the girl was taken away was no guarantee after all. The Q'eqchi' man is ordered to lay the matter to rest, lest he be killed and his daughter/granddaughter never returned. According to Luis, whether the girl is alive and hostage of the FBI or has been killed is an open question. There is *no doubt* that *either* the FBI holds the girl *or* they may have killed her, in a context where certainty is inherently ambiguous. Nevertheless, Luis resolves that it is more likely that the girl was murdered.

Gender constructs seem to be established in terms of a system of unequal exchange and indigeneity seems to be articulated (from Luis' own ladino perspective) in terms of instrumentality and commodification. To an extent, both gender-in-the-feminine and indigenous ethnicity are first reified and then circulated as part of an exchange system. As their worth is inherently instrumental, they should be valued, nurtured, and "developed" *because* of their potential instrumental worth. The story acknowledges that the process of commodification of difference in terms of gender and indigeneity is inherently violent. According to Luis, death and annihilation have marked the histories of the relationships between indigenous people and state and/or imperial institutions. This history of violence, vilification, and abuse, however, is indicated as the point of convergence between disenfranchised and violated indigenous and ladino subjects, as ladinos rise with indigenous subjects against the injustices perpetrated against indigenous people to challenge the ways in which archaeological artifacts, people, knowledge, and secrets are stolen through deception by the Guatemalan Army and foreign powers. Nevertheless, it seems clear that the FBI, the Guatemalan Army, ladinos in solidarity, and elderly Q'eqchi' men are all laying claims to "Maya secrets" harbored by a young indigenous woman. It is these secrets that seem to lie at the center of the controversy, as they engender antagonistic relations between masculinist international, national, and local powers.

El Aparato/The Apparatus

Luis elaborated further on the powers of indigenous bricoleur abilities, the accusations of subversion they unwittingly attracted, and the violence thrust upon them in a second parable whose main character was a young K'iche' man.

> In the same year, about 1970, this happened around 1970, before the story I have just told you, there was another indigenous person (*indígena*), but he was of the K'iche' race (*de raza K'iche'*). This happened in 1970 and the indigenous person (*indígena*) was twenty years old. He was young and in the area of Quiché, near Santa Cruz Barillas, in the direction of Chiapas, that is where he lived in a village (*aldea*), I have forgotten the name of the village, but the truth (*verdad*) is that this indigenous man (*indígena*) went to the capital of Guatemala. He was illiterate (*inalfabeto*), of his own intelligence (*de su inteligencia*), he liked the matter of radiotransmission (*radiotécnico*) and he stayed in the capital for about a year, and from there he then went back to

his village. In his village he started repairing radios for his fellow villagers, at the time there were record players (*tocadiscos*) and radios, there were no tape recorders (*grabadoras*). So he started repairing record players and radios, so that after two years working in this trade, on the wall (*pared*) of his house (*casa*), which was made of wooden sticks (*varas*) like that one over there, he started placing/arranging (*colocar*) record player and radio parts (*piezas*) and he started connecting (*connectar*) them and covered the wall, which was about six square meters in size.

I ask Luis skeptically, that big?

Yes, it was indeed as large as that. The man covered the wall with pieces/parts (*pedazos*) of radios and record players and he made them work (*las puso a funcionar*) and the people were very impressed (*admiración*) so much so that when someone would come to see him to get some radio or record player repaired, he would turn on (*encender*) his apparatus (*aparato*) and the apparatus (*aparato*) would play what one was saying (*este aparato sonaba lo que uno platicaba*).

I ask whether the machine could record (*grabar*).

Yes, it could record and there one could hear (*escuchar*) the telephones of the country (*los teléfonos del país*).

Really? I say.

Yes, there one could hear the radio stations/frequencies (*difusoras*) of the country.

I ask Luis whether he means the radio stations and he says yes. I am very surprised and say, really?

Luis replies that that much he could detect (*agarrar*) with that thing he had put on the wall, just like that, with mere wooden sticks (*puras varas*), he had no education (*no tuvo escuela*), he did not have a teacher (*maestro*) to have the opportunity to learn (*poder aprender*). It was his very own intelligence (*pura inteligencia de él*), and you know what happened? When the Army (*ejército*) realized (*se dio cuenta*), a gossipy *campesino* (*campesino chismoso*) who was *comisionado* went to denounce (*dar parte*) that man who was making apparatuses (*haciendo aparatos*).[8] Some officers (*oficiales*) came with a multitude of soldiers (*cantidad de soldados*) and went to take a look (*fueron a ver*). Yes, of course, it was an apparatus (*aparato*) he had made out of pieces of radios and record players. Well, the officers [were] in good spirit (*de buena onda*) and good people (*buena gente*), because they saw (*vieron*) that it was nothing bad (*nada malo*), they were impressed (*admiraron*) when they saw the radio, they were Army officers, but the accusation (*denuncia*) that had been made against him was a bad accusation (*se la hicieron mala*), because he was being accused of being a rebel (*lo acusaban de rebelde*), and he did not even know what that was (*él ni-siquiera sabía que era eso*). So, those officers left, but after about eight days, the Americans (*los gringos americanos*) arrived there with him, they were from the FBI, they investigated the apparatus (*investigaron el aparato*) and asked him who was it who had taught him that (*que quien le había ensañado eso*), where had he gone to learn that (*que donde había ido a aprender*), whether he had gone to Cuba, whether he had gone to Russia, and I, I, the man was saying, I did not even know Chiapas, Mexico! Because a poor person (*pobre*) cannot go round traveling, can he?

Of course, I say.

Well, then, says Luis, those Americans (*esos americanos*) were there with about five hundred soldiers of the Guatemalan Army, and what they did was to tell him that the apparatus was going to be the cause of his misfortune (*la causa de su desgracia*) and the man replied, here I, he said, I repair radios and record players, I am not harming people (*haciéndole daño a la gente*), I am not stealing off anyone (*no le estoy robando a nadie*), I am not causing harm to the government (*no le estoy haciendo daño al gobierno*). So they replied that that apparatus (*aparato*) that he had, well that was against the government, because only the government could have such an apparatus to be aware (*darse cuenta*) of telephones at the national level and of radio stations/frequencies (*difusoras*). So, he said, well, why is not the government making the apparatus (*por qué no hace el gobierno el aparato*)? If it is in the government's interest (*le conviene*), it is its privilege/competence, if only the government can do it (*solo él lo puede hacer*), well then, let the government do it (*pues que lo haga*) but I did not make it for any specific reason (*pero yo no lo hice para nada*), I made it because my thought/mental capacities (*pensamiento*) was/were helping me. So, they said to him, we will be back, and they left, and after eight days they came back, at about five in the afternoon, and he was not heard of again (*no se supo de él*), if they killed him or what (*si lo mataron, o qué*).

Did they take him away (*lo sacaron de su casa*)? I ask.

Yes, the Americans of the FBI and the Guatemalan Army were there (*andaban los americanos del FBI y andaba el ejército de Guatemala*), about five hundred soldiers.

I say, for one unarmed man?

Yes, unarmed. These two stories (*historias*) that we know (*sabemos*), it is only few of us [who know them], because many people do not like these stories, I don't know why, I don't know the reason (*razón*), people don't record (*grabar*) the stories that are important, people don't like to know them, but for me/in my opinion (*a mi manera*), yes, they are important, because in my view (*a mi ver*), if the government had been intelligent (*inteligente*), the government would have [taken] the *indita* as much as the K'iche' man to develop (*para desarrollarles*) their memory/intelligence (*memoria*), for the future of the country, but rather than developing them (*en vez de desarrollarlos*), they destroyed them (*destruirlos*).

I ask whether perhaps the government felt threatened by such intelligence (*será que se sintieron amenazados de tanta inteligencia?*).

Luis hesitates.

So I add, perhaps people who are doing/making things (*haciendo las cosas*), who can (*pueden*) do/make things, don't need anybody (*no necesita a nadie*) and have strength (*fuerza*) and independence (*independencia*), and that the government may not like.

This is correct (*correcto*). Perhaps, the [Guatemalan] government has an agreement/arrangement (*compromiso*) with the United States, what is it called? Because not all of the United States is bad (*no todo Estados Unidos es malo*), it is only the White House (*Casa Blanca*), the CIA, who try to destroy (*destruir*) rather than develop (*desarrollar*).

Luis' parable constructs indigenous instrumental reason as a "bricoleur" ability (Clifford 1988) to manufacture wonderful creations through one's talents alone, without having to be formally or informally taught. This emphasis might be seen to contain the traces of patronizing ladino attitudes toward indigenous subjects, but the narrative exceeds the frames of ladino racism. Defiance marks the exchange between the K'iche' man and the FBI, as he argues his point and tries to illustrate that he is within his rights to assemble the magnificent apparatus, and that there is no malice or harm in his creation. The FBI's position is, however, that possession of such an apparatus can only be the prerogative of the authoritarian regime and for anyone else to own it amounts to an implicit threat to the government. To have access to the private conversations taking place nationwide, on phones and radio frequencies, is the exclusive right of the repressive state. To no avail does the man point out that if it is the government's prerogative to be in possession of the apparatus, surely they could have manufactured one themselves. There was no malicious intent in the assemblage, only the man's intelligence and creativity. The FBI and the Guatemalan Army leave unconvinced and on their next visit the K'iche' man is taken away and never heard of again.

I suggest that the status of the wonder apparatus manufactured by the K'iche' man be considered in terms of its relation to secrecy. What the apparatus does is allow access to private, semipublic, and public information that one would not be aware of, unless aided by one's talents to assemble such a makeshift technology. Fortuitous access to private and public secrets, and to networks through which secrets circulate, amounts to a transgression that is severely punished by the neo-imperial foreign power and the repressive Guatemalan military state. It seems that only the latter have rightful access to secrets through surveillance, and anyone else intervening in the process of secrecy management can only be a rebel. This coincides with a recurrent theme in my conversations with ex-combatants, namely that it is the very nature of the repressive state to manufacture to a significant extent the subject position of the rebel, and thus draw unwitting individuals into a spiral of accusation, exposure, and punishment. Interestingly, accusations very often come from fellow villagers who are enmeshed in a social fabric that quite literally produces insurgency through practices of denunciation, despite the fact that underneath the production of insurgency, there are only individual intelligence and ingenuity. The fashioning and functioning of the apparatus occurs in the public domain, as the K'iche' man makes his fellow villagers participate in the appreciation of his wonderful creation. Through the production of audibility, the right of access to information and networks is made public, which directly threatens the repressive state's seeming exclusive right to surveillance and secrecy management. Likewise, it is the intelligent generation of audibility that induces the violent repression at the hands of national and foreign power. Luis' narrative is elegantly structured, so that each episode he recounts leads to another. As the parables unfold, they turn progressively more personal, and a third story deals with Luis' own experiences. As the young K'iche' man had the talent to assemble a wonderful apparatus out of discarded parts, thus unexpectedly intercepting telephone and radio transmissions, Luis had similar bricoleur aptitudes.

El Rifle/The Rifle

Luis had applied creativity and ingenuity to the assemblage of a marvelous creation of his own fashioned out of the debris of a plane crash. He had collected the fragments of the wreckage and made a rifle. Having accidentally fired a shot, he attracted the attention of his neighbors, who reported the matter to their authorities. Like the K'iche' man, Luis was drawn into a spiral of accusations and was soon visited by Army soldiers.

Personally, I like to mess around (*traviesar*) with weapons (*armas*). In Sayaxché in 1967, I started assembling/making a 38-caliber rifle (*hacer un fusil calibre 38*) out of some pieces of pipes (*tubos*) of a plane (*avión*) that had crashed (*caer*), and when I had nearly finished it, my father hit it hard and a shot was fired (*meterle un tiro*), he hit the trigger and it exploded. The next day the Army came to the house because the neighbors (*vecinos*) had gone to denounce me (*denunciar*), [saying] that I was making weapons to kill (*armas para matar*). At five in the morning the Army got us out of the house (*nos sacó el ejército de la casa*) and what the officer said to me was that in Guatemala it was prohibited outright (*prohibido terminantemente*) that a person develop one's knowledge whatever that person's inclination might be (*que una persona desarrollara inteligencias de la índole que fuera*), that in Guatemala nobody could invent anything (*nadie podía inventarse nada*) not even the slightest thing (*ni lo más mínimo*) because it was forbidden (*por que era prohibido*).

Where did they take you? I ask.

They did not find it on me, because I, being wise (*como sabio*), during the night I put the rifle in an old water well, nineteen meters deep. I tied it to a string (*pita*) and I hung it there (*lo guindé*), they did not find it (*no lo hallaron*), because if they had found it, they would have killed me. What the lieutenant told me was that if the Army realizes (*se da cuenta*) and they find a weapon on you (*te encuentran un arma*), that you may have made (*que tu la haigas hecho*), they will burn you alive (*te van a quemar vivo*), because that is the law of the government in Guatemala, because that is an offense (*delito*). I said to him, well, I did not do anything to anybody, those people lied to you (*mentir*), I did not, and how would I know how to do/make things, when I am a *campesino*, I told them, I was raised in the *monte* (*me he criado solo en el monte*), I did not even have any education (*yo no tuve ni escuela*), that is what I told them, that was a lie (*mentira*), but he said to me, you were making that rifle (*el rifle tú los estabas haciendo*), because they came to tell, they saw you (*por que los que fueron a decir, te vieron*).

I say to Luis, ah, somebody went and told them, somebody accused/denounced you (*la denunció*).

> Yes, Luis confirms, and no, I said to them, I did not do anything (*no he hecho nada*). Didn't you (*cómo no?*)? He said to me, you did make the rifle (*tú lo hiciste*) and at five in the afternoon you fired a shot (*reventaron un tiro*). Well then, I said to them, you look for it/find it (*aquí, pues búsquelo*), if you can find it! And that is what he said to me, never again make/do anything else (*nunca más vas a hacer otra cosa*) or try to make/do it (*intentar hacerlo*), because they will kill you/you will be killed (*matar*), this is the law (*ley*) and it is in this way that in Guatemala, the very same governments (*los mismos gobiernos*) have destroyed many intelligent people (*gente inteligente*). So, I do not agree (*estar de acuerdo*) with this destruction (*la destrucción*) because if some people are intelligent (*si una gente es inteligente*) one should use that (*usar*) to see whether they develop more (*desarrollar*), but if one kills them (*matar*), that is not right (*correcto*).

Luis' tripartite narrative illustrates how a climate of suspicion and threats of accusation muddled the truth and produced a social context in which secrets were harbored, accessed, intercepted, exchanged, stolen through violence and deception, and fashioned through creativity, intelligence, and ingenuity. While secrets engendered the constant threat of exposure, the repressive system of secrecy management seemed to take on a life of its own and intervened even when (or precisely because) there was no secret to protect, no malicious intent to gain access to secrets. Violence, on the other hand, never appeared to be "mindless." In Luis' account, the repressive neo-imperial and/or national state apparatus of surveillance actually engaged in argumentation and allowed for people to make their case. In the last instance, however, violence or the threat of violence was always imminent, and served the appropriation, management, and control of secrets. Yet, one resorted to telling lies to protect oneself and hid the evidence of one's ingenuity, and hence of guilt, inside a well.

Binaries: *¡A Vencer o Morir!*

In post-demobilization times, Luis and his fellow ex-FAR associates were identified as "ex-combatants" by international agencies, the Misión de Verificación Naciones Unidadas Guatemala (United Nations Verification Mission in Guatemala; MINUGUA); they also self-identified as "ex-*combatientes*." The term *combatiente* (combatant) suggests that guerrilla life was about military strife. While many forms of engagement actually qualified as guerrilla activities,[9] military operations were foundational experiences for many men and women involved in the organization. My interlocutors in the field often reminisced about *ataques* and *ofensivas* (attacks and offensives). Narratives focusing on the occurrence of military operations presented such temporally defined materializations of the conflict in terms of a whole consisting of a binary oppositional relation between discrete parts. Tucán, a Kaqchikel ex-*guerrillero*, recalled his participation in combat in the course of our conversation.

> This is something I cannot forget because those really are moments when one's conscience (*conciencia*) is born, of one being a revolutionary (*revolucionario*) and fighting (*luchar*) against an army. This is no easy task. In all instances, it really is a case of Victory or Death (*allí sí, que a Vencer o Morir*). At that moment in the war (*guerra*) we had to endure it (*aguantar*), we had to do it, because that is the idea, to change the situation of Guatemala (*de cambiar la situación de Guatemala*), so at that time of the war, between different groups (*grupos distintos*), it is a matter of life or death (*vida o muerte*), so that I will never forget, because I participated in many battles against the Army (*ejército*), and not only against the Army, but also against the Army Air Force.

Tucán recalled his participation in military actions as foundational for the articulation of political conscience and the conviction that social change ought to be fostered in Guatemala. He envisioned the struggle as occurring between distinct groups, namely the Army and the guerrilla, and involvement in military confrontation and political mobilization more broadly as regulated by the seemingly irrevocable alternative between *Vencer o Morir*, Victory or Death. While the conflict appeared to be structured according to the binary distinction between the Guatemalan Army and the guerrilla, the guerrilla ethos appeared to depend on the all-too-significant difference between triumph and annihilation. Many accounts, however, problematized the status of totalities, emphasizing instead the partibility of subjects, their course of action, and their effects.

A Desire to Exceed (Oneself)

Carlos was thirty-six years old. He was born in the eastern region of Jutiapa and lived in Escuintla in infancy. During our conversation Carlos told me about his family's move to Petén and noted how, as a young man, he had joined the insurgents, moved by a desire to improve his own condition and that of the people of Guatemala.

> When I was about seven, we moved to Petén, and we lived in the village about twenty kilometers from here. My father was looking for land, and he found a place around Melchor de Mencos, here in Petén. That's where I lived until I was sixteen. It is at the age of sixteen that my involvement in the revolutionary struggle (*involucramiento a la lucha revolucionaria*) began, first as support (*apoyo*), so to speak, to the organization (*organización*). In this case, the very first form of involvement was to disseminate propaganda (*regar propaganda*), during the night, because this was all clandestine (*clandestino*), and no one was supposed to see how we were intervening (*andar interveniendo*), in information gathering, purchase of foodstuff, and such. Well, we did it, before joining the fronts (*incorporación a los frentes*), which came later. . . . When I took the decision of joining (*incorporarse*), I decided to communicate this to my parents, but this when it was already the decisive moment of my *incorporación*. So I met with them and I told them, well, I need to speak with you both. Well, they were surprised (*ellos sorprendidos*). He surely must be thinking of marrying/being in a relationship (*acompañarse*) [they thought]. Marrying the revolutionary struggle (*lucha revolucionaria*), I said. They were very surprised. In the end, they realized that the decision I was taking was the *incorporación* for the development (*formación*) of the guerrillas in Petén. That was something that surprised them immensely, but at the same time they said to me, well, it is very satisfactory for us that you may be taking this path (*camino*), because, for your information, since 1972 we also have been participating in this struggle (*venir participando en esta lucha*). I did not know that. It is something sad (*triste*) [they said] that you may be off, because we know that you are going to a war (*guerra*), and a war, as you know, is of casualties (*muertos*), injury (*heridos*), and suffering (*sufrimiento*). But we know that you are going to do it for all of us, the poor (*los pobres*) who are suffering (*padecer*) in our country. So we wish you good luck (*buena suerte*), behave yourself (*pórtate bien*), with complete discipline (*toda disciplina*) as you have always done. We know you will have many successes (*éxitos*), and do not forget us. These are the words that they said to me in the end. So that with their support, I took the decision to join, although of course I had come to that decision already, as I was saying to you before, despite the fact that I was a minor (*menor*

> *de edad*). Age was not a limit that could keep me (*detener*) with them. Instead, I longed for something more (*desear algo más*), which was not only to fight for them, but also for the people (*pueblo*) who have always needed it (*necesitar*).

Carlos commented on his decision to join the guerrilla at the age of sixteen, noting the youthful fervor and political conviction through which he was able to transcend the restrictions and bounds of village life. When he reached the guerrilla camp for the first time, Carlos told me, he found he was not the only one who had willingly exceeded himself and his condition. Through separate routes, over twenty new recruits who had known each other previously, but were unaware of their respective guerrilla collaboration, came together on the occasion of their first guerrilla training. As they became acquainted with weapons, they began to experience a newly fashioned sense of commonality.

> I have to tell you that it was something very pleasurable (*muy agradable*), because in the end we realized that many of us who joined (*incorporarse*), and it was a group of over twenty of us, in the end, we had all known each other before (*conocidos*), but because of the clandestinity (*clandestinidad*) of the organization, we did not know what each of us was (*en que estábamos cada uno*) and only there we finally realized. So, there were people from different villages there, and that is how we started and it was very nice (*bonito*) to see the first rifles (*fusil*), although very few of them, of course. For we had to have weapons to confront the enemy (*enemigo*), and the enemy in this case was the Army. So it turns out that there [were] about twenty rifles, and in addition there were only rifle carbines (*carabina*), M1s, and there were also some shotguns (*escopetas de un tiro*), 16 and 20 millimeter caliber. Well, I was lucky because in the end the one who was in command there knew me and on some occasions he had made use of me as instructor to train (*entrenar*) *la milicia*,[10] so in view of the degree of trust (*confianza*) that there existed, he allowed that a rifle were given to me, one of the automatic rifles! [laughter] I was lucky in that instance, and certainly we began to feel the warm manner (*manera tan cálida*) of brothers (*tan de hermanos*), which was common among us.

According to Carlos' recollections, military training posited the Army as the common enemy for the new recruits. Nevertheless, inasmuch as there had been multiple and discrete paths leading individual recruits to the guerrilla camp, there would be manifold, complex, and secretive practices of simulation and dissimulation through which the coherence of parts, wholes, and their relations might periodically be sought or, indeed, undermined as they became embroiled in the partialities of the conflict.

Doubling and Insurgent Dissimulations: *Dos Caras* (Two Faces/Faced)

Nicolás was a Q'eqchi' ex-combatant whose ex-combatant status was that of "*disperso*," that is, in the aftermath of demobilization he had returned to his family. I met him by chance, as we converged in the same village. Nicolás was visiting his daughter, while I had gone on this trip with Flor, who wanted to visit a relative said to be critically ill. Flor introduced me to Nicolás' family and in the evening we sat outside the house to converse in the dark. Nicolás recounted the episodes that led to his involvement in the organization, noting strategies devised to undermine the guerrilla/Army binary.

> In 1985 there was strife (*pelearse*) in my *parcela* between the Army and the guerrilla,[11] and there were deaths, about thirteen Army casualties, and for this reason they [the Army] were angry (*tenía coraje*) with them [the guerrilla]. They took me to the *parcela*: "Here is where the *postas* [the observation/surveillance posts] were yesterday." Ah, okay, I said to them, but I did not understand (*entendía*) them, I did not get the point (*no le agarraba el rollo*), for, what were "*postas*"? We say "*postas*" when a tree is planted (*sembrar on palo*), I said to them. Well, you do not understand, now this is going to be your downfall (*te vas a caer*), son of a bitch (*hijo de la gran puta*). He [the Army officer] was angry (*enojado*). Look, I said to him, I did not go anywhere (*no salí*). And still you have the face to tell me that it's not true (*todavía tenes cara para decir que no es cierto*), he asked. Yes, of course, I said to him, I am not involved in anything (*yo no estoy metido a nada*).

On that occasion, the Army officer was satisfied that Nicolás was not involved in insurgent activities. Nicolás was thus taken to Poptún to receive training as a *patrullero*, that is, as a member of the Civil Patrols. As Nicolás told me, the Army entrusted him with the role of Civil Patrol Coordinator of his own village.

> When I got to Poptún, they even gave me a duty/official post (*cargo*)! Civil Patrol Coordinator (*coordinador de patrulleros*)!
>
> Of the Civil Patrols? I ask, in disbelief.
>
> *¡Ándale!* confirms Nicolás emphatically.[12] They gave me that job but I would work two faces (*pero yo trabajaba dos caras*)[13] so that they would not pay attention to me, but what I was most sure of was that we have to be part of the guerrilla struggle (*lucha guerrillera*). Well, since that time I joined the guerrilla struggle (*me incorporé a la lucha guerrillera*). In the Civil Patrols we would just go around (*pa' arriba y pa' abajo*), what's going on, there is nothing happening, and if anyone armed comes, what do we do, *muchá* (pals)? Well, we don't do anything (*no hacemos nada*). In any case, today we see this hamlet (*aldea*) is free, but the day will come when the war will plunge upon us (*va a llegar la guerra sobra de nosostros*), and that was how it was (*así fue*). It always arrived/got there [it came upon us] (*llegó siempre*). I went to *la montaña* in 1985. As I was already asking questions about what was happening/may happen (*qué se pasara*), well, I am clear in my mind (*estar claro*), for there are times one does not know what to think (*hay veces pues que no halla como uno*), but when one is clear (*entonces de estar claro*), we decided to go, as we already used to go and visit the *compañeros* (*siempre me pasaba a ver con los compañeros*). My family knew that I had stayed behind [*en la montaña*], but they did not know whether I was alive (*mi familía sabía que aquí me quedé, pero no sabía si todavía vivía*). I was in the Mardoqueo Front, with Comandante Pedro. About twenty-five *compañeros* [Q'eqchi'] from the same hamlet, we all joined (*nos incorporamos*). Some were able to endure it (*aguantar*), some left.

As a guerrilla sympathizer, Nicolás infiltrated the system of counterinsurgency. As he described it in the course of the interview, for a time prior to joining the guerrilla ranks *en la montaña*, he would "work two faces" as apathetic *comisionado militar* and as active guerrilla informer. Practices of dissimulation were in fact not exclusive to the guerrilla, and rather a domain of counterinsurgency artifice extensively deployed by the Army.

Doubling and Counterinsurgent Simulations: *Botas de Hule*

The Commission for Historical Clarification (CEH 1999, 347–411, Case Study No. 31, Annex 1, Volume I) notes that the village Las Dos Erres was founded in 1978 under the aegis of the Empresa Nacional de Fomento y Desarrollo de Petén (FYDEP) and its colonization policy. In early 1982 the guerrilla entered the neighboring town of Las Cruces to hold a political meeting and purchase supplies. The Army responded by installing a military outpost (*destacamento*) in Las Cruces. Following the massacre in the village Josefinos in April of the same year, the area became progressively more militarized. Army recognizance actions in the village of Las Dos Erres also became more frequent. In September 1982 FAR carried out an attack against military objectives in Las Cruces. The *comisionado militar* of Las Cruces requested that the village of Las Dos Erres put forward individuals who might take part in the activities of the Patrullas de Autodefensa Civil (PAC; Civil Patrols), but the request was rejected. Rumors begun to spread that the villagers of Las Dos Erres might be guerrilla sympathizers. The Army searched the village and found a sack with "FAR" inscribed on it. The sack belonged to one of the founders of the community, Federico Aquino Ruano and thus bore his initials. Nevertheless, the sack was said to amount to proof of guerrilla activity in the village (CEH 1999). About a month later, and as recalled by Nestor in the course of our conversation, FAR carried out an ambush on the road to Palestina. The Commission for Historical Clarification notes that the Army responded by sending a platoon of eighteen men of the Kaibiles Unit, that is, the special branch in charge of commando operations. These were joined by forty other Kaibiles. On 6 December 1982, the fifty-eight Kaibiles entered the village dressed as *guerrilleros*. The Commission for Historical Clarification notes that the order was that the fifty-eight Kaibiles wear olive-green shirts and civilian trousers and that they carry ordinary weapons. The massacre began in the early hours of 6 December, as the Kaibiles disguised as *guerrilleros* killed the infants first.

Nestor told me that he was absolutely certain the Fuerzas Armadas Rebeldes had no links whatever to the site of Las Dos Erres, where the Army massacred the entire village in December 1982 (CEH 1999; ODHAG 1998). Nestor said:

> We had a camp (*campamento*) north of Palestina and we had planned an action (*accionar*) on the Libertad-Subín road, and thus we had to pass in the vicinity of Las Dos Erres, which we would habitually pass by. But what we would do was avoid it (*evadir*) [the settlement], so that we would not be seen (*ver*), or we might go by at night, but we never let ourselves be known there (*nunca nos dimos a conocer allí*) and people never knew about the guerrilla (*la gente nunca supo*). Nevertheless, they had desire/intention to collaborate in practice (*deseo práctico*) because the Army really tested them (*probar*). According to

> the information we have, the Army dressed themselves up as *guerrillero* (*el ejército se vistió de guerrillero*), entered the community, the people welcomed them (*recibir*), they gave them food (*le dio comida*), and the Army, in order to confirm (*confirmar*) that they were *guerrilleros*, grabbed the *comisionados militares* and they killed them right in front of the people [villagers]. When the soldiers who had dressed up as *guerrilleros* retreated (*retirarse*), they go and dress as the Army (*vestir de militares*) and return (*regresar*) to suppress the people/village (*reprimir el pueblo*) saying why had they allowed their *comisionados militares* to be killed (*por qué habían dejado que mataran sus comisionados militares*). This was the justification (*justificación*) for further violence.

The narrative of the Army dressing up as the guerrilla was a common theme in my conversations with people in Petén. Many had commented on the indeterminacy and ambivalence in the Army/guerrilla distinction. Arguments were common that while there might be *guerrilleros* in the Army ranks, the guerrilla might be made up of Army officers. In my conversation with Nestor, I spoke of an "image confusion" (*confusión de imagen*) and Nestor set out to qualify how any confusion was the product of specific counterinsurgency tactics deployed by the Army to confound the population and, crucially, to mystify the *guerrilleros/as*. As Nestor said:

> There were other cases. In the guerrilla we used *botas de hule* (rubber boots)[14] exclusively and the Army used *botas de hule* to confound (*confundir*) people, or to confound us (*nosotros mismos*), that it had not been the Army that had passed by a certain place. Or else, they would dress [like us] or would arm themselves with the same arms as us. But many succeeded (*lograr*) in identifying/discerning/discriminating (*identificar*) [between the two], because the Army soldier (*soldado del ejército*) and the guerrilla soldier (*soldado guerrillero*) were not the same (*igual*) in the way they treated people (*forma de tratar la gente*). There was a form/manner (*forma*), it was the form/manner that people would identify (*identificar*), and how people would identify the Army. Because while the Army might be dressed like a *guerrillero* (*estuviera vestido de guerrillero*), the manner (*trato*), the form of address (*forma de dirigirse*) [toward] a *campesino* and [toward] poor people (*gente humilde*) was completely different. For we never threatened them (*amenazar*), we never pointed a rifle at an unarmed civilian (*civil desarmado*), we would speak with them in a

form/manner (*forma*), like this, soft (*suave*), without affecting them (*afectarlos*) [detrimentally]. On the contrary, soldiers address (*dirigirse*) civilians undermining them (*hacer de menos*), they treat them with contempt.

Practices of simulation and dissimulation complicated the binaries on which the conflict was predicated, chief among them the distinction between the guerrilla and the Army. Nevertheless, Nestor was adamant that the practices of simulation deployed by the Army failed complete mimesis. Despite the cunning deployment of guerrilla attire, the Army never mimicked guerrilla ethics correctly, and that is where the categorical distinction lay.

Doubling in Combat: Brothers

Nicolás had a brother who also joined the guerrilla. As he noted, their fates were remarkably different.

> I had a brother, he stayed [in the guerrilla] and died. He was working (*trabajar*) [in the guerrilla], he was working with some *compas* [*guerrilleros*] of the village. They were carrying a sewing machine (*máquina*), to sew waterproof clothing (*costurar ropa de repelente*) that was being used for the war (*guerra*). This took them a few days, but they did not realize, or perhaps someone went to tell (*avisar*), and when they came out they fell in the trap (*caer en la trampa*). The military got them. I looked out for them for fifteen days. I looked for them again in the capital when the Peace [Accord] was signed, but I could not see them, we never saw them again.

Nestor also had a brother, Rafael. I got to know them both, and one day I asked whether they would like me to interview them together. Nestor and Rafael kindly agreed, and on the day of the interview we all went to their home and conversed together for a while. Rafael, whose background I was not well acquainted with, began by recounting his experiences.

> We used to live in a village in Petén [the site of a massacre] at the time, [and] I was a bit off the rails (*desacarrilado*) we could say, I liked drinking too much. My brothers were already organized (*estar organizado*) [in the guerrilla], we used to talk a bit, we celebrated the triumph of the *Sandinistas*, which was taking place in Nicaragua, and

we would identify with that war (*guerra*) and would comment that it would be good if something similar would occur in Guatemala. However, my brothers were already organized [in the guerrilla], but they never said anything to me, perhaps because of the situation, and for the fact that they had to be very discreet (*muy discretos*). They thought it was impudent (*descocado*) that I should be so drunk (*pasado de copas*). They feared I would talk to people who might harm us (*jugar una mala pasada*), so they resolved to never say anything to me. That is how in 1979 I left the village and headed south. I was twenty. And where I was, in the south of the country, in the course of an action of the Army, they captured me (*capturar*) to go into military service, and my brothers stayed on in Petén. I was in the Army for thirty months. Army training was a bit rough (*brusco*). The reality is that in the Army the training is not very professional (*professional*), I don't know if things are different now, but at the time the training was quite rough. My brothers in the guerrilla had training that was superior to that of the Army. I took a course (*sacar un curso*) in Jutiapa, in the military zone there. The course was called *Curso de Tigre* (Course of the Tiger). In that course one would learn some elements (*elementos*), for instance, what they called "*Sonido de Olores*" (The Sound of Smell/Scent). One would be taken to a place and they would play things (*sonar cosas*), and they would put meat to roast (*asar carne*), and grass (*hierba*), and one would have to identify the smells. But this was not an intense course. Afterwards they sent me to the area of operations, which is what they called it, they sent me to Nebaj.[15] We were in Nebaj for six months between 1979 and 1980. We were the first soldiers to get there, on the landing strip north of Nebaj, and that is where we installed a *destacamento* (outpost). We had no contact with the guerrilla. We would be told that they would come, they would send us papers/messages (*mandar papeles*), and people would inform us that the *guerrilleros* were over there; but our *compañía* never had a confrontation (*enfrentamiento*), with the exception of an unsuccessful attempt (*conato*), where they [the guerrilla] placed a *claymore* (Claymore mine) and slightly wounded a soldier. Afterwards we went to look for them, but there was no trace (*rastro*) of them. That was all. The matter got progressively more intense (*agudizarse*), our *compañía* was called "The First Fusileros Tojiles" (*la primaria de fusileros Tojiles*),[16] and was relieved by "The Third Fusileros Jaguares" (*la tercera fusileros Jaguares*), from Jutiapa. Of those 660 soldiers who made up the Jaguares, only fourteen returned to the

> military zone. The rest were annihilated (*aniquilar*) by the *compas* [the *guerrilleros*]. Luckily I did not take part in any counterinsurgency action, because now I would regret it (*doler*), if I had done it. That is, my ideal has always been a revolutionary one (*mi ideal siempre ha sido revolucionario*), but where I was I could not do anything against the current of the Army (*la corriente del ejército*). Now I am happy that I can be of use in some tasks related to the party. I think that the best thing my brothers did was not allowing me to join (*incorporarse*) [the guerrilla], because I might not be alive today if I did.

Following Rafael's account, Nestor confirmed that many of the reasons he and his brothers had not involved Rafael in the organization were related to the fact that they would not willingly recruit a relative into the organization unless the relative displayed the necessary will and conviction. Nestor then recounted how they had reunited in the mid-1990s.

> We met in front of McDonald's, El Tecolote, in Guatemala City in 1995. And since the day we met, we have not parted (*cuando nos juntamos, no nos despegamos*). At times, when I was in combat (*estar combatiente*), I remembered them, not just him [his brother, who is present], but also my other brother who was also taken to military service (*el servicio*). When I was in the combat line (*línea de combate*), I would remember them and as I was in the midst of combat, I would think, I might be shooting one of my brothers (*a lo mejor me estoy tirando con uno de mis hermanos*). As there were many [soldiers] from *Oriente* (*orietanos*) in the military ranks in Petén,[17] I would often hear the eastern inflection in their voice (*la voz caballita*). And one day I had an altercation (*maltratar*) with one of them, there were about five meters between us, and *cabal*,[18] I worked out (*atinar*) that he was from *Oriente* (*orientano*), and he even told me his name. I did not want to tell him mine, but he was mistreating me (*maltratar*), he would say, with you, I will kill ten *guerrilleros*. I have already killed five, and with you it will be six. *Dále, pues, dále* (get on with it), I would say to him, and I left him there. What I would think was, that the likelihood (*a lo mejor*) was that it was my brother in front of me (*con un hermano estaba yo en frente*). He [the soldier] was from the *compañía Tojil* and in 1983 we annihilated a whole *compañía*, and it was the Tojiles. We had a three-hour-long combat, we [the guerrilla] were two *compañías*, and they were one. We rounded them up and annihilated them (*aniquilar*). Some got out alive because they fled,

> or rather, the platoon (*pelotón*) who was with the head (*jefe*) of the *compañía* managed to escape the confrontation, and the rest were left there (*el resto se quedó allí*).

Nestor recalled how in the midst of combat he had seen his own brother in the enemy standing about five meters away from him. Through a merographic analogy, he had seen his own kind in his nemesis. The merographic analogy created a connection between two seemingly discrete entities, namely the Army and the guerrilla, through the image of his brother facing Nestor during combat. The merographic effort was one of envisaging a connection and sameness, in what presented itself as difference, that is, as a connection from another angle (Strathern 1992a).

Proximity and Adjunction

Carlos told me that following demobilization procedures, some ex-combatants had gone to meet Army officers they had fought against during the war. Accompanied by MINUGUA military personnel, they entered the *zona militar*, that is, the military base. The encounter between the ex-*guerrilleros* and the Army officers engendered the articulation of merographic analogies by both parties, and produced a series of reciprocal revelations.

Strathern has coined the neologism "merographic," an adjective that combines etymologically "meros," Greek for "part" or "share," and "graphic," to stress "the way ideas write or describe one another; the very act of description makes what is being described a part of something else, e.g. description" (Strathern 1992a, 204, note 21). In her discussion of English kinship, Strathern points out that domains imagined as discrete, for instance, "nature" and "culture," may appear to be connected "by virtue of being at once similar and dissimilar" (Strathern 1992a, 72). Similarities are engendered through an effort to "recognize" connections, while dissimilarities emerge out of "recognition" of difference, making difference to be a connection from another angle (Strathern 1992a, 73). Merographic analogies and the connections on which they are predicated are partial in the sense that they presuppose "that one thing differs from another insofar as it belongs to or is part of something else" (Strathern 1992a, 73). These models of relationships Strathern calls "merographic."

Ex-*guerrilleros/as* deployed a "merographic capacity," insofar as "merographic capacity" refers to the ability to envision partial analogies. As argued by Lury (1998),

> Analogies are partial not only in the sense that they imply perceived difference as well as similarity in the making of comparison between wholes and in that sense are not complete or total, but also in that they make wholes (including persons) out of parts in particular ways. In this making, while parts of a person are part of that person as a whole or a system (such as the individual), they are also, from another perspective, conceived as parts of other wholes, such as, for example, society or nature. In this sense, things (including the individual, nature and society) are seen to be constructed or determined and to be inhabiting what might be termed synthetic culture or a culture that constructs (Lury 1998, 13).

Disclosures revealed how the parts of seemingly discrete entities had been in complex relations to each other. Early on in our conversation, Carlos posited a series of distinctions between the guerrilla and the Army, and the Army officers and the soldiers. Carlos said:

> Well, I think that in our case, [in the aftermath of demobilization], the majority of people could talk to them [the Army] (*la mayor parte de la gente, sí, venimos y nos podemos platicar con ellos [el ejército]*), we shook hands (*nos estrechamos la mano*), because in the end, as far as I am concerned, the point was to understand that in those times, to undertake/sustain an offensive activity (*actividad ofensiva*) was just and necessary (*justo y necesario*), to be hostile to them (*pues hostil en contra de ellos*), but today this is no longer possible, although one never stops carrying on (*mantener*) feeling that anger (*coraje*), in the memory of all they did/perpetrated, right (*verdad*)? But in this case, this is more toward those high-rank officers (*altos oficiales*). For instance, if you meet a high-ranking officer you know that he intervened (*intervenir*) in that war that is no longer (*finalizar*), and that in one way or other they are responsible for many instances of violations of human rights (*hechos de violaciones de los derechos humanos*). And it is not the same for the soldiers (*soldados*), because soldiers go [into the Army] for three years and then they leave, whereas the officer, in order to graduate as an officer, they spend a period of seven years directly in the Army for their training (*formación*). So this is where, in the end, in one way or another, one feels rejection (*rechazo*) toward another, a rejection we still hold, because we know that in one way or other, we have to carry on erasing it (*borrando*).

Carlos then proceeded in his account of how he had met high-ranking Army officers in post-demobilization times.

> So I recall that soon after I demobilized (*desmovilizarse*), I met some colonels of the military zone of Cobán [Alta Verapaz]. Indeed, there I met the second in command (*segundo jefe*). And then I also met another colonel who was third in command (*tercer jefe*). I had that opportunity. So, they tell me, okay, but where exactly were you mostly, and at that exact moment a friend approaches and calls out "Oswaldo." They knew of "Oswaldo" [one of Carlos' pseudonyms], so, you are Marvin Herrera [his first name] [they ask]? Correct (*cierto*), I reply. In that case, we have heard of you (*hemos sabído de vos*). Of course, I say to them, for you keep your intelligence (*inteligencia*), you of the military still have it intact! We know you move around a lot, they say to me. Of course, that's correct, I say to them. And when are you going to come and visit us? When the opportunity may arise, and indeed, rest assured, we come and visit there (*llegar*). And that's how it was, I arrived there some time later. And when I got there and was there with them, only the second and third in command were present. Of course, I was accompanied by an official of the military corps of the United Nations Verification Mission in Guatemala, should problems arise. And so we got there and when they saw us, well, [they were] happy, well, welcome, they say, here we are, did you want to speak to us? Of course, we come to visit you, not just to see (*ver*) you, we come to converse a bit (*platicar un poco*). And after three minutes that we were there talking, everything stopped, the colonel sprung up, the second in command, and left to welcome the colonel of the military base, first in command. He had been told we were there. Go, bring them to the office, he tells them, and so we went all the way there, inside their office, inside the *comandancia*.

I sensed the strained and chilling aspect of the story and said to Carlos, you entered the lion's den. He replied, "Yes, that's where we stayed for a time, in the *comandancia*, that's where we conversed and they were, I can tell you, very cordial. The only provocation came from the second in command, who says, you, were you ever here? For good or ill (*ni a buenas, ni a malas*)? Never, I say to him. Never did they send me to carry out an action here, I say to him, my superiors never sent me. And neither did you have the capacity to bring me here by force (*traer aquí a puro huevo*)." Carlos was an extremely confident and charming man, with a characteristic propensity for irony and wit.[19] But when he recounted his visit to the military base, he seemed, suddenly, profoundly vulnerable. Nevertheless, he pressed on with the story and proceeded to reflect how merographic connections between the two discrete domains of the guerrilla and the Army were articulated in post-demobilization times. Carlos referred to a merographic analogy from the perspective of the Army.

> That's exactly how I said it to them/what I said to them (*así se lo dije, va*) [that you cannot bring me here by force]. So, as I was saying, the second *jefe* was the one who [asked whether I had ever been there], not the third *jefe*. The first *jefe*, what he expresses is that a lot of work was needed at the level of the Army officials, because there was still great rejection (*rechazo*) toward us and he asks me if on our part this is also the case. Well, yes, I say to him, there is also that, but that is what one has to work on to strengthen this process we are currently experiencing, it is a commitment (*compromiso*) that in the end we have to uphold, you and us, and contribute toward with our attitude (*actitud*) so that it may progressively get stronger (*fortalecer*). Excellent, he says to me. But I want to tell you something very special, he says to me. Of an opportunity that arose when we were called, he tells me, to a meeting in Honduras, they called us, and they did not tell us with whom we were going to meet, but when the plane was about to land, they tell us, you will now have the opportunity to meet officers of the guerrilla, of the URNG [Unidad Revolucionaria Nacional Guatemalteca; Guatemalan National Revolutionary Unity], who come to dialogue with us. I was very surprised, he says (*yo sorprendido, dice*). And it transpires that this is a meeting of Army officers (*oficiales del ejército*), I am talking about colonels, about officers, some captains (*capitanes*), so he says that his surprise was that there he meets some of his very best friends, of a time when he was a student in an institute, and that best friend of his then is whom we know as El Moreno Méndez, Rodolfo Sanchéz.[20]
>
> Manolo! I cry out, and Carlos and I laugh.[21]
>
> So then, he [the Army officer] says, it is incredible (*increible*) to see you [the friend] here, and imagine, he says to me, I would have never believed, after all that, that he would be so totally leftwing (*totalmente de izquierda*), and I would be rightwing (*derecha*), because he was in the guerrilla, and I was integrated here in the Army.
>
> We [Carlos and the others visiting the military base] stayed there with them for a good spell (*bonito rato*), drinking soft drinks (*aguas*).

> In what we can, here we are going to help you, and here in the vicinity, with trust (*con confianza*), here are the telephone numbers of the military zone, should you need them, and with that, we get ready to leave. On our way out they stop us, there, at the checkpoint at the entrance, and again, for the two of us who were demobilized combatants (*desmovilizados*), Tucán and I, they say, your identity papers (*su identificación*)? Look, I say to them, I am Marvin Herrera. And what is your profession, they say to me (*y su profesión, me dicen*). Well, up to not long ago, it was *guerrillero* (*bueno, hasta hace poco tiempo, era de guerrillero*), I say to them. Now, I don't know, because I don't know exactly to what profession I will dedicate myself. The guy laughed. So then, what? Are you going to keep us here detained (*detenidos*)? No, *qué les vaya bien*. Okay, *gracias*. And so we left.

Carlos recalled how during a secret meeting between officers of the guerrilla and officers of the Army, the guerrilla and the Army had revealed themselves by a merographic connection as marked by both their proximity to each other and their respective belonging to different domains. Carlos concluded thus:

> There was also another opportunity, which also was very interesting, during the phase of demobilization (*desmovilización*). Having already demobilized, and the *compañeros* being [back] in the hamlets (*aldeas*), there were some provocations (*provocaciones*) on the part of some units of the Army (*unidades del ejército*) against some *desmovilizados*. So they came and informed our *compañeros*. We then spoke to the Army and the Army expressed a commitment to patrol (*hacer una gira*) the various areas and gather (*reconcentrar*) again the *desmovilizados*, the populations who may be there and who may have been *incorporados combatientes* (active combatants), in an attempt to begin establishing and maintaining a contact (*contacto*) with the population and specify to them what the functions of the Army would be from then on. So, we went, we went with them, there were two colonels (*coroneles*), one who was second in command, Ricardo Saguierre, was the second in command of the military zone of Puerto Barrios. There was also the second in command Lieutenant Colonel Gonzales, who was the second in command of the Naval Base of the Atlantic.
>
> They were very impressed by the fact that the population, when one stopped to observe, would come to hug me (*abrazar*), would take off my rucksack to carry it themselves, and could not stop conversing

> (*platicar*) with me. And they said, Carlos, you are well known around here (*eres conocido por acá*). No, not really, I reply. No, they say, one can see they know you (*se conoce que te conocen*), and that they appreciate you (*apreciar*) very much. And how did you achieve (*lograr*) all this? It has been an enormous sacrifice (*sacrificio*), I say to them, I think that what is most exact (*exacto*) is to have fought for reasons so just (*justo*) and because this population has suffered (*padecer*), that is how. Well, I can tell you that they [the Army officers] did not feel too secure (*tranquilo*), how shall I say this? They were feeling bad (*mal*), for the fact that although they were the highest authorities (*autoridades máximas*), they were not regarded and treated in the same way. But it was obvious/inevitable (*lógico*) that the population would express this, you know (*verdad*)? And on we went together, and with MINUGUA. Yes, we know we are under surveillance (*controlados*), but this I can tell you, that the conditions that have been created in our country have to be strengthened. And I think that this is the process in which we have been, to the extent that should they not respect us, this may cause a new conflict. But I think that the conscience (*conciencia*) has been, on our part and on the part of the Army, that it does not suit us (*corresponder*), that we do not really have the conditions, nationally or internationally, to develop a new war (*guerra*).

Guerrilleros and Soldiers, Sons of the *Campesinado*

Esteban, an ex-combatant in his fifties, told me about his conversion to Roman Catholicism in post–Peace Accords times. In his account, merographic connections between the domain of the Army and that of the guerrilla conjured up the effect of a different domain where the distinction was no longer valid. Esteban referred to "*el campesinado*," the "*campesino* people," and noted how both *guerrilleros/as* and soldiers belonged to it. In the scale of the "*campesinado*" different orders of connection of affinity and difference appeared. Esteban said:

> *Bueno*, now I am going to tell you. I am persevering (*perseverar*) in the Church, albeit with some sorrow (*pena*). Because those people who are more backwards (*la gente que es más atrasadita*) are already saying, look, he is in the Church because he is afraid (*tener miedo*), but I don't know fear any longer (*y yo el miedo si ya no lo conzco*), I am no longer afraid (*miedo yo no le tengo*). Respect (*respeto*), yes, for everyone. I talk to soldiers, to anyone, I respect anyone, but I no longer

fear anyone (*tener miedo*). But, respect, yes (*mi respeto sí*). No anger (*coraje*). Everyone is free, and God will give to everyone, depending on his or her life on earth. And more so/worse with the Army (*peyor con el ejército*). If I reach the knowledge that the Army, the soldiers were not culpable/guilty (*si llego al conocimiento que el ejército, los soldado no tuvieron la culpa*). No. They put the soldier there, they told him, this needs to be done, and it's an order. Well then, those who are truly responsible for that are the governments of the time, those who were in office at the time, and the high military ranks (*los altos jefes militares*). The soldier is below (*el soldado está abajo*), executing orders issued by superiors (*cumpliendo ordenes a los jefes*). If he does not execute orders, they think he is politically on the left; because he does not do his duty (*porque este no cumple*), this is a sign (*seña*) that he supports the *guerrilleros*. But the soldier is son of the *campesinos* (*pero el soldado, es hijo de los campesinos*), it is not his fault (*culpa*), while the superior is son of the rich (*el jefe es hijo de un rico*), and orders are executed and are not to be challenged (*y ordenes se cumplen y no se discuten*). Hence, this is my dialectics (*dialéctica*), it is not the Army's fault because they are humane people (*gente humana*) and all soldiers come from the *campesinado* (*y todo el soldado viene del campesinado*). That is where they come from. Soldiers come from the *campesinado* (*del campesinado viene el soldado*). Yes, this is how I explain this to you (*sí, eso yo se lo comento así*).

Conclusion: Merographic Analogies

Guerrilla struggle, as Tucán, Nicolás, Carlos, Nestor, and Rafael imagined it, was not strictly a confrontation between discrete entities, such as the Army and the guerrilla. In the account of violence and conflict offered by Luis, violent political repression was said to develop as a response to individuals' displays of talents and aptitudes, which were deemed to contravene arbitrary and hastily fashioned rules and/or interdictions. The perpetrators of violence materialized in specific guises, namely as the FBI and the Guatemalan Army. Some episodes of violence were, on occasion, precipitated by the interventions of indiscreet neighbors, that is, by the incitement of relationalities of disclosure, predicated on the production and revelation of secrets. Such positive relationalities of disclosure involved the institutions of the nation-state and of neo-imperial powers, and unleashed violent reprisals. The multiple embodiments of the perpetrators of violence featured plasticity and ability to multiply, as Army soldiers swelled in numbers. Nevertheless, episodes of violence were preceded by an initial propensity for debate, leniency, and understanding. Guatemalan Army soldiers, for instance, were characterized as having the capacity to appreciate the value and accomplishment of people's intellectual talents and creative actions, despite the fact that these would ultimately be deemed to deserve punishment. In all three episodes recounted by Luis, the perpetrators of violence were eventually equated with, and/or made to stand metonymically for, the nation-state and the United States government, both envisaged as apparatuses of surveillance, control, extraction, and destruction of human talent. Beyond any debate and appreciation, they ultimately quashed human intellectual and creative endeavors. In sum, whatever the materialization, action, and consequence, all subjects were granted the faculty to discern human ingenuity, but in the last instance violence linked to the management, incitement, and production of secrecy prevailed.

Violence and ambivalence often coexisted, and occupied the same intellectual and experiential frame in ex-combatants' accounts and were implicated in the production of entities or parts viewed as discrete, with augmentation and reduction of distinctions between parts featuring as a common theme in ex-combatants' narratives. The instantiations of connectivity, plasticity, and porosity in subjects and relations are the product of the merographic capacity of subjects as much as of performative operations. Working beyond totalizing forms of contextualization, merographic connections performatively open up wholes, to reveal incompleteness, including gaps, from different perspectives. Further, merographic analogies summon up the partiality of the whole and the conditions of possibility of other perspectives, but rather than being exhausted in mere pluralization of value, merographic analogies conjure new wholes, always displacing and deferring the idea of totality and totalizing perspectives.

In the case of the material presented here, a number of partial analogies performatively produce merographic connections between parts. Parts such as "the soldier" and "the *guerrillero*" were made to appear to belong to different and discrete wholes, namely "the Army" and "the guerrilla." Simultaneously, however, multiple relations were imagined between such parts in multiple scales. In my analysis, I have highlighted how distinctions between parts figured in ex-combatants' narratives, and argued that they generated doubling effects that constantly summoned up other subjects and other relationships. Parts and their relations engendered instances of duplication and diminution and may be said to function in post-plural scales. Indeed, despite suffering and violence endured at the hand of state agents and state-controlled technology, experiences of militancy in the insurgency were not exhausted in binary understandings of the conflict. Distinctions were deployed and exceeded through dissimulation, as well as being periodically dissolved. This is most apparent in the occurrence of doubles, doubling subjects, and doubling relations in ex-*guerrilleros/as*' accounts. Doubling was associated with merographic connections between entities such as "the Army" and "the guerrilla" as they were linked by practices of dissimulation, which in turn engendered ambivalence and indeterminacy. Merographic connections also appeared in ex-combatants' discussions of their relation to their own siblings. Rafael and Nestor, two brothers, discussed their distinct experiences in the Army and in the guerrilla, respectively. While presenting themselves as discrete subjects with different experiences of the conflict, and positioned within discrete entities, Nestor recounted how during combat he would imagine his brother Rafael at the receiving end of the shots he fired. He was able to see his own kind in the Other.

For Carlos, secrecy and doubling produced instances of revelation. Carlos recounted how in post–Peace Accords times, ex-combatants met the Army officers who had been their enemies during the conflict, and how each party was revealed to the other as proximate and adjunct. Doubling, simulation, and dissimulation established different orders of relations between different parts and wholes. These merographic connections established relations that functioned in post-plural scales, conjuring up new wholes such as the *campesinado*, the collectivity of *campesinos*.

In guerrilla representations of the conflict, violence and ambivalence were closely linked and produced numerous connections. Guerrilla subjects displayed merographic capacities, as they negotiated connections between and among discrete domains, with Nicolás belonging to both as a *comisionado militar*, guerrilla informer, and later combatant. These *guerrilleros* noted how the Army had attempted to mimic guerrilla merographic abilities, and as part of counterinsurgency tactics tried to appear as the guerrilla, to confound the perception of domains of the population, and the guerrilla themselves. The merographic abilities of the guerrilla and the population were greater than those of the Army, in their capacities to see and replicate connections *and* distinctions. The sensory training Rafael received in the Army aimed to prepare him to both smell and hear distinctions, but as he conceded, the guerrilla surpassed the Army in this respect. Through merographic connections, domains were augmented and supplemented, revealing them as adjunct. When Carlos and his parents revealed (to each other) their distinct trajectories of participation in the guerrilla, the "guerrilla" as a domain widened. In turn, in post-demobilization times, it was revealed to Carlos how those who had been his leaders in the guerrilla struggle had been close to the same Army officers he had fought against. The latter was not only Carlos' revelation of adjunctiveness and connection: the experience of the high-ranking Army officer who recounted the story had at first been merographic—he met the *comandante guerrillero* only to find they had been best friends at school.[22] Merographic connections and the ability to entertain partial analogies generated new domains, in which connections were reconfigured. Thus, according to Esteban, the soldiers and *guerrilleros/as* both belonged to the *campesino people*, while Army officers and the rich occupied a different domain. The ability to imagine merographic connections has an important performative dimension, in that merography opens up wholes, expanding and contracting domains, enabling relations. In the next chapter I explore the expansion and contraction of value in guerrilla moral orders and scales of relatedness.

5
Sociality, Substance, Moral Order

Introduction

In this chapter I explore processes of constitution of guerrilla sociality and relationality. I argue that from accounts given by members of the Fuerzas Armadas Rebeldes (FAR) there emerge a number of perspectives on their experience of guerrilla life. Different perspectives may be said to offer different scales through which guerrilla sociality was imagined—by those who participated in it. Plurality of perspective and of scale reveals guerrilla practices through which multiple socialities and moral orders were brought into existence during the struggle, each entailing distinctive forms of differentiation and conjunction among combatants. Guerrilla sociality was constituted through multiple modes of relatedness, and guerrilla perspectives on sociality generated multiple relations. The analysis proceeds by juxtaposing a range of perspectives that relationally produce a sense of partiality and excess, while simultaneously highlighting how figurations of difference were central to the articulation of sociality and a range of affective practices of relation and connection.

Las Trés Puntas de Lanza/The Three Tips of the Spear

I sought a meeting with one of the *comandantes* of FAR for some time, and finally managed to arrange to see him. I approached the meeting with a degree of apprehension, and prepared as thoroughly as I could. The *comandante* in question had lived for over sixteen years in Petén, *en la montaña*. Many ex-combatants had mentioned his name and had described him as the man who, while not strictly at the forefront of the organization's public profile, was in fact the one who knew the history of FAR in Petén in greater depth than most. For years he had been the strategist of guerrilla operations and had spent more time in clandestine life with the *frentes guerrilleros* (guerrilla fronts) than many other members of the *mando* (military command). The *Comandante* had been a member of the first FAR. His political biography stretched back to 1962. Early on in our long conversation, the *Comandante* offered his views on the nature, goals, and means of the guerrilla struggle, and specifically of the political and military program of the Fuerzas Armadas Rebeldes. The guerrilla struggle undertaken by FAR was made up of "*trés puntas de lanza*," three tips of a spear. Each tip of the sharp implement amounted to a great task, an undertaking that the guerrilla had to carry out. Each task provided *nutrimiento*, or nourishing for the organization and the struggle. The first nourishing substance was "information," the second "supplies," and the third "combatants." As the *Comandante* argued,

> There were three great tasks (*tareas*) during the war that people had to carry out. First, information (*información*), all possible information. For our people (*nuestra gente*) lived in hamlets, in villages, in cities, in towns, everywhere, and they would mix with the Army (*y se mezclavan con el ejército*), somehow they would intermingle (*entremezclarse*) with the institutions of the state (*las instituciones del estado*), and in other places (*lugares*) where we would not be able to get access (*tener acceso*). So, in this manner we were able to organize networks of information (*redes de información*). The other great task (*tarea*) was logistics (*la logística*). In the rural areas we were able to develop what we used to call "war economy" (*la economía de guerra*). So we would organize the people to plant crops (*siembra*), to plant rice, beans, etc., and also to have logistics brokering (*corredores logísticos*) that may bring all production (*producción*) where we may need it, and specifically to sustain (*mantener*) the combatant forces (*fuerzas combatientes*), the military units (*las unidades militares*). And the last great task out of three was to have new combatants (*tener nuevos combatientes*), because the development [of the insurgency], we were not going to achieve it on our own (*porque el desarrollo no lo íbamos a lograr nosotros sólos*), it was not going to be a guerrilla of twelve men (*no éramos una guerrilla de doce hombres*) who were going to achieve it all. No. We did not think that would be the case. A guerrilla has never triumphed in this manner (*nunca una guerrilla ha triunfado tampoco así*), but rather with the mass incorporation of the population (*incorporación masiva de la población*). On this account, then, we were able to sustain ourselves (*mantenernos*) over decades,

> and were able to recover in the aftermath of hard blows (*golpes duros*). For we always had new combatants (*nuevos combatientes*), always. Many would join (*porque teníamos nuevos combatientes siempre. Se incorporaban mucho*).

According to the *Comandante*, the third tip of the spear, namely the incorporation of new combatants into the struggle, was a structured and graded path. New combatants had to undergo a scrupulously rigid process, with ascending steps that were sealed off from lower ones. First, individuals would become *milicianos*, that is, civilian recruits who would be deployed for tasks deemed by the *comandancia* (the command, or the *cúpula*, the small group of top guerrilla leaders) to be paramilitary in nature. The process allowed only those deemed to be the most trustworthy and able of individuals to progress to the higher echelons. The next step led to the "*guerrilla locales*," or local guerrillas. These groups were entrusted with the task of carrying out military operations that were local in scope. Members would work the land during the day, and would not leave their village of residence. Finally, there were individuals who were selected from the local guerrillas. They made up a more permanent, better-trained group whose operations were not tied to a village or community and could instead move across local jurisdictions. Although there was coordination among the levels in the instance of specific operations, each grade was, in principle, independent and closed off from its respective lower counterparts. Comandante Manolo explained the process to me as follows.

> We were able to carry out a graded scale of activities (*escala de actividades*) with the new combatants. First, [they would be members of the militia] *milicianos* and would do all the paramilitary work (*trabajo para-militar*), from distributing flyers (*lanzar volantes*), to aiding us as guides, or developing collateral activities (*actividades colaterales*) related to all military activities. That was their first step/grade (*escalón*) and we always tried to ensure that they passed through all the steps/grades so that they may reach our combatant ranks (*fuerzas combatientes*) as persons who had been already tested (*personas ya probadas*). We did not grab the first person who might say, I want to come with you, and put them in a regular unit (*unidad regular*). No. Never. . . . That was a basic requirement (*requisito muy básico*) for us. So they would first be members of the militia (*ellos primeros fueron milicianos*). Then, in an ascending scale (*escala ascendente*), the local guerrillas would be organized (*se organizaban guerrillas lo-*

cales). The local guerrillas were *compañeros* who would already take part in combat (*combatir*), but at the level of their own communities (*a nivel de sus comunidades*). These local guerrillas worked in their communities (*comunidades*), and, for example, if there were five localities (*localidades*) or five hamlets (*aldeas*), then each one would be part of a general plan/the planning (*planificación general*) and would undertake some specified activities, but already with arms (*pero ya con armas*). So they would engage in some small disturbance to the Army (*pequeños hostigamientos al ejército*), they would place some landmine (*mina*) where a truck would pass by, or they would undertake whatever sabotage activity (*actividad de sabotaje*), but always in their own jurisdiction (*jurisdicción*). When we would draw a general plan (*plan general*), each one of them would undertake some activity within the whole of that general plan, but at their own level (*nivel*), at the level of their own hamlets (*aldeas*). Then we would somehow organize the territory in various smaller territories (*el territorio en varios territorios pequeños*), for instance . . . let's say that there were localities (*localidades*) scattered everywhere, there were small hamlets (*pequeñas aldeas*) everywhere. We could divide the territory within a general plan and each one of them [the smaller territories] would undertake some activity (*actividad*). This territory would then have numerous hamlets (*y luego este territorio tenía varias aldeas*). Of the best local *guerrilleros* (*guerrilleros locales*), of the very best we would make up a military unit that would be much better trained (*unidad militar mucho más preparada*), [a unit] much larger and much more permanent (*permanente*), you know (*verdad*). Conversely, the communities/villages (*comunidades*) would undertake military activities (*actividades militares*) and during the day they would work the land (*trabajar la tierra*), they would carry on in their communities (*seguían en sus comunidades*), while the others made up a chosen/selected unit (*unidad*) of the best [combatants]. This unit was more permanent. But it would still have a jurisdiction (*jurisdicción*), and we would call them territorial troops (*trupas territoriales*). Then, we had a much larger unit made up of the best combatants out of the territorial troops, and these made up the principal ranks/forces (*fuerzas principales*), *verdad*, so, as you can see, these were various categories of forces (*varia categorías de fuerzas*) . . . This mobile-strategic force (*fuerza móvil-estratégica*), that is what it was called, could act in any of the territories, in accordance with the characteristics of the operation (*operaciones*) that they would be planning to under-

> take, in accordance with a number of other things. For instance, if it [the mobile-strategic force] was to act in this territory, then the permanent force (*fuerza permanente*) would be of support, with all the local communities/villages (*comunidades locales*). In the end we would design (*deseñarse*) everything in such a manner. As you can see, this presents you with a plan (*esquema*) that does not allow just anybody who might want to try to reach just any point, because here one needed people tried and tested (*gente experimentada, probada*), who would not run away at the first Army bombardment (*bombardeo del ejército*), say. We needed experts, we needed specialists, we needed talented people, good officers, good combatants, and good troops more generally, who would be able to achieve their objectives.

According to the *Comandante*, combatants, that is, one of the three substances of the guerrilla, represented a whole that was divided into parts. Parts were graded in ascending order. Through a process of selection, grades led to a force that, while decreasing in numbers, would be assigned greater mobility and scope of action. In the descending direction, the grades augmented in size to encompass larger numbers of associates, but became both more localized in terms of their operations and less intense in the kind and rate of insurgent activities allocated to them. By division and grading of combatants, one of the three guerrilla substances contracted so as to be preserved as much as it was possible. In turn, through graded multiplication, agency and movement of guerrilla substance was maximized. From the holistic perspective deployed by the *Comandante*, division and multiplication of substance nourished the organization and the struggle. Processes of division and multiplication of combatants, forces, and territory revealed in the *Comandante*'s master plan were secret. They were not envisioned by the combatants I spoke to except partially. Nevertheless, awareness of substance permeated the accounts offered by ex-combatants. They revealed the perspective of one part of what the *Comandante* had deemed a whole, and specifically the perspective of a part constitutive of one of the three guerrilla substances Comandante Manolo had imagined. Some combatants spoke of substance and nourishing when recalling their guerrilla experiences. Carlos, for instance, had told me how guerrilla military and political training constituted nourishing.

> We would establish what we would call political, politico-military schools (*escuelas políticas, político-militares*). There we would form/train (*formar*) all our combatants militarily. One would have to know

> how to carry out an "annihilation ambush" (*emboscada de aniquilamiento*), a "curbing ambush" (*emboscada de contención*), an "ambush of provocation" (*emboscada de ostigamiento*), all those types of military action. So we would train (*capacitarse*) and at the same time, we would study the tactics of the Army. The better our knowledge of them, the easier it would be to hit them (*golpear*). They would do the same, they would study us, how we would act, and if we were not proficient/alert, they would inflict damage on us. That would happen when we fell into a routine of doing things. In the schools they would also talk to us about the conjuncture the country was in (*la coyunctura que en el país se manejaba*). We would gain awareness of the economic problems, the social problems that in one way or another affect or affected the population. So we would consider all this and history as well (*historia*), so our consciousness would increase and rise (*elevar la conciencia*), as would the morale of the revolutionaries. I can say to you that this was our chief source of nourishment (*nuestro principal alimento*). And this is what still keeps us here at present, you know (*verdad*)?

Carlos noted how guerrilla training nourished military dexterity, political conscience, and revolutionary conviction among the *guerrilleros/as*. Interestingly, however, despite the common idiom of substance, no other ex-combatant I had the opportunity to meet spoke in terms that might resemble, in part or in its entirety, the master plan of the *Comandante*. In our conversations, ex-combatants seemed never to have envisaged the whole frame, or used the same lexicon and repertoire deployed by the *Comandante* in his remarkably integral and all-encompassing vision. Up to this meeting, my vision too was an ensemble of fragments, as were the visions of the *compañeros/as*. By the time the conversation with the *Comandante* had come to an end, I began to think that, despite the illusion of wholeness, partiality imbricated his account.

> As I was saying to you at the beginning, we needed to feed ourselves/to nourish ourselves with information (*necesitábamos nutrirnos de información*), nourish ourselves with new combatants (*nutrirnos de nuevos combatientes*), you see (*verdad*), hence it was in the more densely populated areas (*zonas más densamente pobladas*) that we had our population (*teníamos nosotros población*). A further element that influenced [the process] was the location of military objectives (*donde están ubicados los objetivos militares*). We would not be making war

> here around these lagoons, where there is nothing, not even the Army (*nosotros no íbamos a hacer la guerra en estas lagunas, aquí no hay nada. No estaba el ejército tampoco*). The Army would concentrate in this area, then where the Army was there would be our war fronts (*ahí donde estaba el ejército, allí estaban nuestros frentes de guerra*). Now, as our organization was a clandestine one (*clandestina*), there were communities where there was never war (*guerra*) . . . The work of recruiting was not one of saying, hey you, are you coming? No (*pero no era un trabajo de reclutar, vos, te venís, no*). It was a political activity, one of training (*capacitar*) the *compañeros* and *compañeras.* One would give talks (*pláticas*) by night, by day, there was nothing [unusual], they would carry on with their usual routines, but the front was there, and they would join that front, or the nearest front. We developed activities of organization (*trabajo organizativo*) in the whole of Petén. . . . We did not expect to achieve all three things everywhere, for instance, in eastern and central Petén, what we had the most of there was combatants, and very little supply of provisions (*abasto*). In the Q'eqchi' villages (*comunidades q'eqchies*) in Alta Verapaz [in the 1990s, when the Frente Panzós Heróico was established there], there was balance. There were combatants, a supply of provisions, and a great deal of information (*allí hubo combatientes, hubo abasto y mucha información*). In San Luis and the whole of that area [southern Petén], what happened was that we did not have many combatants, for a very straightforward reason. Because those were the last organizing efforts that were undertaken, and there was no longer time to train combatants. Those were the last places where we achieved [political] organizing, because they were going to be deployed as the starting point to penetrate Izabal (*penetrar a Izabal*). But in order to penetrate Izabal, we had to go through these places, and we needed to meet bases of support (*bases de apoyo*) . . . Within the military forces, there were excellent *compañeros* who were not combatants, but who would penetrate the communities (*penetrar a las comunidades*). And they would be the ones who would be there for months on end, politically working through the people (*trabajando políticamente la gente*) [organizing people politically].

Comandante Manolo deployed the expression "three tips of the spear" on different registers. The "three tips of the spear" referred to the triad of nourishment and substance: information, supplies, and combatants. Further, the expression referred to the three different components of the struggle, namely armed struggle (*lucha armada*), the political struggle of the masses (*lucha política de las masas*), and the diplomatic struggle (*lucha político-diplomática*). Despite coordinating efforts, the different parts at times proceeded at different paces. The different fronts of the struggle produced different subjects of struggle.

> We thought the political strategy (*la línea política*) had three important axes (*ejes*). The first was armed struggle (*lucha armada*), for which we endeavored (*pretender*) to have people join (*incorporarse*) the struggle in increasing numbers. The second axis was the political struggle of the masses (*lucha política de las masa*), and the third was the participation of our organization in the political-diplomatic struggle (*lucha político-diplomática*). The axes were three tips of the spear. We were discussing the *trés puntas de lanza*, let us return to the issue (*tema*). The other line of action, within the political strategy (*línea política*), was the political struggle of the masses (*lucha política de las masas*). All of those sectors (*sectores*) that in one way or another we had influenced, they headed (*encabezar*) the mass movement [social movements] in the countryside and in the cities: the unions' movement (*movimiento sindical*), the movement of colonists (*movimiento de pobladores*), the movement of the churches (*movimiento de las iglesias*). All that, the masses could do. Why, then, was I saying "*trés puntas de lanza*"? Because each had its own objective in the struggle (*objective de lucha*) and each of them would develop its activities independently (*separado*) of the others, but in coordination (*coordinación*). Each had its own way (*su propria forma*) of doing things, those of the military struggle with arms and the masses with their political revindications. The third tip [of the spear], was the political-diplomatic struggle/diplomatic politics (*la política diplomática*), that is, to tell the world what was happening in Guatemala because here there was a circle (*cerco*) of misinformation (*disinformación*), and to obtain support. So, each of them in its own direction (*cada uno por su lado*) would undertake its own effort (*esfuerzo*). None was more important than the other; all went toward the same goal (*tema*). What would happen, however, was that at times armed struggle would go very far ahead (*la lucha armada se nos iba muy adelante*). Or at times it was the struggle of the masses (*la lucha de las masas*), or the political-diplomatic work (*trabajo político-diplomático*) had its objectives and would achieve them. The idea was to stimulate each other (*estimularse entre si*), because the *compañeros* of the masses/social move-

> ments would be happier (*más contentos*) to take to the streets knowing that there was a war and that we were supporting them. They would have more of an incentive (*propósito*) to get out [overtly struggle] knowing that inside there would be a whole range of activities that would support them (*respaldar*) vis-à-vis the international community. And beyond the *trés puntas de lanza*, there was the fourth stage, namely negotiation (*negociación*), negotiation as a further weapon of the struggle (*una arma más de la lucha*). But this was within URNG [Unidad Revolucionaria Nacional Guatemalteca; Guatemalan National Revolutionary Unity]. We turned the negotiating table (*mesa de negociación*) into the continuation of the battlefield (*la continuación del campo de batalla*).

In the account provided by a FAR *comandante*, the guerrilla was envisaged as an entity composed of three substances, namely information, supplies, and combatants. A tripartite distinction was also drawn between different aspects and modalities of struggle, namely armed struggle, the political struggle of the masses, and the political-diplomatic struggle. Each substance, like each strand of insurgent activities, was part of an all-inclusive vision provided by the *Comandante*. The *Comandante* also commented on the necessity of managing production, reproduction, and circulation of substances, and the difficulty of coordinating the pace of different fronts of struggle. I argue that the management of the three substances, which were envisioned to make up the guerrilla, coincided with the articulation of multiple socialities and moral orders. The comprehensiveness that characterized the vision of the *Comandante*, with its distinctive lexicon and modalities of division, multiplication, and connection, was never replicated in part or as a whole in my conversations with ex-combatants. Conversely, the *Comandante*'s vision may come across as partial and incomplete when contrasted with and complemented by the vision of guerrilla sociality offered by ex-*guerrilleros/as*. Switching from the scale inherent in the *Comandante*'s perspective to that of the combatants, it appeared that ex-combatants envisioned guerrilla sociality through idioms of relatedness, and as a moral order based on sameness and sharing.

Guerrilla Sociality and the Inception of Relatedness

Multiple fronts and subjects of struggle presented the guerrilla with the task of ordering the relations among themselves and with others, notably with the population. This gave rise to the establishment of social relations of "affinity." Affinity came to be qualified in multiple ways, and progressively, the guerrilla was envisaged in terms of family relations. Comandante Manolo explained:

> I am going to tell you about a case (*caso*), which is also funny (*simpático*). One day we met some persons who were cultivating crops (*siembras*). This was in a territory where the Army would not venture, where nobody would venture, we alone had control over everything (*el control de todo*). They were planting crops (*sembrar*). Obviously, they got very frightened (*asustarse*) because they saw us coming wearing uniforms (*nos vieron uniformados*). So, we asked them what they were doing there, why they were sowing, and in Guatemalan territory, when they were Mexican, they were indigenous Chol (*cuando ellos eran Mejicanos, ellos eran indígenas choles*). So they told us that they had been evicted from their communities, large landowners stole (*robar*) their land and they evicted (*expulsar*) them from Mexico, and they arrived at the border (*línea fronteriza*), on the Usumacinta [river], and what were they doing? Moreover, here there are laws that prohibit logging (*talla de los arboles*),[1] and one was not allowed to plant crops. In any case, they would see that over to the other side [of the river Usumacinta] there was plenty of land, so in clandestine manner (*clandestinamente*) they started to cut down the forest (*tumbar la montaña*) and began to plant crops (*sembrar*). It had been some time since they had started doing this. But what else could they do, they had nowhere else to go. So, we told them that it wasn't a problem, that they could carry on doing it, however there were no guarantees that we could guarantee their life there (*garantizar su vida allí*), because the Army would reach the area and they would annihilate them (*porque el ejército llegaba y los iba a aniquilar*). Well, with the understanding/agreement (*compromiso*) that they could carry on planting, they became our friends (*se hicieron amigos nuestros*). Well, there was an interest (*interés*), namely planting crops, but this allowed us to be able to cross to their side [of the river] (*pero esto nos posibilitó a nosotros pasar al lado de ellos*), you see (*verdad*), and establish a good neighborly relation (*relación de buena vecindad*). On the side where they had their village, one day a woman was about to give birth (*estar dando luz*), and there was nobody who could assist her (*atender*), and we had a doctor with us, so we crossed the border and took him to the hamlet and he helped with the delivery (*atender el parto*), *verdad*. From that moment onwards, relations of mutual help (*ayuda mutua*) were es-

tablished in many respects, *verdad*, that resulted in many of them crossing the border (*frontera*). They would come to plant crops over here. But we were worried that if the Army arrived, they would experience problems there, so they asked us whether we could defend them (*nos pidieron que nosotros los defendiéramos*). But we could not do that, we would go back and forth, of course, that was an area that we controlled, but we could not dedicate ourselves to looking after/protecting people, could we? So they asked us that we teach them how to use arms, and whether we could give them some for them to defend themselves (*defensa*). That we could do, so [we passed on] a few *escopetas* (shotguns), a few little rifles (*riflecitos*), so that they could feel a bit safer, mostly for defense, because they weren't war/combat arms (*armas de guerra*), and we would not have given them combat arms anyhow, but with a rifle, an *escopeta*, they were feeling better already (*ya se sintieron mejor*). We taught them how to use them, and gave them some ideas as to how they could defend themselves in the event the Army should get there. This established an excellent relation (*una excelente relación*) with them. Later we would go by, and they would guarantee some sort of corridor to get the things (*cosas*) for the guerrilla through from Mexico. At times they would volunteer to help us with their animals, with their mules, that is, a very good neighborly relation (*relación de buena vecindad*), as we would say. But as this was the area where our *guerrilleros* would get to on occasions following a combat, there we had a hospital, a school, and a training camp (*campo de entrenamiento*). We had everything there. That was our base (*zona base*). So our *guerrilleros* would get there, and these *compañeros* began to cross the border more often, in groups, with families. There was coming and going of people, back and forth, and it became more and more our base. A daring *guerrillero* (*osado guerrillero*), I would say, fell in love (*se enamoró*) with a *Mejicanita* [young Mexican woman] on the other shore, and would go and see her. They fell so much in love that the *guerrillero* brought her over to Guatemala. So the family of the *guerrillera* wondered what had happened. He had taken her with him, so that established some familial ties of support (*lazos familiares de apoyo*) to the *compañera* who was going to Guatemala, and of course for the son-in-law (*yerno*). Those familial ties were always very good, because they identified people with the struggle (*esos lazos familiares siempre fueron muy buenos, por que identíficaban a la gente con la lucha*). At the same time, in those places, there was great [Army] repression (*represión*), to the extent that entire families (*familiar enteras*) would go to *la montaña* to hide. That is where we developed plans of defense and production (*planes de defensa y de producción*), because we could not be left there with no food (*estar sin comer*). Further, one had to defend oneself from the Army, so we made plans for these families. At the beginning, we defended them, but it was best to teach them how to fight (*luchar*) so that they could defend themselves. We could not carry on defending people, or we would not have reached our objectives. In that way, entire families joined (*integrarse*). In the villages, in the local guerrillas (*guerrillas locales*) and even in the permanent forces (*fuerzas permanentes*), one would see entire families there . . . Each family would grow, to the extent that it would then mix (*mezclar*) with the other families (*las demás familias*) and you would see the nephew married to the daughter of Fulano,[2] so one would become related [through kinship ties] (*emparentarse*). That was common and I don't think it was negative. On the contrary, it was very positive, it established ties (*lazos*) that would allow us to win over that large family (*ganar esa gran familia*), to attend to it politically (*atenderla políticamente*), because not everybody would be in the guerrilla front, they would disperse across the organization. The only negative aspect was that information might run up and down, that would happen and it was inevitable (*inevitable*). Occasional leaks of information (*fuga de información*) were managed, but those ties of friendship (*lazos de amistades*) and family links/ties (*nexos familiares*) we were able to make good use of (*aprovechar*) to establish corridors of organization (*corredores de organización*). . . . And we carried on considering ourselves a large family (*gran familia*), because not only ties of familiarity (*lazos de familiaridad*) were established, but also, through political work, we would make the *compañeros* see the fraternity/amity (*hermandad*) that we had among us all (*tener entre todos*), to establish a series of moral values (*valores morales*) that would allow (*permitir*) that the relations among *compañeros*, between couples (*parejas*), and with the population would be excellent (*excelente*). For instance, it was absolutely forbidden to touch even a single fruit of a tree that would not be ours, or that would belong to a person who had not given it to us. In all instances one had to buy it. If the *campesino* would give it to you, that was different. And still, it would be shared among all (*y aún así se compartía entre todos*). *Hermandad* (fraternity/amity) was the affection (*afecto*) and the affinity (*afinidad*) that existed among the *compañeros*. For instance, I was in Petén for very many years, and

> that was my people (*esa fue mi gente*), although I was born elsewhere. But imagine spending sixteen years *en la montaña*, and having numerous combatants as I did, combatants whom I saw (*ver*), formed (*formar*), educated (*educar*), trained (*entrenar*), and those I took to combat (*llevar al combate*). By necessity (*necesariamente*) nexuses of great friendship (*amistad*) are established. Clearly, it is a very healthy friendship (*amistad muy sana*), as it does not hinder (*obstacular*) the military line of command that exists (*la línea de mando militar que existe*). But one ultimately holds great fondness for them (*llegar a tener mucho cariño*), affection (*afecto*). As times goes by, as they say, they had children and their families, and their children were also my combatants. I had two generations of combatants (*dos generaciones de combatientes tuve yo*), the parents and the children (*los padres y los hijos*). So I would see a young man (*muchacho*) and I would ask, how is your father, perhaps his father was older, or had a problem with his leg or something and could no longer be the combatant he had been before. He is living in a certain village and he sends his regards, [the young man would say]. And I would later visit the ex-combatant, as my brother (*ya como mi hermano*). We had been together (*juntos*) for a long time, and he had his children and they were now combatants, even officers (*oficiales*). So the relation/relationship (*relación*) extended over generations (*generaciones*). How could one not have fondness (*cariño*) for these people? Moreover, that was your family for so many years (*además esa fue tu familia durante tantos años*).

The *Comandante* noted the multiple ways in which the guerrilla was akin to a family. For one, guerrilla forces established kinship ties with civilian populations that would converge in the areas under guerrilla control. Further, following violent counterinsurgency actions, the population of entire villages sought refuge in the forest, leading to families joining the guerrilla ranks. As families mixed with each other and became kin, a specific form of guerrilla relatedness developed. Guerrilla *hermandad* (fraternity/amity) provided a further mode of articulation of relatedness, to the effect that the guerrilla itself may be thought of as a large family. As noted by Carsten (2000, 2), "relatedness" may be usefully deployed "in opposition to, or alongside 'kinship' in order to signal openness to indigenous idioms of being related rather than a reliance on pre-given definitions." "Relatedness" conveys a distancing "from a pre-given analytic opposition between the biological and the social on which much anthropological study of kinship has rested" (Carsten 2000, 2). Framing guerrilla sociality in terms of relatedness thus seems particularly apt, as it allows for different deployments of idioms of "family ties" as they occurred simultaneously in guerrilla discourse. As the *Comandante* noted, there were parents whose children had also joined the guerrilla. Thus, there were two generations of combatants and as the *Comandante* pertained to the generation of the parents, he considered them to be his siblings. *Hermandad*, in the sense of fraternity and amity, permeated the sociality of guerrilla relatedness. In point of fact, guerrilla sociality and relatedness developed a distinctive and enduring moral order based on sharing. In turn, practices that involved sharing of substance functioned in complex ways and produced effects of sameness and difference.

Tamales Guerrilleros and Sharing Substance

Rubén spoke of a memory common to many ex-*guerrilleros/as* when he noted that some activities in the guerrilla were predicated on sameness. He recounted how tasks such as washing one's clothes and preparation and consumption of food had to be carried out by all.

> Nobody would wash the clothes (*ropa*) of others. There were beautiful (*lindo*) things in the guerrilla. To go to combat (*ir al combate*) and do work in the kitchen (*trabajo de cocina*) was the same (*era lo mismo*), you know (*verdad)*, and serving others (*sevir*) was forbidden (*prohibir*). That is, we had to share (*compartir*), everything was shared (*en común*). Furthermore, in the case of Cande, she was an expert in making tortillas (*hechar tortillas*), nevertheless, she was never viewed as a person who would make tortillas. My brother was also an expert at making tortillas. One would share everything, in all instances (*en todo caso se compartía*), *verdad*, one would help out, one would contribute so that activities might be undertaken and accomplished. Many things would thus be undertaken on the grounds of physical reconsiderations (*reconsideraciones puramente físicas*), let us say, not everything would be strictly the same. That is to say, well, the load is of fifty *libras*,[3] are we going to distribute it to everyone the same (*miramos parejo*)? No. Instead, at times, for physical issues (*cuestiones físicas*), there we would reconsider, where that *compañero* is able to carry fifty *libras*, he will carry fifty *libras*. The *compañeras* are able to carry twenty-five *libras*, then they carry twenty-five *libras*. Alternatively, there would be a standard measure, where the *libraje* (weight in pounds) would be thirty, and from there one would ask for volunteers, for those who would manage (*aguantar*) five *libras* more,

> those who would bear twenty more, would carry twenty more. Because by the same token (*igual*), there were some *compañeros* among us, including myself, who were physically much weaker (*debil*) than a woman, for there were *compañeras* who were much stronger than any of us. Things would be measured (*medir*) that way, so that there would be equity (*equidad*) and no mistreatment (*maltrato*). The *compañeras* would work in communications (*comunicaciones*), in medical service (*sevicio médico*), they had greater talents (*mejores abilidades*). There were excellent *compañeros*, but one would notice (*notar*) that the *compañeras* had better abilities to do that kind of work. Likewise (*al igual*), there were excellent women combatants (*excelentísimas combatientes*), and many of them died in combat. It was the same. Merly, for instance, died in combat.

As both the *Comandante* and Rubén had noted, food was scarce, but it was always shared. Cande commented on this as follows:

> It was very difficult, because at times, we had to carry *bolas de masa* to eat.[4] They were cooked *bolas de masa*, we would call them "*tamales*,"[5] but it was only cooked *masa*, and at times there was no food at all . . . At times we would eat, at times we would not. It was the same with water, sometimes we would find water, and sometimes we would not. We would set up camp for one or two days, but most of the time we would walk and walk and walk, carrying one's food (*comida*). Because in the beginning, in the years from 1981 to about 1986, we would not have the luxury to eat some beans (*frijol*), or sugar or oil. It was mostly cooked *bolitas de masa*, small balls of boiled corn, which we would call "*tamal peludo*." There [*en la montaña*] everything was shared (*compartido*). There were squads (*escuadras*), each with six combatants, and each platoon had four *escuadras*. So everyone would take turns (*era turniado*). For instance, if it was that platoon's turn, they would arrange tasks with the *escuadras*. Everything was shared, the work in the kitchen (*trabajo de cocina*), guard (*la posta*), gathering wood for fire (*ir a traer leña*), anything really, everyone had to do what it was their turn to do.

Despite scarcity, ex-combatants recalled how any available food was shared and a sense of commensality established. In the case of food, and *tamales guerrilleros* in particular, to share meant to divide one substance of the guerrilla, as well as the activities related to its production, among all. Through division and distribution of equal parts, the effect of sameness was achieved, regardless of other scales of difference such as rank, gender, and ethnicity. Thus, division of substance in this instance created sameness. Rubén commented on other practices related to circulation of substance, notably those aimed at making substance move and circulate with the guerrilla forces. With regard to transportation of a load, Rubén noted how to share was to divide the load among the combatants, but not to do so strictly in equal parts. Instead, to share weight was to begin with a standard unit and increase or decrease the load carried by individuals by an established part, to accommodate differences among them. The differences at stake were not those in the scale of rank, status, or gender, but rather those of a perceived capacity/ability to physically endure an increase and/or decrease in load. Furthermore, individuals would take on increases in load voluntarily. With this scale, the guerrilla created difference of an embodied kind, as in the distinction between physically stronger and weaker combatants, and a mode of agency, as in the acquisition of greater quotas of load for transportation by those who would be able and willing to do so. The circulation of that composite guerrilla substance that was "supplies" was thus made possible. Further, related production of scales of sameness and difference conjured up an overall effect of equity. From the perspective of the ex-combatants, these practices were foundational to the establishment of guerrilla sociality. Insofar as guerrilla sociality was grounded on specific practices of sharing and on the establishment of related dimensions of sameness and difference, the ex-combatants acknowledged the partiality of the sociality they endeavored to create and maintain during the years *en la montaña* and of the moral orders that sustained it. Guerrilla socialities and moral orders based on sharing substance differed from the socialities and moral orders that connoted the lives they had led before joining the struggle, and those they were to live following demobilization. Sociality predicated on sameness and equity was partial in a further sense in that it coexisted with other guerrilla moral orders that produced sameness and difference in different scales.

Matrimonios por las Armas/Marriages by Arms

Rubén discussed the moral order based on sharing substance and the effect of sameness, equating both with an ethos central to guerrilla life. However, he also commented on other coexisting moral injunctions, notably those that concerned scales of gender and sexuality, and gender and sexual relations among combatants in particular. He noted that gender and sexual moral orders had changed over time. Rubén said:

> As I was saying, [in the guerrilla] there were beautiful things and others very hard (*duras*). At the beginning, it was forbidden (*prohibido*) to disrespect (*faltar de respeto*) a *compañera*, for instance, talking to her about sex (*hablarle de sexo*) or asking her to sleep with you (*pedirle que se acostara con uno*), you know (*verdad*). At the beginning there were rules (*principios*), that one could not disrespect a *compañera*, one would have to maintain a boundary (*límite*). I did not live in that time (*esa época yo no la viví*), but I have been told about it. Many of the *comandantes* would joke about what used to happen as a result [of the rules]. One day, someone was nearly executed by firing squad for something like that. Well, someone was nearly executed because he had sexual relations (*relaciones*) with a *compañera*. He was already on his way to trial (*juicio*), because then FAR had a very tough (*fuerte*) set of disciplinary rules (*reglamento*) that would be upheld (*respetar*). Well, luckily (*de buena suerte*), he was rescued by the *compañera* who took it upon herself to save him. She said to the other officer (*oficial*), *sos un cabrón*,[6] you are a *cabrón* if you execute the boy (*el patojo*), and I will tell everyone that you also slept with me (*acostarse*), ah, so you are screwed (*te jodiste*)! So no, he must not be executed (*no hay que fusilarlo*) [laughter]. All these things I am telling you, they all fit within a trajectory (*trayectoria*). Later on, in my era (*en mi era*), in my time (*época*), this continued in the same manner, but perhaps a bit more flexible. You could talk to a *compañera*, but you cannot talk to the *compañera* who is already in a relationship with a *compañero* and you have to learn to respect her (*respetar*), *verdad*. That is why the *casamientos por las armas* (weddings/marriages by arms) occurred (*para eso se dan los casamientos por las armas*). That is what they were called. They were symbolic (*simbólico*) and somewhat juridical (*algo jurídico*), so to speak, among ourselves (*dentro de nosotros*). It held great honor (*honra*) and great respect (*respeto*) for us. So we began to do that, to marry by arms.

Rubén recalled how a young man who was later to become a prominent leader of FAR had come close to being executed for having slept with a *compañera*. So strict were the rules of conduct ordering gender and sexual relations in the early FAR, that a breach would have been punished with death by firing squad. The *compañera* in question, however, had come to the rescue of her lover and manipulated the strictures of the rules to her advantage and to the benefit of her young *compañero*, whose life was spared as a result. By the time Rubén joined the guerrilla ranks, Rubén argued, rules of conduct had been relaxed. Sexual relations among men and women were allowed, and yet, they still required some ordering. That is why *casamientos por las armas*, that is, "marriages by arms" were instituted. Marriage practices in insurgent movements are well documented (Barnes 1999; Bhebhe and Ranger 1991; Kampwirth 2002; Kriger 1992; Randall 1981; Urdang 1979; West 2000; Wilson 1991),[7] but with the Fuerzas Armadas Rebeldes, *casamientos por las armas* were a type of union destined to soon be discontinued. Alma, a combatant in her late thirties, had been one of the few who got married "by arms."

> I asked Alma whether she had a relationship *en la montaña* (*se acompañó en la montaña*) and whether she did something akin to *la pedida*.[8] In Petén, it is customary but not obligatory for the family of a young unmarried man or young unmarried woman to visit the house of prospective suitors and "ask" (*pedir*) a man or woman in marriage for their offspring. I asked Alma whether when she got together with her partner they [the couple] informed anyone (*es decir informaron a alguien*), such as a military chief (*jefe militar*) of the event. Alma replied that she did. I asked whom she informed, whether she informed Nestor [the *comandante* of Alma's front at the time], and she replied that no, at the time Nestor wasn't there, he was down south. I said to Alma that I understood many informed Nestor. Nestor was like a father (*papá*) for many people. In her case, at the time, it was Comandante Méndez, as he was still alive and was there, so there were marriages then, marriages by arms, but there also was free union too (*entonces, allí existían casamientos también, por las armas, y existía unión libre tambíen*). This was the first time I heard of "marriages by arms" (*casamientos por las armas*) and I hesitated, repeating, "marriages by arms" . . . who got married by arms, that you may remember (*quíen se casó por las armas, que usted se acuerde*)? Alma replied, someone whom people would call Magalí got married, Magalí and, I don't know who it was, Noemí, I don't remember who else was there. I also got married by that (*yo también me casé por eso*). She added that yes, it was like a marriage similar to that which occurs in civil life (*sí, o sea que allí era como un matrimonio parecido a lo que se da en la vida civil*), that is, if an unmarried woman goes just like that,

without any formal support, (*que si una muchacha se va solo así*), well, she has much less, less support (*pues tiene menos, menos apoyo*), as she has not respected her elders/superiors (*o no respetó a sus mayores*), we could say (*podríamos decir*), so the matter there was the same (*entonces la cuestíon allí era lo mismo*), you see (*verdad*), it was similar to that (*era parecido a eso*). I asked Alma whether it was for that reason that there were "marriages by arms" ("*matrimonios por las armas*") and she replied yes. I asked what the name of her *compañero* was and Alma replied it was Eagle (*Águila*). So she had a marriage by arms (*así que hicieron un casamiento por las armas*) and everyone was there, everyone (*todos estuvieron allí, todos estuvieron*), the whole front.

I asked Alma whether in civil life, with her current partner, Alma did something similar to *la pedida*. Yes, [she said], when we met, we were *novios* (a couple) for a time (*sí, y cuando non conocimos, estuvimos un tiempo de novios*), although it was known to my parents (*aún que estaba a conocimiento de mis padres*), but I always had the idea that they would give me the opportunity to converse more [with him] (*pero yo siempre mantenía la idea de que ellos me dieran la oportunidad de platicar más*),[9] that I would relate myself to him more to see whether it was to my convenience/liking or not (*relacionarme más con el para ver si me convenía o no*), because in some cases what happens is that the unmarried man enters directly (*porque en algunos casos, lo que se da es que el muchacho entra directo*), and the parents decide for her (*y los papás deciden de ella*), *verdad*, so in my case (*entonces en el caso mio*), it wasn't like that (*no fue así*), *verdad*, they gave me the opportunity (*me dieron la oportunidad*) and when I considered that it was to my convenience/liking with the [unmarried] man (*y cuando yo consideré de que me convenía con el muchacho*), I told my father, I told him (*yo le dije a mi papá y le dije a él*), *verdad*, so, his parents went to talk to the house [of her parents] and all that (*entonces, ya los papás de él fueron a hablar a la casa y todo*), we reached an agreement (*ya nos pusimos de acuerdo*), well, first of all, *el permiso* (permission) (*bueno, más que todo el permiso*), already formal (*ya formal*), since then we were officially *novios* [officially engaged] and all that (*que ya fuimos novios oficiales y todo*), *verdad*, that is the first time they entered [the house] (*fue cuando la primera vez que entraron*). The second time [they visited] it was already to establish the dates for the wedding (*ya la segunda vez fue para poner fechas para el matrimonio*). I asked Alma whether she thought *la pedida* was something that was in the woman's interest or not. I explained that on occasions I had been told by women who were not ex-combatants that the event of *la pedida* was something they had endured (*la pedida mucho le costó*), because they were not allowed to decide (*porque ellas no pudieron decidir*), what I meant was that a person entered to ask for them and spoke directly with the father and mother (*la persona entró a pedirlas y habló directamente con el papá y la mamá*) and the women I had spoken to felt they did not have any part in the process (*ninguna parte en el proceso*), they were simply handed over (*y que solo ellas fueron entregadas*). There were some such cases (*hay unos casos de esos*). Yes, this did happen, but not in her case, Alma noted. I added that in other cases/instances it [*la pedida*] was a guarantee for the woman (*garantía para la mujer*), because, I was told, if something happened between the couple (*la pareja*), for instance, if there were episodes of violence (*episodios de violencia*), the parents had the right to get their daughter out (*los padres tienen derecho a sacar a la hija*), that is to say, that in that case/event, it was like a form of security (*seguridad*) for the daughter, the fact that the parents had handed her over (*la entregaron*), right (*verdad*)? Alma confirmed that was indeed the case, *verdad*, that was why *la pedida* existed, because one leaves under the gaze of the parents (*por que uno se va en vista de los papás*), because in any event that may occur in one's life (*porque cualquier cuestión que sucede, ya en la vida de uno*), in the event that the man made a mistake/got the wrong partner (*que a lo mejor el hombre se equivocó de pareja*), then in this case the woman (*entonces aquí la mujer*), she has the aid/protection/guardianship of her parents, because it is under their gaze that she left in the first place (*puede, tiene el amparo de los papás por que en vista de los papá se ha ido*), *verdad*?

According to Alma there were similarities between civilian and guerrilla life, but there were also differences. She stated that in a life like the one that one lives here (*por que una vida que se vive acá*) [in the ethnographic present], one has friendships and all that, one gets on well with people and all that (*uno tiene amistades y todo, se lleva con la gente, y bueno*), *verdad*, but during the life *en la montaña* one would see oneself as brothers and all that, very united (*ahí uno se veía como hermanos y todo, muy unidos*), yes, what one would have and what the other would have would be shared, everything (*sí . . . lo que tenía uno y lo que no tenía el otro se compartía, todas las cosas*).

According to Alma, "marriages by arms" were akin to *de jure* and *de facto* unions in civil life in which individuals were accompanied and supported by their parents and families in their choice of a partner. In Alma's account, "marriages by arms" augmented the sense in which the guerrilla was a family. The assent and witnessing of the union on the part of the guerrilla family represented a guarantee for the partners, notably for the woman. As in civil life, eloping with a partner or entering a *relación informal*, that is, an "informal relationship," was considered reckless in that the partners, notably the woman, would not be able to count on the support of their families in the event of a dispute between them, domestic violence, or other issue that might be grounds for separation. Through *matrimonios por las armas* a number of merographic analogies were articulated, for instance, the merging of the two domains of "guerrilla life" and "civil life" and the establishment of a sense of contiguity of the moral orders relating to both. According to Alma, marriages by arms constituted a safeguard for women combatants, as they would be able to appeal to the parental authority of the *comandante* in the event of a crisis. Nevertheless, as Rubén noted, *matrimonios por las armas* were a short-lived practice. Rubén explained:

> So we began having marriages by arms, but soon afterwards, the couples would begin to fight/argue (*pelearse*), they would split up (*dejarse*), and so we simply could not continue on such a course. So, it was announced, okay *muchachos*, what we really do not want is that one day someone might shoot somebody else (*alguien le meta un tiro a alguien*) because of such a matter. So we will maintain the same principle of respect (*principio de respeto*). As for the *compañera*, well, let her decide whether she wants to be with her *compañero* or not, if she wants to leave him, but nobody should be duplicitous (*hacer el duple*). Rather if they want to split up, let them split up, but they should make it public (*que lo publiquen*), and if they later want to be in a [formal] relationship (*juntarse*) with someone else, they may do that if they wish. So there would be public announcements (*anuncios públicos*) about who was splitting up and who was not (*dejarse*) and some of them were very funny (*chistosos*). I will tell you an anecdote (*anécdota*). There was a *compañero*, a veteran, whom we would call Chano, and there was a *compañera* who was much older (*muy avanzada de edad*), you see (*verdad*). So we would call this Chano "*el clandestino*" ("the clandestine one"), because of his clandestine relations (*relaciones clandestinas*). So, Chano, in clandestine manner (*clandestinamente*) and so that no one would realize (*percatarse*), began hav-

ing sexual relations (*relaciones sexuales*) with the *compañera*, and she was responsive to this (*corresponder*). One day, however, for sure she must have sent him away (*de plano ella lo cachó*), saying that he was simply amusing himself (*simple y sencillamente estaba pasando el tiempo*). So, during a gathering of the forces, and with the procedure we used to use, she said, I ask to speak (*pedir la palabra*), and she was told, do speak *compañera*, come to the front (*pase al frente*). So she stepped in front and said, *compañeros*, I just want to declare/inform you that as of today I am the wife (*esposa*) of the *compañero* Chano, and please, nobody bother me from now on (*y que por favor nadie me moleste*). That was the joke of the year (*la broma del año*), and Chano did not know what to do with himself (*no hallar donde meterse*). In any case, they were not together for long after that. So, one would say, *compañeros*, we inform you that, or, I wish to inform you that I have finished my relationship with Fulano, that is, with so and so, so that there would not be problems. But the point was not, oh, so that someone else may follow (*para que venga otro*), someone else may come and speak to me (*hábleme otro*).[10] No, the point was simply, it was a manner (*forma*) that the *compas* [*guerrilleros*] adapted (*adaptar*), their own manner (*forma propria*), so that they would not be disrespectful to anyone (*para no faltarle de respeto a nadie*). So if people wanted to be in a relationship, they would no longer tell the *comandante*, but they might announce it in public. Okay, so the *compañero* has come to the decision of being in a relationship with the *compañera* and that was it. This was to avoid that any other *compañero* might be disrespectful to her by mistake (*equivocadamente*). Now, as for couples splitting up, announcements were not very common. Everyone would realize very quickly that they had split up, or that they had an argument/fight (*rápido todos se enteravan que se habían dejado, se habían peleado*), *verdad* [laughter], but that is how it would happen. Marriages by arms were abandoned because one could not go around marrying people, and one could not make fun of authority (*no se podían estar casando, no se podían estar burlando de la autoridad*). So to avoid that authority should be undermined (*evitar que se burlaran de la autoridad*), it was best not to marry (*era mejor no casarse*). Lead your life (*hagan su vida*), behave according to the regulations (*compórtense de acuerdo al reglamento*), be careful in making mistakes (*cuidado con cometer errores*), and nothing would go wrong (*y nada pasa*). We don't bother you (*molestar*) and you do not bother the collective (*colectivo*), the organization (*organización*)

> and the *compañeros*. That is how that changed, according to the circumstances (*fue cambiando palautinamente*).

Comandante Manolo had performed marriages "by arms" of combatants, and he commented on the marriages and the reasons for their quick demise as follows:

> Comandante Manolo is surprised by my question about marriages by arms (*matrimonios por las armas*). He says, well, that occurred at the beginning, it did not work out (*funcionar*). What happens when you have an area under your complete control (*zona de tu completo control*), you have to organize the economy (*la economía*) there, production for the war (*producción para la guerra*), not just the combatants, but the people who produce [supplies] in the very same space (*allí mismo*). That also makes you consider what to do with all those children, for instance. For children are not going to be left in the wild (*niños no van a quedarse de silvestres*). You have to make plans for their education (*educación*), their training (*formación*), because these people will join/be part of (*integrarse*) society. And how could they, without an education? Then, that made us consider social life (*vida social*), it made us think about the children, the elderly, women, hospitals, schools, and many other things. And we resolved to create (*formar*) our own institutions (*nuestras proprias instituciones*) in those living conditions (*condiciones de vida*), you know (*verdad*)? So, as they were many people, we had to organize (*organizar*) and regulate/establish norms for (*normar*) the life of everyone. And that is how we, leading on from a certain tradition (*a partir de cierta tradición*), and this has not been written/recorded anywhere, we had to elaborate our own civilian laws (*leyes civiles*), you understand. Those civilian laws allowed us to have a degree of control (*tener un control*) over our people. However, these civilian laws, this control, was established not merely to organize our own people, but also to avoid (*evitar*) any infiltration from the enemy (*infiltración del enemigo*). Anyone who would violate those norms, was also violating security (*seguridad*), and that could not be (*eso no podía ser*). For instance, we could not allow that a girl (*muchacha*) from around here should arrive and marry (*casar*) a *guerrillero*. And who is that girl? Why does she come to the guerrilla? Who sent her? What for? (*¿Y quíen es esa muchacha? ¿Y por qué viene a la guerrilla, y quíen la mandó? ¿Con qué propósito?*). Could she not be someone who has infiltrated the ranks (*infiltrada*)? We had

every right (*tener el derecho*) to ask those questions and we had every right to guarantee the security (*garantizar la seguridad*) of our organization, you understand. So that is why those norms (*normas*) were not written down (*estar escritas*) almost anywhere. They were forged (*plasmar*) in our military regulations (*reglamento militar*) . . . Those norms safeguarded us (*garantizarnos*) over many years; they gave us a degree of organization (*cierta organización*), a degree of coordination (*cierta coordinación*), and a degree of control (*cierto control*) over our people . . .

As for civil laws, the *comandantes* had the authority (*potestad*) to carry out marriages (*hacer matrimonios*), I held them myself, the task was deemed to be my responsibility (*a mi me tocó*). And "*pasar por las armas*" (undertake the "marriage by arms"), don't think it meant that I was executing them by firing squad (*que los estuviera fusilando*). No, it was a symbol (*símbolo*). The *comandante* of the guerrilla unit married the *compañeros* who had decided to live together (*vivir juntos*), to be a couple (*ser pareja*), well, they had the right to do that. We did not deny (*negar*) that to them. Of course, they had to uphold many rules (*cumplir muchas normas*). But later on, "*pasar por las armas*" also meant a festivity of the guerrilla (*festividad de la guerrilla*). Two lines of *compañeros* would assemble, and they would hold their arms [weapons] up, and the *compañeros* [who were getting married] would go by underneath [the weapons]. [That meant] that the whole of the guerrilla accepted the fact that they were a couple (*ser pareja*), in other words, the whole of the guerrilla gave them their blessing (*darle su bendición*) and accepted the fact that they were husband and wife (*marido y mujer*). That is what it was. I did that twice, we did it twice. However, we then realized that very often our combatants and our people who would join (*integrarse*) the guerrilla, they brought their whole villages (*aldea*) to the guerrilla. That is, they went to the guerrilla with their customs (*costumbres*), with their traditions (*tradiciones*), with everything. Something important should be said about this, and I will illustrate it with an example, so that we may understand each other . . . In a village the *compañera*, or the woman, has very few options (*opciones*) to be free to choose whom she is going to marry (*casar*), very few. Because the villages (*aldeas*) are very dispersed/far apart (*dispersas*), or because Fulano, that is, so and so has already eyed her (*hecharle el ojo*) for her to be his wife (*su mujer*). But the first requirement (*requisito*) is that he should have a good cultivated plot/harvest (*siembra*), that he should have money (*dinero*), that he should be able to support her financially (*mantener*). In other words, it is a contract (*contrato*). And although she does not love him (*querer*), she goes with/follows him. But she goes to live with him because he can support her financially (*mantener*). He will give her clothes, he will give her many things, that is, it is a relationship (*relación*) that is not grounded in affection (*cariño*) and love (*amor*). As you know, in relationships (*relaciones de pareja*) in everyday life (*muy corrientes*), well, they first get to know each other (*empezar conociendose*), they go out together (*salir juntos*), and then they feel that they are having a relationship (*sienten que están teniendo una relación entre ellos*). It is a process (*proceso*). In this case, however, it is not like that. Thus, a *compañerita* who has not had many options in her own village,[11] now can choose (*escoger*) whom she will marry [*de jure*] (*casar*), with whom she will marry [*de facto*] (*juntarse*), because there would not even be *de jure* marriages (*por qué nisiquiera había matrimonios*). So, in the village of the [guerrilla] front there was a young man (*muchacho*) who eyed her (*hecharle el ojo*) and he said to her to go with him. Before, she could not choose among many, there were no options, due to the repression/violence (*represión*), for whatever reason. And they would get to a village in resistance (*aldea de resistencia*),[12] and they would relate (*relacionarse*) to everyone there, and there they would truly live a community life (*vivir en comunidad*). So she would see all those handsome young men (*hermosos muchachos*) who were there, and she would look at her husband, and she would realize that he did not meet all the conditions (*condiciones*) of someone she would like to have as a husband. So the next day she would get together with someone else. Just like that, she had compared her husband with the others, and she realized that he did not meet all the requirements, that she had no other option than marrying him [*de facto*] (*juntarse*) in civil life (*la vida civil*), *verdad*. So, what would happen was that as these were relationships that were not grounded (*cimentadas*) in affection (*cariño*) and love (*amor*), and rather in material conditions (*condiciones materiales*), the first marriages [held in the guerrilla] were among these people, more or less, and would fail (*tronar*). And eight days later the marriages (*casamientos*) had dissolved (*disuelto*). And all that, of having got them to "*pasar por las armas*," that had been all in vain. So we opted for not doing it like that. In time, the *compañeros* would choose their partner (*pareja*), and those were more stable relationships (*relaciones más estables*), but we never again ventured into being ridiculed (*quedar en ridículo*) even [laughter]! In do-

> ing marriages that were not going to last for anything (*durar nada*)! With the effect that the political authority (*autoridad política*), the authority of the organization (*organización*), of the *comandante*, of the people would be compromised (*comprometer*)! Well, no, we resolved not to have them [marriages by arms] again. After that, the relationship was different, if there were people who had lived together for some time and they decided to get married [*de facto*] (*juntarse*), and wanted to have a ceremony (*ceremonia*), well then, they could get married (*casarse*), so the *comandante* had the necessary authority (*toda la autoridad*) to marry them (*casarlos*). That was the history (*historia*).

Through marriages by arms one of the guerrilla substances, namely "combatants," was divided and combined according to scales of gender and sexuality. Marriages by arms joined a male and a female combatant into a couple, thus setting the individuals concerned apart from the rest of the combatants inasmuch as gender and sexual relations were concerned. Through a merographic analogy, guerrilla sociality and relationality were imagined to be akin to a family. Moral orders based on sharing were articulated in conjunction with familial practices such as marriages by arms, wherein an authoritative figure, usually a *comandante*, would take on the parental role of witnessing and sanctioning the union. The community would also be joined in familial and communal terms, as they witnessed the union of the couple in the celebrations. Marriages by arms were short-lived and only a handful of these types of union were sanctioned by the *comandancia*. While the merographic analogy of "family ties" continued through the years of struggle, as did the ethos of *hermandad* (fraternity and amity) and sharing, gender and sexual relations demonstrated a certain unruly quality. As they transgressed and undermined the moral order(s) placed upon them, guerrilla moral orders adapted to mold themselves in accordance with the excess of gender and sexuality. To safeguard the authority of the *comandancia*, rules progressively relaxed and were replaced by a more flexible notion of "respect." "Respect" suited the merographic image of the family, but extended it, as respect was due not only to superiors, but also to any *compañero/a*.

Alma, Rubén, and the *Comandante* had offered different perspectives on marriages by arms. Alma had noted that they provided a degree of continuity between the experiences of social life within and outside the guerrilla. Rubén pointed out that they had juridical validity insofar as the combatants were concerned. Through humorous anecdotes, however, he argued that in matters of emotional and sexual relations between men and women, flexibility of moral orders was more appropriate than strict codes, rules, and procedures. The *Comandante* had also downplayed the significance of the practice and noted that marriages by arms had been ephemeral and ultimately unsuccessful. Nevertheless, Alma, Rubén, and the *Comandante* converged in their consideration of marriages by arms as part of a much broader and significant undertaking, namely that of fashioning social institutions in the guerrilla. They all acknowledged to have been engaged in the creation of a doubling of the society they had left when joining the insurgency. They attached different values to this process of creation of sociality, and to the unions and separations thus engendered. The duplicate society of the guerrilla may resemble the society they labored to protect themselves from. Nevertheless, the guerrilla replica was distinct, in that it functioned on moral orders based on commensality, *hermandad*, and respect. While there may be replication, there was also reinvention. Guerrilla reinvention, however, presented itself to me as marked by melancholy. In Butler's reworking of Freud's work on the subject, melancholia connotes a "refusal of grief and the incorporation of a loss, a miming of the death it cannot mourn" (Butler 1997, 142). "If melancholia designates a sphere of attachment that is not explicitly produced as an object of discourse, then it erodes the operations of language that not only posits objects, but regulates and normalizes objects through that positing. If melancholia appears at first to be a form of containment, a way of internalizing an attachment that is barred from the world, it also establishes the psychic conditions for regarding 'the World' itself as contingently organized through certain kinds of foreclosures" (Butler 1997, 143). Overwhelmed by melancholy and harboring my own secrets as a post-plural subject, I ventured to ask Rubén about the heterosexual logic that seemed to mark any discussion of gender and sexual relations in his account and in the accounts of other excombatants. I asked Rubén whether the logic that regulated sexual relations in the guerrilla was primarily heterosexual (*lógica de heterosexualidad*). Rubén replied:

> There was only one case he could recall, of an excellent officer (*excelentísimo oficial*). I respect him very much as an officer. In how he presented himself, he was not homosexual (*su presentación, pues no era que fuera homosexual*), *verdad*. We experienced a very delicate situation, because the *compañero* joined in the capital, and arrived in the guerrilla fronts [in Petén] and gained prestige (*cobrar mucho prestigio*) on the grounds of his personality (*antes su personalidad*),

> his respect (*su respeto*), and attitude (*actitud*) toward women and toward the *compañeros*. So he got to graduate as lieutenant (*graduarse hasta de teniente*) and headed a front in the area of Naranjo, La Libertad. This *compañero* was an excellent officer, but while an officer he made undue propositions (*algunas proposiciones debidas*) to a *compañero*, and this *compañero* denounced him. So when this happened, the whole unit was very indignant (*la unidad se indignó demasiado*), knowing that a homosexual was in command (*un homosexual los estaba dirigiendo*). The *compas* felt betrayed (*se sintieron como traicionados los compas*), there was lack of political maturity (*falta de maduréz política*). So the *compañero*, for having made an improper proposition (*propuesta inadecuada*) to this other *compañero*, turned into such a red-hot topic (*candente*) that the *comandante* had to intervene, and those of us in charge of security had to take him out of Petén, because the *compañeros* were very angry (*muy molestos*), because of that *machista* attitude (*por la misma actitud machista*), or whatever you may want to call it. But the *compañero* was an excellent (*excelentísimo*) and extremely good officer (*calidad de oficial*). We suggested (*pedir*) to him that it might be best that he got out (*salir*), in order to avoid problems, and he himself said that he would prefer to leave Petén. Work for him was arranged in the city, so he carried on working as our *compañero* in supplies. That was the only case we had then. Later on, with the others, things were very different. In the case of the *compañero* whom you know well, nobody was bothered or offended (*reprocharse*).[13]

Moral Disorders: Mourning the Dead in the Ethnographic Present

Cande was thirty-nine years old. She was born in Santa Rosa and was one of the first women to join the guerrilla struggle in Petén. She told me that her parents came to Petén between 1960 and 1968 and settled in a village where they spent years working the land, at times renting a plot, or *agarrando* (that is, occupying the land illegally or with no clear or secure land tenure), with no security of any sort in terms of land tenure.

> My parents (*mis padres*), one was unaware of many things (*uno ignoraba muchas cosas*), but my parents and their siblings (*pero mis papás y sus otros hermanos*), they had been working in that [the guer-

> rilla] since before (*desde antes venían trabajando en eso*), and gradually they started disclosing to my mother (*declarandole a mi mamá*), well, my father [began disclosing] what he was working on. And as we grew up, it was explained to us what he was working on, and they started deploying us (*utilizar*), that is, unconsciously we were already contributing to that work (*o sea, inconscientemente ya nosotros aportábamos en ese trabajo*), but we didn't know what we were doing. Afterwards, my father began to explain to us to what ends/why we were fighting, so that in Guatemala there may one day be a better life for the people (*el pueblo*), not only for those who fought, and that is how they gradually deployed me as messenger (*mensajera*), I was first a messenger delivering correspondence to a place, and learning a few things concerning arms (*algunas cosas de armas*), like that, guns, things like that, I worked on that for a time, that was my beginning. And as I was saying to you, my father used to converse a lot with us, he would gather us and explain to us what the causes were, and why [the struggle] was undertaken (*nos reunía y nos esplicaba cual eran las causas, y el porque se hacía*), because of the situation, that is, power in Guatemala is held by few, isn't it (*por la situación, o sea el poder en Guatemala lo tienen unos cuantos, no*)? And that every day it kept getting worse for the poor, and that is how I started, I could say that all my family, for the whole of my family got involved in it, in those things (*y así es que yo pues empezé, podría decir que toda mi familia, por que nosotros, toda mi familia se metió en eso, en esas cosas*). I was fourteen, between fourteen and seventeen years of age when I was working on that, I would make tortillas, I would deliver mail, I would make purchases for the *compañeros* who were already *en la montaña*. It was in mid-1982 that I joined (*incorporarse*) the clandestine struggle directly, it was in mid-1982. No, I am sorry, in 1980. Because at the time, before the beginning of 1980 there was a group who went abroad to train (*preparase*), so in that group was me, and then the group went to the *monte* (high vegetation) to train more people. So I joined one of those groups, with a *compa* (colloquial form for *compañero* or *compañera*) who died, whose name was Androcles, whose pseudonym was Androcles. And with Nestor, whom you know.

Cande trained in Cuba and when she returned to Petén she was a combatant and also worked in communications. When she got in a relationship with a *compañero*, she told the officer in her platoon. During her years in the guerrilla she said she had always commanded respect.

> I have to tell you about respect (*respeto*), of how one may command the respect of others (*como uno se da a respetar*). When I started, there were no women. In the group where I was there were only men, I was the only woman. I would go round in a small patrol (*patrullita*) and when we would get together with the other groups to train, I felt at ease (*sentirse lo normal*), nobody disrespected me ever, I felt the *compañeros* of my patrol and the others appreciated me greatly, they admired me (*admirar*) because I was involved [in the guerrilla]. When I went to Cuba, the group who went with me was very fond of me (*cariño*) and they would support me. During the training we would stand in huge trenches (*trincheronas*) and I could not jump high enough and get out, so the same *compañeros* would help me so that I could get up.

I asked Cande what it had meant for her to be *en la montaña* and her grief and melancholy submerged us both.

> What did it mean for me to be *en la montaña*? Look, as I said, at the beginning my father would tell us many things, the majority of us who were *en la montaña* believed so strongly (*creer tanto*) in [revolutionary] triumph (*en el triunfo*), and we were so resolute (*decididos*) and had so much conviction (*convencidos*), that if in any instant we should commit (*ortorgar*) our lives, this would have been for something just (*justo*). That is why I tell you, it gives me sadness (*tristeza*), I start to cry, at times out of anger (*coraje*), at times out of sadness (*tristeza*), for all our *compañeros* who gave their lives (*vidas*), they gave their lives out of conviction (*convencidos*), so that those of us who would survive would continue [in the struggle], and would serve as examples among our people and among all the people. All of us who were there were moved by this ideal, that there would be change (*cambio*), for our children and for everyone's children. Regrettably, for reasons I do not entirely understand (*comprender*), that was not achieved (*llevar a cabo*), because other countries who had the revolution already, lost it, and that did not help us. I believe that if we had triumphed, we would not have been allowed to live either, because the powerful (*poderosos*), they have the power (*poder*), and what rules is money (*lo que manda es el dinero*). That is why I tell you that I was confident of and convinced of [the necessity of] the struggle, of change, but now I am upset (*molesta*), because when the Peace was signed, there was an item [in the Peace Accords] that said that we would be able to go and look for our combatants who were left dead (*quedarse*

> *muerto*) and that we would be able to give them Christian burial (*cristiana sepultura*), and now that is not possible. . . . They say there is no money for it, and that the established deadline to carry out this work has already passed. What really hurts (*doler*) is that while our *compañeros* gave their lives for the people (*mientras nuestros compañeros dieron su vida por este pueblo*), now "*traga quien tiene más galío*,"[14] and the [deceased] *compañeros* lie forgotten (*olvidados*), and I am left with nothing. . . . I don't know how to explain it (*no sabría explicarme*), I don't know, handing over the weapons (*entragar las armas*) caused something like emotion/sentiment in me (*me causó como una cosa de sentimiento*), and since then I began to feel for those *compañeros* who died, I began to feel, like the one who says, I will go there, and you stay here (*yo me voy acá, y tu de quedas allí*). I cried when I left *la montaña* (*salir de la montaña*), I cried because I also had taken such fondness/appreciation to the forest (*le agarré tanto aprecio a la selva*), because the forest gave us a roof, gave us food, gave us water and the weaving that was part of our life (*por que la selva fue lo que nos dio techo, quien nos dio comida, quien nos dio agua, quien nos dio el téjido parte de nuestra vida*), and when the demobilization happened, and we got out from there, it was difficult for me (*costar*), it was difficult for me to accept this life change (*cambio de vida*), because one does not know what one will find here [in civil life], exiting a system (*sistema*), so to speak, and entering a new one. For now it would be very difficult for us to go and visit these *compañeros* who were left buried (*enterrados*), some of them, at least. For others the Army took with them, and who knows what happened to them.

For Cande, leaving *la montaña* was to leave a "system" to enter a new one. Cande discussed her experiences at demobilization as entailing a detachment or parting from a complex set of relationships to persons, objects, and the environment, all of which had participated in the interlacing that was guerrilla life *en la montaña*. At this point of dissolution and disassembling, guerrilla sociality and relationality appeared as a whole constituted by parts that included the deceased *compañeros* buried in the forest. Their death had not marked the end of their relationship. Rather, death marked a sense of permanence and durability of guerrilla relationality and its continuity, so long as those who survived carried on in the struggle spurred on by,[15] and on behalf of, those who had been killed. Guerrilla sociality between the living and the dead was made possible by their mutual coexistence *en la selva*, that is, in the forest. The connection could be sustained and reproduced as long as the sociality in the forest might itself be maintained. Other ex-combatants had implied that what was also necessary was that there exist those who may recall where the dead lie. On demobilization, Cande envisioned the inception of dissolution of guerrilla sociality as a moment of splitting, as in the division between the deceased *compañeros/as* who were left in the forest, and those moving on to a life and a system outside of it. The temporality of this perspective conjured up assemblage, as in the dead increasingly appearing as bundles of guerrilla relationships, and disassembling, with guerrilla relationality progressively resembling a "vanishing whole" (Strathern 1992b). I have argued that *guerrilleros/as* envisaged their experiences *en la montaña* as grounded on moral orders based on sharing, commensality, and relatedness. Cande argued that the process of disassembling of guerrilla subjectivities and sociality entailed forgetting the dead with the relationalities and moral orders they had come to stand for. Unwilling to partake in what were for her progressively more ravenous and greedy times, and unable to sustain her relations with either the living or the dead, Cande felt she had been left with nothing. Cande had labored strenuously to avoid the disclosure of this sense of diminution. For months she had amiably and yet firmly exerted ethnographic refusal (Ortner 1995) and rejected any relation with me. Encouraged by her brother, she eventually agreed to speak of the scale of disappearance and diminution through which her attachments to the guerrilla whole were articulated at the time.

Conclusion: Post-perspectival Reinventions of the Social

In the account provided by a FAR *comandante*, the guerrilla was envisaged as an entity composed of three substances, namely "information," "supplies," and "combatants." Each substance, like each strand of insurgent activities—"armed struggle," "the political struggle of the masses," and "the political-diplomatic struggle"—was clearly structured and overseen by the *Comandante*. In my analysis, the management of the three substances that were envisioned to make up the guerrilla coincided with the articulation of multiple socialities and moral orders. Interestingly, the comprehensiveness that characterized the vision of the *Comandante*, with its distinctive lexicon and modalities of division, multiplication, and connection, was never replicated in part or as a whole in my conversations with ex-combatants. Conversely, the *Comandante*'s totalizing vision might come across as partial and incomplete when contrasted with and complemented by the vision of guerrilla sociality offered by ex-*guerrilleros/as*. Switching from the scale inherent in the *Comandante*'s perspective to that of the combatants, it appeared that ex-combatants envisioned guerrilla sociality as a moral order based on sameness and sharing. This point was made with reference to the ways in which activities were organized in clandestine life. As I have illustrated, most ex-combatants remembered enduring hunger and malnutrition during the war and commented on the constant lack of proper food provision. Nevertheless, they recalled how all available food was shared. Food preparation was also referred to as an instance in which everybody was truly the same, as men and women regardless of rank had to partake in food preparation. Ex-combatants recounted how *tamales guerrilleros* were made with just maize and water, often not even with slaked lime to properly cook the corn. *Tamales guerrilleros* often had no salt, as salt was difficult to acquire unless funds and channels for purchase and delivery were available. Life in the guerrilla was remembered as a moral order established through homogenizing practices based on sharing. Such a moral order was one of many that coexisted simultaneously, some enduring in time more than others.

As an example of an ephemeral moral order that did not endure over time, and one geared toward the regulation of specific scales of difference of gender and sexuality, I have discussed marriage practices among *guerrilleros/as*. A small number of ex-combatants spoke of how they or others had married "by arms." Alma, for example, was one of the *guerrilleras/os* who were married "by arms" and she illustrates very clearly how guerrilla sociality was envisioned through a specific idiom of relatedness and was said to constitute a family. "Marriages by arms" were ultimately abandoned, however, and I conclude by noting possible reasons for their fleeting character. While life in the guerrilla was often qualified through the merographic analogy of "family ties," gender and sexual relations were recognized to be unruly and to constantly exceed moral orders placed upon them. Further, their ordering need not have aided in the management of the three guerrilla substances. Rather, attempts at regulating gender and sexual relations potentially undermined guerrilla sociality and relationality, as well as the parental authority of the *comandancia*.

Some ex-combatants reflected on their experiences of struggle, highlighting a shift from the moral order based on sharing, which they saw as distinctive of social life *en la montaña*, with the rise of an individualistic post-demobilization ethos. Cande connoted the post–Peace Accords times as entailing a certain moral disorder, as in a disregard for guerrilla moral orders based on equality and sharing. The transition from a communal to an individualistic form of life that punctuated her account was exemplified in her sense of betrayal of those *compañeros/as* who had died *en la selva* (in the forest) without even having been granted proper burial. Guerrilla socialities and their substances and moral orders emerge as multiple and complex, revealing pliability and multiple temporal dimensions. They supplement the perspective on sociality and subjectivity of a post-plural account within the horizon of performativity. In other words, in ex-combatants' accounts, guerrilla sociality and relationality were predicated on multiple merographic analogies and intersecting moral orders. Through production, reproduction, and circulation of guerrilla substances, central dimensions of guerrilla social relations were generated. Equitable distribution of scarce food provisions among all produced relationalities of homogenization, and a moral order based on sameness. Merographic analogies that established connections between domains such as "the guerrilla" and "the family" provided the ground for further moral orders grounded on interdependence *and* authority. With short-lived practices such as "marriages by arms," idioms of familial relatedness grounded an attempt at ordering gender and sexual relations. Nevertheless, gender and sexuality appeared to be connoted by excess and instability, and any attempt at disciplining them was acknowledged to ultimately challenge the parental and military authority of those entrusted with the task of governing them, and thus the guerrilla project as a whole. "Marriages by arms" were supplanted by a notion of "respect" that was sufficiently permeable and flexible to accommodate the excess of scales of gender and sexuality, and that ensured the authority of the *comandancia* would not be ridiculed and undermined. *Guerrilleros* and *guerrilleras* with their different perspectives and scales produced multiple models of sociality and relatedness. Guerrilla models appeared to depend on division and connection of parts and wholes, and disassembling and reassembling of the social realm. Insofar as these processes occurred in temporal frames, they also conjured up the effect of malleability, as the guerrilla replica displaced the broader society and periodically reinvented itself. The labor of imagination at stake in these processes, with its models of sociality and relatedness, replicates and is replicated in the post-perspectivism imagined through the notion of performativity. Eschewing simple enumeration of a plurality of discrete wholes, both guerrilla imagination and the ethnographic imagination elicit a multiplicity of interpreting subjects marked by the immediacy of their encounters, the deferrals inherent in their constant shifting in perspectives, and thus in constant rearticulation. There thus seems to be a partial, tentative, and provisional correspondence between guerrilla merographic analogies and the break with context of postplural knowledge practices and rearticulatory performativity. In the next chapter I recast these questions in terms of ethnographic post-plurality and antifoundationalism and reflect on the aesthetics of ethnography and performativity through the concept-metaphor of "prosthetics."

6
Secrecy, Prosthetics, Aesthetics

> Gaps seem to give us somewhere to extend: space for our prosthetic devices. Absent expertise, the features of a distant kinsman, a glimpsed spirit elicit their imagining while also eliciting the perception that all images are borrowed images. A sense of excess or insufficiency, then, of lack of proportion, of connections being partial suggest[s] we could extend the perceptions themselves.
>
> —Marilyn Strathern 1991, 115–6

> —We can understand phenomenology only by seizing upon it as a possibility.
>
> —Martin Heidegger [1962] 2002, 39

Introduction

This chapter is intended to be a reflection on *forms* of description and theorizing, that is, on the aesthetics of knowledge practices. The aim is to provide a "cultural description" of cultural categories such as "subjectivity," "personhood," "embodiment," and "agency," and not to be a "sociological analysis" (Strathern 1988, 274). I envisage the task by reflecting on the aesthetics that underpin theoretical models and the processes through which theoretical models emerge. To address the labor of imagination that theory and ethnography entail, I propose an engagement with "prosthetics," as a critical tool and a concept-metaphor (Moore 1999; 2004) of considerable imaginative potential for an analysis of secrecy and insurgency in Guatemala, and one that lends itself to a series of performative (re-)inscriptions and (re-)articulations.

There exist numerous sites of articulation of "prosthetics" in the imagination of cultural theory. "Prosthetics" evoke debates over relations between the organicity of the body and the in-organicity of technology (Downey et al. 1995; Gray 1995; Haraway 1991; Stone 1996; Zylinska 2002). From this perspective, "prosthetics" suggest meditations on the status of the nature/culture boundary usually resulting in both augmentation and excentricity of the agentic prosthetic subject. In point of fact, prostheses mark the liminal space between the organic and the inorganic, the animate and the inanimate. The relation between inorganic prostheses, more or less permanently attached to organic bodies, points to a series of questions concerning the type of sociality that may be established between organic humans and inorganic technology and the kinds of embodied subjects that may be said to emerge in the context of organic/inorganic interactions. Further, through a questioning of dualisms, prosthetics invite reconfigurations of what may be understood by "embodiment," "subjectivity," and "agency."

Donna Haraway (1989; 1991; 1997) offers a groundbreaking attempt at rethinking the relationality of humans and machines. It is Haraway's contention that the interaction between the two is not unidirectional or, indeed, anthropocentric. Rather, Haraway suggests that humans and machines are *both* produced through mutuality of interaction. Agency is thus posited as a product of mutual interworkings of the human subject and the machine, and this insight in turn leads to a reconfiguring of the subject in terms of a cyborgian imaginary: "A cyborg is a cybernetic organism, a hybrid of machine and organism, a creature of social reality as well as a creature of fiction. Social reality is lived social relations, our most important political construction, a world-changing fiction . . . The cyborg is a matter of fiction and lived experience that changes what counts as women's experience in the late twentieth century. This is a struggle over life and death, but the boundary between science fiction and social reality is an optical illusion" (Haraway 1991, 149). In Haraway's cyborgian imaginary, the hybrid cyborg is enmeshed in fact and fiction, to the extent that the boundary between lived reality and representation appears to be a perspectival effect, an optical illusion. The cyborgian subject is further defined as a normative, if simulated, effect of Foucauldian bio-power (Haraway 1991, 163) and Western hegemonic teleology. The cyborg's hybrid and illegitimate conception engenders the possibility of a counter-hegemonic political strategy.

> By the late twentieth century, our time, a mythic time, we are all chimeras, theorized and fabricated hybrids of machine and organism; in short, we are all cyborgs. The cyborg is our ontology; it gives us our politics . . . The cyborg is also the awful apocalyptic *telos* of the "West's" escalating dominations of abstract individualism, an ultimate self untied at last from all dependency, a man in space . . . The cyborg skips the steps of original unity, of identification with nature in the Western sense. This is its illegitimate promise that might lead to subversion of its teleology as star wars. . . . The cyborg is resolutely committed to partiality, irony, intimacy, and perversity. It is oppo-

> sitional, utopian, and completely without innocence (Haraway 1991, 150–1).

The cyborg is thus a subject who/which, having merged the organic/mechanic interface and transgressed speciation narratives, allows for reconfigurations of subjectivity and agency that are not entirely dependent on, but may be still spuriously related to, Western metaphysical traditions. The cyborgian subjects presented by Haraway eschew dualism and naturalism and are endowed with cyborg heteroglossia, that is, a condition and a capacity not determined by dualisms but, rather, moving between and thus reconfiguring entities, domains, and traditions, in post-plurality.

Haraway's (1991) conceptualization of the human/mechanic interface has been very effectively explored in the work of the performance artist Stelarc (Smith 2005; Zylinska 2002). In the context of the "Third Hand" project, for instance, a mechanical limb is grafted onto/into the artist's stomach and leg muscles. During the performance, Stelarc's body is also attached to a computer system so that Internet users can remotely determine the movement of Stelarc's prosthetically enhanced bodily extension. The overall effect is that of decentering Stelarc's control over his own movements, so that the artist's body is no longer "his own." Fleming (2002, 95) argues that Stelarc's performances with "the body-as-an-action-system" subvert Cartesian notions of control and centricity through "corporeal decenterings" enacted in the complex and multiple spatial and chronological site of the wired environment. The subversion of the autonomous agent is said to amount to "subversion without inversion." Partly in reference to Stelarc's work, Moore (1999, 162) notes that "all forms of technology are, of course, prosthetic and, this accounts, in part, for their symbolic role in the construction and mediation of identity, particularly gender identity." The mutuality of articulation between the organic and the inorganic, the human and the mechanic has its confluence in the figure of the cyborg and its hybrid, illegitimate, and heterodox condition. In its complex relation with Western metaphysics, that is, both within the horizon of Western metaphysics and also substantively and ideationally beyond it, the cyborgian subject is a performative subject animated by what Barad (2003) calls "post-humanist performativity." From the perspective of post-humanist performativity, the world comes into being and is continuously restaged performatively through matter's agentic force of intra-action, thus revealing the contours and boundaries of cyborg—and both humanist and post-humanist—entities and forms of embodiment as evanescent.

In a rather different exchange, "prosthetics" have been conceptualized in terms of notions of presence and absence, with factual or imagined prosthetic extensions as supports to a body that is understood as lacking factual or imagined limbs/bodily parts (Hogle 2003; Kurzman 2001; Nelson 2001a; 2001b). "Prosthetics" have thus been deployed to illuminate a number of trajectories such as the prosthetic role played by the *mujer maya* (Maya woman) in propping up the Guatemalan state (Nelson 1999; 2001b), or the prosthetic body of workers as the sites of capital accumulation (Haraway 1991), and related to the latter, the prosthetics of supervision in *maquiladora* factories (Nelson 1999; Wright 2001). Objecting to the deployment of the term "prosthetics" in these analyses, Kurzman (2001) notes that the metaphor of "prosthetics" presupposes certain normative ideas of bodily wholeness and completeness, thus implicitly relying on the body of amputees as the ground, "or silent site of creative discursive frameworks" (Kurzman 2001, 374). Instead, Kurzman proposes to think critically about the way "we all naturalize able-bodiedness as a subject position tied to one particular body" and develop instead frameworks that, by thinking about impairment, may allow for theorizations of "multiple bodies, subjectivities, forms of ability and mobility, and ways of being whole" (Kurzman 2001, 383–4), and, I wish to add, ways of being in parts.

If, as Haraway (1991) suggests, the cyborgian subject operates as fact *and* fiction, science fiction *and* social reality, in the prosthetic subject, presence and absence may come to presuppose each other in complex existential embodied trajectories so that subjects may exist in composite wholes, or indeed in parts. Through the concept metaphor of prosthetics, with the recovery of gaps, cyborgian interactions, and performative intra-action that the concept-metaphor allows, it may be possible to hold within the same frame the phenomenology of the prosthetic subject and the scales of her supplementation.

Prosthetic aesthetics were conjured up during my fieldwork in different contexts and scales of engagement. The "ethnographic moment" that connoted the realization of multiple and complex naming practices and related relationalities among ex-*guerrilleros/as* revealed that names amount to a prosthetics of guerrilla subjectivity and sociality.[1] Through the deployment of different names, (ex-)guerrilla subjects were able to extend themselves to fashion different orders of agency and connection. Further, through names, presence and absence presupposed each other in specific ways. Discarding a name may make a subject disappear so that she may be able to embody a new pseudonym, and hence a different incarnation. With nicknames, "the same" subject may acquire a further prosthesis and one that mainly functioned within guerrilla secret socialities and relationalities. When Mosquito recovered his guerrilla nickname in the course of our conversation, he activated a guerrilla prosthetic extension that pertained to the realm of guerrilla secrecy. Just as swiftly, through ethnographic refusal (Ortner 1995), he deactivated it. In a different scale, ex-combatants often referred to joining the guerrilla organization as a moment of *incorporación* or "incorporation,"[2] evoking a process of joining a collectivity. The term "incorporación" was to me extremely powerful in that it also evoked a sense in which each *guerrillero/as* might be part of a corporeal guerrilla whole and might in turn represent a part of a larger whole, *la guerrilla*. Through the many accounts of their *incorporación* offered by the ex-combatants, I was made to imagine bodies in parts, embodied/corporeal parts and wholes, and multiple orders and scales of attachment and connection. In other words, I imagined the guerrilla through prosthetic aesthetics.

In what follows, I wish to highlight a further aspect of prosthetic aesthetics, and one that is presupposed in the performative cyborgian subject as much as in the subject marked by presence and absence, namely the prosthetic subject and her phenomenology. Csordas (1994, 11) argues that "[t]he dominance of semiotics over phenomenology, and hence concern with the problem of representation over the problem of being-in-the-world" has marred analysis and is reproduced in the pervasive and seemingly categorical distinction between "language" and "experience." Drawing on Husserl (1964), Heidegger ([1962] 2002), and Merleau-Ponty ([1962] 2002), approaches informed by phenomenology foreground the experiential and embodied quality of subjectivity and sociality (Csordas 1994; 1999; Jackson 1996; Rapport 2002; 2003). As argued by Rapport,

> It is important to reiterate that these three kinds of knowledge—self, world and other—are bound up together, mutually implicated. Also, that these knowledges are personally embodied; they are the possession and creation of distinct individual organisms. Also that such mutually implicated, personally embodied knowledge is not a fixed or stationary phenomenon but one in continuous process of being and becoming. Finally, the identity of the organism and its environment—the organism-plus-environment—can be said to be dependent on the ongoing process by which that organism comes to know itself. The organism is the knowledge of the world, is the order it creates of and around itself (Rapport 2003, 220).

Within the horizon of phenomenology, strong categorical distinctions between "experience" and "representation" are weakened. Moreover, with Heidegger's specification that "[w]e can understand phenomenology only by seizing upon it as a possibility" (Heidegger ([1962] 2002, 39), I wish to discuss phenomenologies of the ethnographic encounter and its prosthetics and forms of being-in-the-world.

In the conclusion of this chapter I suggest that the relation between guerrilla prosthetics and anthropological prosthetics may be tentative and temporal replicas of each other. Through the establishment of a relation of equivalence between the ethnographer's prosthesis of the tape recorder and the guerrilla's prosthesis of the rifle, the *guerrilleros/as* and the ethnographer borrowed each other's images, to constantly and performatively extend, reinscribe, supplement, and defer to each other and their relations. Such temporal processes of corporeal reinscription make subjects and descriptions prosthetic. Subjects and their descriptions may be always incomplete, ever partial, and yet constantly augmenting and diminishing in and through their prosthetic aesthetics. Prosthetics thus allow for (re-)figuring and (re-)configuring linkages and sites of analysis, representation and experience, thus (re-)casting prosthetics in anthropological and cultural theory, and as a detour, in the practice of ethnography.

Prosthetics and the Phenomenology of the Ethnographic Encounter

Alma and I meet again, about two weeks after our first brief encounter. Alma was allocated her own *lote* (plot of land) and *vivienda* (house), but prefers to live with her mother, father, siblings, partner, and her own children on her father's *lote*. The family built a large kitchen with wooden walls and *techo de corozo* (palm roof). The sleeping quarters are large enough to accommodate everyone, including visiting researchers. For our conversation, however, Alma takes me to her own house. We walk through the village for about five minutes, and then stop, while she undoes the knots of the rope that keeps the wooden door shut. There is ash in the *fogón* (hearth), a sign that fire has been lit at some point in the past, but a hen is now sleeping in it. It is clear that people seldom come by or use the premises. There are no utensils or items of everyday use. We sit on the benches whose stilts are buried in the ground. I set up the tape recorder, take out the cigarettes, and Alma and I smoke, while I explain the nature of my visit in greater detail. The long conversation that ensues is punctuated by our smoking Rubios Azules.[3] Alma recounts several episodes related to her time *en la montaña* and I am mesmerized by her gripping storytelling. While Alma's house and the cigarettes mark the inter-subjective space of our encounter, and the tape-recorder placed between us grants all manner of prosthetic extensions to us both, there are other items that gain prominence as her narrative unfolds.

In order to reroute concept metaphors and meta-theories of prosthetics, I propose to consider this ethnographic encounter with Alma, the ex-*guerrillera* engaged in giving *form* to embodied subjectivity in my presence. The analysis therefore takes its lead from a conversation with this ex-*guerrillera* intent on the act of telling stories about her time *en la montaña* during our encounter. The fictional quality that I hope to highlight is not that of the content of what is being said, or what is being remembered. Rather, I wish to point to the phenomenological dimensions of the ethnographic encounter and the multiple processes through which embodiment, subjectivity, agency, and anthropological knowledge come into being and are supplemented through a number of prosthetic mediations.

The labor of ethnography entails the deployment of self (Ortner 1999) as much as the use of distinctive paraphernalia. The place of objects in the practice and representation of ethnography has been noted by Stocking (1983) and Clifford (1980; 1988; 1992; 1997) in their insightful remarks on the role played by the tent in Malinowski's fieldwork in the Trobriand Islands. Clifford (1988, 28; 1992; 1997, 20, 54) notes that Malinowski's tent functions in his work as a defining icon of ethnography, producing a regulatory conceptualization of ethnography as a "practice of co-residence." Conversely, the paraphernalia of my fieldwork was mainly the stuff of travel. Rucksack, hammock, mosquito net, toothbrush, and toilet paper marked the itinerant and transitory quality of the ethnographic encounter as much as a clinging to specific "technologies of the self" (Foucault 1988). The items were also suggestive of multiple conceptualizations of the experience of ethnography in the way they seemed to figure a shift from "single-sitedness" to "multi-sitedness" (Marcus 1998).

The *chiclero* hammock I borrowed was made of thick enough *lona* as to be impenetrable to insects and was often remarked to be the token of Petenero identity.[4] The Petén and the Petenero identities in question were those of the early- to mid-twentieth century, namely times characterized by the mass extraction of chicle. The sap of the chico zapote tree (*Achras zapota*), also known as *oro blanco*, or "white gold," made the fortune of the United States chewing gum industry. It also allowed for the accumulation of wealth and status for a number of prominent Guatemalan/Petenero families (Schwartz 1990; see Chapter 2). The *chiclero* hammock, as a prosthetic attachment to the resting body of the *chiclero*, was a reminder of the bodily practices associated with the extraction of labor and resources for the purpose of capital accumulation (Jameson 1991; Limón 1994; Martin 1992; Taussig 1980; 1987) characteristic of Petén up to the mid-twentieth century. That the *chiclero* body and its prostheses were of archival rather than contemporary ethnographic relevance was signaled in the ethnographic present by the diorama exhibit one could view in the former INCAP museum in Flores. There one could find the display called "Disappearing Petén," including the *chiclero* hammock arranged in a taxidermic, faux-jungle setting for the consumption of tourists as much as for justification of the work of the "environmentalist" non-governmental organization that financed it and maintained it. Nevertheless, the prosthetics of labor and human and natural exploitation have changed. The *motosierras* (chainsaws) and *los camiones* (trucks) of the illegal logging industry were more topical and relevant prosthetics of capital accumulation in Petén in the ethnographic present and featured prominently in people's everyday discussions and preoccupations.

During my time in Petén, I also acquired a "*hamaca guerrillera*," or "guerrilla hammock." Acquaintances told me that a group of ex-*guerrilleros/as* disabled by injuries suffered during the conflict were putting the skills they had acquired during their time in the insurgency to use in post-demobilization times and were making hammocks. I said I would very much like to buy one and weeks later the hammock arrived from Guatemala City. This *hamaca guerrillera* was a large rectangular piece of waterproof fabric, which, I was assured, would keep out rain and insects, and regrettably retain the heat and humidity within. I never used the *hamaca guerrillera* while traveling to and from communities, because I thought it would be safer to conceal obvious signifiers of insurgency.

Rucksack, hammock, tape recorder, cigarettes, and camera and the other prostheses of my fieldwork were loci of multiple mediations. Their activity and idleness defined the prosthetic quality of my ethnographic practice. For instance, my propensity for "hearing" rather than "seeing" seemed suited to my activities on the routes of guerrilla secrecy and determined the primacy of the tape recorder in my exchanges with the ex-guerrilla. The tape recorder seemed to function in less intrusive and more intimate ways than the prosthetic eye of a camera would. Unlike with images, I felt I could produce anonymized recordings self-sufficiently in collaboration with my interlocutors. Nevertheless, my prosthetic hearing entailed its own anxieties, mainly having to do with that disturbing and most prosthetic of associations with *orejas*, in the literal sense of "ears" and the metonymical sense of "informer." With the story of the apparatus recounted by Luis in mind (see Chapter 4), and the implicit warning that (anthropological) bricoleur abilities to hear and record the conversations of post–Peace Accords ex-guerrilla secret socialities might provoke violent reprisals, I took Luis' advice seriously and hid the evidence, namely the tapes, "inside a well." The tape recorder of my fieldwork functioned as the prosthetic extension of the ethnographic embodied subjects whose agency now extends beyond the immediacy of the encounter. My interlocutors in the field fully realized the prosthetic potential for augmentation and extension inherent in the ethnographic encounter and its prostheses. Ex-*guerrilleros/as* redrew the boundaries between us subjects and our prostheses accordingly. They conjured up the image of technologically enhanced guerrilla subjects and extended this, to show how a prosthetic embodiment also pertained to anthropology. In so doing, they gave a *form* to the phenomenology of the ethnographic encounter.

Guerrilla Phenomenology and Its Prosthetics

As Alma and I smoked Rubios Azules in her abandoned house, she began to recount stories about her time in the guerrilla. Guerrilla phenomenology and its prosthetics slowly emerged in Alma's storytelling. I was captivated.

> I am going to tell you [a story] (*contar*), I remember that once, when I left, once I went to Mexico, I got back in [into Guatemala], and when I got back in, I thought I was going in the direction of Dolores, but at that time they were going to establish the Panzós Heróico Front in Alta Verapaz, so the Captain who was in that front would say to me, let's go. The Captain was in love with me (*enamorado de mi*) and was courting me (*me estaba enamorando*) but the truth was that I had not yet decided what to do about him (*estábamos en veremos con él*). We passed by a camp (*campamento*) and I realized that he had, well, he had a girl (*chava*), well, before, and there he met up with the girl and I saw that he stayed on (*se quedó*) with the girl there and I did not like that, so I told him, definitely no (*ya no*) [nothing would happen between them]. Then we left that camp and proceeded on our course (*marcha*) and he tells me, let's go [to join his own front] and I tell him no, and he asks why and I tell him it is not in my interest (*no me conviene*) to go, and he was a bit hard pressed (*presionado*) because he wanted to take me there, but as I was stubborn (*necia*), I would jump (*brincaba*) [in frustration and anger] when I considered that I had my reasons, I would say no, I want to go the other way, to the FAR Front, my front, I won't leave it for anything (*yo no lo dejo ni por nada*). And he, obstinate (*terco*), as obstinate as that. In the end, I did not go [with

him]. Two to three months went by and eventually he let the matter rest (*se convenció*). I went as far as the river Santa Isabel, and from there I made my way back to the FAR [Front]. That's where I stayed. With time, something like eight to ten months later, I can't remember well, the other front needed to be strengthened and they sent almost everybody [in the FAR Front] that way. We went and I was the one in charge of setting the route (*rumbera*) because I knew the area, I was leading all that crowd (*gentío*) with me in that direction, feeling quite sad (*triste*), as at times I would forget the routes (*rumbos*), and we would proceed kind of lost (*algo perdidotes*) at times, but we would carry on nonetheless. We got together with the others, and on one of those occasions there were some *compas* who were ill with *dengue*,[5] and I had a problem with my tonsils, and they had to go and attack an Army base (*destacamento*) that was there in Fray [Fray Bartolomé de las Casas, Alta Verapaz], so they told me, you are not going, you are staying behind. So we stayed on with those who were ill, all of those who were ill and a medical officer who stayed with us. Three days later, the guys were supposed to be back on the fourth day and most of us were already feeling better and I was also feeling quite well again, so they sent us, go and wait for the guys. We went. I remember we were picking *nances* [wild berry-like fruits], and while we were doing that a girl came out on her way to fetch water, and the *compa* who was with me started courting the girl (*enamorar a*), but the girl would not take much notice of him (*le daba lado*), and we were carrying our handful of *nances*, we gave some to the girl as a present and carried on. So, I say, there was a house in that direction, I say to him, I will go there to try and get a bag because my little hat, the hat that we would wear, that's what I was carrying the *nances* in. I am going to look for a bag, I say to him, and I left my ammunition belt (*cinturón*) behind, my rifle, and everything, and I go just like that (*me voy así*), as I was wearing a brown t-shirt, a civilian one (*particular*), I put that on and that is it, when I get this close to the house I see a woman approaching and she says to me that [one word is unclear in the recording] and she keeps on looking at me (*me quedó viendo*), and I notice that behind the house, that's where the soldiers are, and I make my way back quickly and I say to the other *compa*, that's where the *cuques* [soldiers] are, I say to him, and we left quickly, we left. So, what of the *nances*? I had a handkerchief, and we left the little wrap with the *nances* tied to a tree, and on our way back we went to pick it up, with some tortillas that that girl had given us as a gift, we went to a hill (*cerro*) to wait for the others and we started to eat, when I see that the group (*grupo*) was over there, that's where the *compas* are, I say to my companion, and he just keeps on looking (*se queda viendo*), I stood up, and I was whistling and whistling at them and they did not even take notice, imagine (*fíjese*), there in the terrain free of vegetation (*allí en lo puro limpio*). Stoop down, my companion told me, that's the *cuques* [soldiers], he told me, and I was stubborn, until finally I threw myself to the ground. He would tell me, it's the *cuques* [soldiers]. We will see, I told him, anyway, we walked down the hill to go and see. We were just getting near when we heard the bangs (*cuentazos*), they [the soldiers] had clashed with the other [guerrilla] group, those who were coming to meet up with us (*venían al contacto con nosotros*). And yes, indeed (*cabal*), it was the Army. And there the noise/exchange of fire (*cuenteyo*) started. So, I say, they fell onto the guys (*le cayeron a los muchachos*), I tell my companion, and they must have caught them by surprise, so I say, let's get in there, and we bash (*les damos*) the *cuques* [soldiers].

From behind? I ask.

Yes, from the rear guard, seriously, so they come up against us and the others were free. So we got in there, and, exactly, from the rear guard we started shooting. So, the other *compa* tells me, here we should proceed by *saltos vigilados* (jumping in with those behind holding guard), because there could be more of them in that direction, and so we were proceeding like this, he would advance a bit and I would stay still supporting him from behind, from there, he would take on guard and I would go ahead, and that's how we were proceeding when, *cabal* (precisely)! We fell right into an Army ambush that was right where we had left the *nances* and where they had seen us! And that's where we went back to!? And that's where they were waiting for us, and precisely when we were going through a nice clean stretch of grazing land (*potrero*), I eyed a little house that was on the small edge, so that people would not see (*para que no fuera a ver la gente*), when I see a shadow this big and I realize that it was the Army, I turn and the shooting is just behind me in my direction (*y son los cuentazos atrás de mi*), and I threw myself to the ground fast (*yo corriendo me tiré a tierra*), there was a fence there, and I threw myself in the direction of the fence, I stand up again and I jump into a stream that was there, and the other *compa* who was with me, well he also started unleashing lead [shooting] (*rempujar plomo*), and so we started, and what? It's when we start to withdraw that another

Army group comes out, just like that, to cover us [in the sense of siege, not protection], and they almost got us encircled/imprisoned (*casi nos teníamos encerrados*). It was just the two of us, and that's when we started unleashing lead [shooting] (*bolarles plomo*) and proceeding ahead, and they were shooting back, we were just about to jump across a huge furrow (*íbamos a cruzar un sanjón bien grande*), because there are very ugly furrows in Alta Verapaz, when they threw a mortar (*tiraron un morterazo*), and I almost fell ahead of myself, ahead of where I was going, so I came back on myself, and the other [*compa*] on his way back from jumping across the stream fell near me, so the expansion wave (*onda espansiva*) [result of the explosion] threw me on my mouth in the direction of the furrow (*me tiró de boca para el sanjón*), and that's where I got the problems with my spine, up to this day I suffer from problems with my leg, and there, I could not get away, I was feeling watery (*me sentía aguada*) [in the sense of unsteady], I felt my feet becoming watery (*sentía que me se aguadaron los pies*), had already no strength left (*ya no tenía fuerza*), and the other *compa* did not want to leave me behind, come, he said to me, he was giving me his hand so that I could get out, and I was not even able to stand (*yo ni pararme podía*), in the end I got across a stretch of land that was there, where there was *milpa*,[6] the *milpa* was nice and small (*chiquitita estaba la milpa*), and on we went, let's go, he said to me, and the *compa* was dragging me (*me llevaba a jalones*), I was feeling that my legs had no strength anymore, and the *cuques* [Army soldiers] behind us unleashing lead (*volandonos plomo*), they almost killed us (*casi nos mataron*), they pushed us toward the Chiniq River, that's what they call it in Alta Verapaz, and I say to the *compa*, you go, I am going to stay here (*yo aquí me quedo*), that's where I am going to stay (*aquí me voy a quedar*) because I don't want to die drowning (*porque yo no quiero morir ahogada*), I say to him, it's better this way and I am going to throw lead from here, you go. He did not let me do that/leave me (*no me dejó*), what he did was to throw me in the water (*lo que hizo me tiró al agua*), and we, I mean, he threw himself and he pushed me, and I was going behind him, and that way, we got to the other side swallowing water (*tragando agua salimos al otro lado*), and we went, the hell with it, and they did not catch up with us again. In the meantime, the unit with which the Army had clashed, I mean, those *compas* started to maneuver, and the row started with them (*y ya empezó el alborote*) and they got them off our backs. But all this was outright chaos (*ah, pero todo eso fue la fregada!*). We did not go through there, the trouble (*tenquello*) started at about two, at about two PM, and it finished at about six PM, as it was already getting dark, and they started, I was really unwell (*yo iba bien fregada*), I recall I got to the house of some collaborators (*colaboradores*) at about eight-nine PM. I recall that they gave us food, and from there the big rumor arose (*y de allí el gran chisme*), that they had killed me (*que me habían matado*), and as in those days the Army started putting women in their ranks, well they started to say that so-and-so [Alma] had been killed (*empezaron a decir mataron a Fulana*) and all that, and as many people, civilian people, knew me, they would say, they killed so-and-so, they killed so-and-so, and the *compas* would say to them, no, that's not true (*no es cierto*), that's where she is, but no, that can't be because we saw her, the Army showed her to us [the people would say], no, that's where the *compa* is, she is around, she is well [the compañeros replied], bring her here for us to see, to see whether it is true or not (*a ver si es cierto*), they [ordinary people] would say. Later, little by little, I started to appear (*después a poco a poco fui yo apareciendo*), Ah! Well, that's true, so who was it that the Army had with them?! They had a girl who looked like you, they would say, and so on, but in reality it wasn't so.

I say to Alma that from what she tells me, it is clear the people in the villages (*comunidades*) cared for (*querían*) her and the other *compas*.

Yes, they care for us (*nos querían*), Alma says. Many people got to know me. I had many acquaintances (*mucha gente conocida*) in those days.

I ask whether this means that one was not in total clandestinity (*a clandestino total*).

No, Alma replies, people knew us, we were not totally *en la montaña* as they said [as it was believed] (*nos conocían, nosotros no andábamos totalmente en la montaña como decían*), we were in there, in the community/village (*nosotros estábamos metidos en la misma comunidad*). . . . There are many, many stories . . . and for that problem that I had there [being injured by the explosion], I already had problems, and later I did not have the same physical endurance I had before (*la misma resistencia física como tenía antes*), the legs were bothering me a lot, I could not run anymore, I was facing considerable difficulties. That's how they later got me out (*así fue como después me sacaron*), I did not want to leave, I remember that, there on the border [the border between Guatemala and Mexico] I met up with Nestor and I told him, I do not want to leave, look Nestor. Yes, man!

> (*sí hombre*!), he said, but if you don't go/get out, you are going to be even more screwed up (*jodida*), I am going to recommend you to the *compañeros* there, learn some job, learn to drive, all that, he said to me, and if it is the case that you really don't like it and you can't get used to it (*si en caso totalmente no te parece, no te vas a hallar*), I am going to send for you, you come back again. With time, I got used to it. There is a great deal I like recounting (*hay una mayoría de cosas, me gusta contarlas*). Sometimes, when I get together with the guys, we start telling these stories, yes, that's the way it is.

I thank Alma for taking time out to speak to me, and I turn the recorder off. However, Alma begins to recount another story. The form or aesthetics of her narrative seems prosthetic, in that it is punctuated by gaps that lead to extensions and further attachments, and connect further images and experiences.

> Once, the news came that a group (*grupo*) [group of *guerrilla* combatants] that had gone in the direction of San Pedro Carchá failed in their mission/got hit (*fracasaron*), and a *compañero* arrived looking for us, saying that they had taken out (*sacado*) a wounded *compañero*, and the boss (*jefe*) said to us, who wants to go that way? So, there was a sergeant there who was the uncle of the guy (*muchacho*) who got wounded, I'll go, I said and he said to me, let's go, it was about ten in the evening, we had just got there, very tired (*bien cansados*), we have to go right now because the *compa* is wounded, so we left there and then, on foot. At about two o'clock in the morning we stopped walking, we rested for a while, and then we started walking again, we stopped again at about two in the afternoon, we were possibly (*quizás*) near the road, and in that place where we were the night fell, then at night we crossed the road and we started walking again in the night (*de noche, a caminar usted*)! At about one in the morning, that's when we stopped for a while, and from there again, up to where the *compa* was, he was in that Sierra Machamá, there in Alta Verapaz, that's where the *compa* had got himself into (*estaba metido el compa*), we went to get him, and we were going back, but when we were on our way back we meet up with the other group (*grupo*) that was around there and when we were about to cross the river, that river, what is the name of that river that is near Fray . . . what's its name? It's the same as the one here, the Pasión River, what do they call it, perhaps I will remember later on, for having crossed it so many times,

I can't even remember now! Anyway, in crossing this river, the river was extremely high (*lleno*), very high, who dared throw themselves to the other side (*quien se avienta al otro lado*)? It is very dangerous for one to throw themselves in a haste like that, because there may be (*a lo mejor*) the Army on the other side, they would stir one up (*se lo atizan a uno*)! Who are the best swimmers? Because I had learned to swim quite well, I tell them, well, I can jump in (*yo me aviento*), and that León was there, I'll jump in too he says, and that Angel says, me too, so good, the three of us. The first one to throw himself in was that León, that one was really good in the water (*ese sí era bueno para el agua*), he threw himself from there, and from there the other *compa* jumps in, and what? He had not even got halfway into the river when he started to shout that he was drowning! Ah! I started to be afraid (*a mi me empezó a darme miedo*), as when a river swells up, it penetrates up into the vegetation (*se mete así entre la palazón*), and there was indeed a big tree (*palo*) there, this size, and I went to climb/hang myself from (*aprenderse*) that tree always looking to the other *compa* and shouting to the others that they got him some help (*que le dieran ausilio*), and I started to climb up that tree, that tree had a hole/cavity like this, and I grabbed the hole to lift myself up, when I see that that's where there was a huge curled-up snake (*cuando veo yo, allí estaba una gran culebrona enrollada*) in there, I lost hold of the tree and fell [in untidy fashion] into the water (*yo me desprendí del palo y cahí amontonada en el agua*), and I say, how do I get out? And León says to me, as the river made a bend and the *compa* was shouting and he was disappearing [in the water] and every now and again he would appear, he [León] says to me, let's go to the bend, perhaps we will still manage to find him, and we said, imagine this [she says to me], there in the grazing field (*potrero*), we were running, and a man (*don*) heard the screams (*gritos*) and he went with his canoe (*cayuco*), and he dragged the *compa* out and he [the *compa*] pulled through (*salió*), but very frightened (*espantado*), horrible, there. Later on with the man's canoe, the man had no idea who they were (*quienes eran*) [who the people he had helped were], ah, they said to him, could you do us the favor of taking us to the other side, and the man (*don*) could not refuse (*y el don no podía decir que no*), out of obligation (*porque obligadamente*),[7] that's where it is, the canoe and the oar, everything, the boys (*muchachos*) went first, and from there we all got to the other side.

I ask Alma whether they had any equipment and she says yes. I then ask her whether they were carrying all the equipment with them when all this happened.

She replies that no, they had left it behind.

I say to Alma that she seems to remember many things.

Many things indeed. Once, but this was here in Petén, they sent us to get some uniforms, here, on the way to Belize, I went with a *compañero*, it was only two of us, we went, and on the shores of the river Mopán we set up camp (*acampamos*), early the next day we left again, the *compañero* got to the other side [of the river] and went to get a canoe, and we both jumped (*nos zampamos*) into the canoe with the rucksack and all, and the rucksacks were very heavy, we were carrying a load of uniforms (*puros uniformes traíbamos*), and the only thing I said, I am going to take off my boots, so there I was only with my equipment when, what the hell (*que púchica*), I see that the canoe capsizes halfway across the river (*a medio rio da vuelta el cayuco*), and we fall in the water (*y nos vamos al agua pues*), and I have no idea how (*yo ni se ni como*), but the only thing I did was grab hold of (*agarrar*), secure (*asegurar*) my rifle, but from there I don't remember (*pero de allí no recuerdo*), get this (*fíjese*) [she says to me], I put a shoulder string of the rucksack here, the other here in the middle, and I have no idea of how I managed to swim, but the reality is (*la verdad es*) that I did manage to get out, and the leather boots (*las botas de cuero*),[8] the two pairs of boots, they were gone, mine and the other *compañero*'s and we were so sad (*y nosotros tristes*)! What are we going to do now?! Well, we'll have to walk barefoot (*nos toca caminar descalzos*), there was that plant (*sarsa dormilona*), how it would scratch one's feet, very bad (*bien feo*). And I say to him, I am not going to be able to withstand walking like this (*yo no voy a aguantar a caminar así*), I am going to get myself into that house, and be it only a pair of old shoes that they may give me (*aún que sea un par de zapatos viejos que me den*), because I am not going to be able to bear it barefoot (*pero yo descalza no voy a aguantar*), so we got ourselves into a *manaquea*,[9] waiting for the late afternoon (*tardecita*), and from there I got near to the house and the group of youths (*la chamaquía*) who were there realized very quickly that I was barefoot, and what happened to you [they enquired]? And to your shoes?[10] I left them [the youths] over there, and from there I spoke to the man (*señor*) and he had a pair of boots, an inside-out pair of boots (*botas al revés*) [laughter], oh my god, an inside-out pair of boots (*a par de botas al revés*), but this is how in the end we managed to get hold of

> some shoes, and that's how we carried on walking, but well screwed up (*pero bien jodidos todos*), at times we had to take off the boots, we would carry them by hand and we would walk barefoot, and on like this . . . There are so many stories from *la montaña*, so many things happened, like these, and many more.

I focus on the aesthetics of Alma's narrative in part to highlight the form that her account and narrative took: every story she recounted conjured up the incompleteness of the account and the narrative movement toward, and a connection to, a further episode, an extension. Through the concept-metaphor of prosthetics, I also want to reflect on the aesthetics of the subject her accounts presupposed. Through Alma's account of her being-in-the-world, Alma gave a sense of the experiential and embodied character of her time *en la guerrilla*. She referred to numerous prosthetic attachments such as her hat, boots, rifle, and ammunition belt and those she found along the way such as the bag to carry the *nances* and the canoe to cross the river. As Alma lost attachments and acquired new ones, her agency was expanded and/or contained. Paraphrasing Strathern (1991, 115–6), gaps and intermittencies gave Alma somewhere to extend. Alma's storytelling also extends the work of ethnography and conjures up a space for ethnographic prosthetic aesthetics, as through this account, perception is extended and made into an augmented sensory field. This is a field of sensory augmentation and extended agency that allows ethnography to borrow images, for instance, those indeterminate images of the Army and the *compañeros/as* that even Alma confounded, the embodied experience of combat, and of guerrilla embodied subjectivity more broadly. This fabling and restaging of the world and of the subject was enabled by and sheltered in the disused dwelling offered by Alma, as much as it was activated through the ethnographer's prosthetic extension of the tape recorder. Seizing upon phenomenology as possibility (Heidegger [1962] 2002, 39), both the *guerrillera*'s and the ethnographer's prosthetics allowed for the articulation, repetition, circulation, and supplementation of guerrilla and description, a fabling that worked through the mutual borrowing of images.

Handing Over Arms and Tape Recorders: The Guerrilla and Ethnography Borrow Each Other's Image

During the course of my fieldwork many ex-*guerrilleros/as* expressed the pain and sense of loss they had experienced in the demobilization camp at Sacol, when the order was issued that they should hand over arms. If it had not been for the weapons, they argued, they would not be alive. Manuel explained:

> To surrender the weapons was the hardest thing (*lo más duro*), for us, to leave them, after so many years that one had carried it (*lo cargó*) [the rifle], one carried it, so, more than any other thing, one would defend oneself with it (*uno con eso se defendía*), if it hadn't been for this, one wouldn't be telling what we really lived/experienced (*lo que vivimos*) and suffered (*sufrimos*). The most arduous of stages (*la etapa más dura*) was when we said, here it is, for that was the hardest part (*lo más duro*).

Manuel handed over his rifle but kept his hammock and his tent (*carpa*). The tent, a rectangular piece of thick waterproof fabric, was spread across his patio when I visited him. It was being used to dry *frijol* (beans) in the sun. Macario also spoke eloquently about the time leading up to the Peace Accords and the eventual decommissioning of weapons. In his concluding remarks, he likened the tape recorder, that is, the prosthetic tool of anthropological labor, to arms, that is, the prosthetic tool of guerrilla labor. This was no simile that restricted its signification to the realm of representation. Rather, it was part of his attempt to evoke the phenomenology of loss and its embodiment at stake in decommissioning, and one in which I was to partake. Macario elaborated on guerrilla and anthropological prostheses thus:

> There were *compañeros* who were "*bases*," they may pass (*pasar*) as combatants now, but in reality they were not combatants, they were *base*, or *milicia*. They would look after the weapons, in the *buzones* (storage), in the ground (*bajo tierra*). They were the contact (*contacto*) with the Mexican border. Look, Silvia, when in 1988 I joined in earnest (*meterse de lleno*), already carrying a rifle (*ya de tomar un fusil*), the vision (*visón*) was to give grounds to profound social change (*profundo cambio social*), to establish a revolutionary government (*gobierno revolucionario*), a government with equity (*equidad*) for all. That was our idea, because we knew that was the only way (*forma*) to bring forth structural change, and that is why I got involved (*meterse*). I saw *compañeros* cry, I saw very sad *compañeras* due to the situation they had experienced (*vivir*). I was young (*joven*), I had not experienced it, but of course, I lived in poverty (*vivir en pobreza*), yes, but had not experienced all that they had experienced. On entering the *campamentos* [guerrilla camps], the situation there was very difficult

(*difícil*) *en la montaña*. They would give you a rifle but they would not give you a uniform (*uniforme*), one would have to see what to do about a uniform, one would get one's boots (*botas*) and would start to walk. But this [hardship and lack of resources] was not important, because what mattered was the spirit of the revolution (*espíritu de la revolución*), to foster change (*cambio*). That is why I joined, because I saw the injustice in which the people (*el pueblo*) lived. So my spirit (*espíritu*) was above all revolutionary (*revolucionario*), to make changes (*hacer cambios*) and so that no more innocent people (*gente inocente*) would die. The years went by, and from 1990 onwards, one began to talk of a possible peace settlement. For us that was very difficult, because we had the experience of the peace settlements in Nicaragua, and in El Salvador. And we would say, will it be the same? But in the end, that idea began to be introduced. What was most difficult was that in actual fact the *comandancia* took very radical decisions in the center, and the combatants and *las bases* were almost not taken into account in signing the Peace Accords (*la comandacia tomó decisiones muy radicales en el centro, a los combatientes, y a las bases casi no se les tomó en cuenta en la firma de la paz*). Nevertheless, the decision [to sign the Peace Accords] was from the bottom up (*de abajo para arriba*). I worked in the area of logistics, and I was a political organizer. We would receive information concerning the [negotiation] proceedings (*procedimiento*) and the contemporary situation. We would go and tell *las bases* and work with them. Of course, we would receive suggestions (*sugerencias*), but the suggestions were very few. We found that very painful (*dolernos*), signing the Peace Accords, that is, with all the problems in our country, and knowing that it was unlikely that politicians would deliver (*cumplir*). The first Accords were signed, and us, still as combatants of URNG [Unidad Revolucionaria Nacional Guatemalteca, Guatemalan National Revolutionary Unity], we would not believe it (*creer*), and we did not feel satisfied (*satisfechos*). The Accord on the Ceasefire was signed, and believe me, when the United Nations [Verification] Mission in Guatemala [MINUGUA] arrived, for us it was even more difficult. They arrived in the *campamentos* [guerrilla camps] and they would tell us that if twenty soldiers should approach, and there were thirty of us, we should not fire at them (*dispararle*), because we would be violating their rights (*violar sus derechos*). And if we captured a soldier, we had no reason to harm him (*hacerle daño*). And this [was said to us] when we knew that if they [the Army] should capture a *compañero* or ourselves, they would dismember us (*hacer pedazos*). It was very difficult, and we would say, is this really how things are (*si esto es así*)? In any case, we were clear (*estar claros*) about our vision (*visión*), and we had to accept that moment (*momento*), Silvia, the whole situation. And believe me, when the signing of the Peace Accords happened on 29 December 1996, instead of feeling satisfied (*sentirse satisfechos*) about that mission, we felt very sad (*sentirse muy triste*). For us that was not a reason to cheer (*gritos*), it was not a happy occasion (*alegrías*), as if to say, good, it has ended (*acabarse*), mission accomplished (*misión cumplida*). No. The tears rolled (*se nos rodaron las lágrimas*), we looked at our rifles (*miramos a nuestros fusiles*), we remembered the *compañeros* who had fallen (*nos acordamos de los compañeros que habían caido*). And believe me, it was difficult, remembering and saying, have we done well (*bien*), have we erred (*hacer mal*)? Well, if it is for the good of the country (*país*), that's fine, but if this turns against us (*si esto llega a dar un giro*), we will be those responsible for it (*culpables*), because believe me, many things can be done with a rifle in hand (*porque creeme con un fusil en la mano, se pueden hacer muchas cosas*).

I say to Macario that many *compañeros* have said that to me. They said that it was very difficult for them (*le costó muchísimo*) handing over the arms (*entregar las armas*), the very act of handing them over, of going to leave them. Some did not go to leave them, they gave their rifle to another *compañero/a*, so that they would leave it on their behalf because they could not face the act. Macario agrees.

What was extremely difficult was that one would remember (*recordar*) *compañeros*, those who had been *compañeros*. I will tell you something. One would remember the *compañeros* who died, and who always, when they were on the point of dying (*que ya para morirse*), would say to you, I am leaving (*yo me voy*), you go, and continue in the struggle (*sigue la lucha*). It is difficult to forget, wounded *compañeros*, hearing them cry (*oirlos llorar*) and say, well *compañeros*, you go and fight (*hagan ustedes la lucha*). That is not easy (*facil*) and we, those of us who had healthy arms (*brazos buenos*), healthy legs (*piernas buenas*), and yet tired of walking, because one would walk, we could carry on with the struggle. We had already gathered (*concentrarse*) in the *campamentos* [demobilization camps] to hand over our rifles (*entregar nuestros fusiles*), but as I was saying, that was something very difficult to believe (*creer*) and to accept (*aceptar*). In any case, there were some *compañeros* who were already very tired (*cansado*), which must be said. I was tired too, but I still had the spirit (*espíritu*). . . . At the same time, the tears (*las lágrimas*) [would roll], because at times one cries inside/internally (*llora uno internamente*), because one cannot hold back (*no puede resistirlo*), let the Peace be signed (*que se firme la paz*). But many *compañeros* would say to me, look *compa*, if the signing of the peace does not happen this year, or next year, I will leave, and indeed, many left. Six months to the signing of the peace, many *compañeros* left. They could not withstand it anymore (*aguantar*), war is not easy (*la guerra no es facil*). That is why when civilians (*gente civil*) at this moment, many have said to me, look *comandante*, because that is what they call me here, and I was never [a *comandante*], and I have told them that, if you need us and if you want to make war, we'll come with you, if this government [the Frente Republicano Guatemalteco/Guatemalan Republican Front government[11]] does not deliver (*cumplir*), let's make war (*hacer la guerra*), we will join. So I say to many of them, *compas*, I am very grateful, but you do not know in earnest what a war is, a war is not fought with conscience alone (*una guerra no se hace solo con conciencia*), in a war one needs strong political training (*formación política*), having a psychology with a view to achieving a clear objective and a clear sense of what you are undertaking (*tener una psicología pero por un objetivo claro de lo que tú estás haciendo*), and not just that they should give you a rifle and that they should teach you how to handle it (*manipularlo*) and how to shoot. Within, it is not a matter of destroying but rather of doing (*por dentro no va aquello de destruir sino de hacer*). . . . We were exhausting ourselves (*nos estabamos desgastando*), militarily and economically and in what were human resources (*material humano*). Every day people had more fear (*miedo*), day by day people wanted less struggle (*cada dia la gente tenía más miedo, cadad dia la gente quería pelear*) because they feared retaliation, given all that had happened and the campaign the Army had undertaken to destroy us. I think that was a political moment characterized by very clear thinking (*pensamiento claro*) on the part of the *comandancia* in this instance (*allí sí*), up to having to kick us out from *la montaña* (*hasta que nos sacaran a patadas de la montaña*), to come out with our heads high (*salir con la frente en alto*), there they [the *comandancia*] really deserve great praise, despite the pain in our heart (*aún que con el dolor en el corazón*), and everywhere (*y en todo*). But I think that it was better this way, than having to leave by fleeing

> (*era mejor así, que salir corriendo*), believe me, the tears flooded out of us (*se nos derramaron las lágrimas*) when it was announced that we were going to hand over our rifle, the rifle that had been our life companion (*nuestro fusil, que había sido compañero de la vida*). The point is that it was not easy to take off your gear (*quitarte tu arnés*), with all your equipment (*equipo*), take out your mosquito net (*pavillón*), your tent (*carpa*), place everything there, knowing that they were going to burn it (*quemar*), handing over your rifle to the point that they would count the ammunition (*balas*). It was very difficult, and one would say, might it be that as I hand over my rifle (*será que al entregar a mi fusil*), it is possible that they could come and kill me (*es posible que me vengan a matar*), a series of things would arise in one's mind (*le venían a la mente a uno*), and that is why many *compañeros*, what they have said to you is true (*es cierto*), one would give one's rifle to one of the new *compañeros* [more recent recruits], and would say to them, look, you go, because I cannot do it.

Macario talked of the pain and sense of loss inherent in the process of decommissioning. The order to hand over arms induced dismemberment, as the *guerrilleros/as* parted from their prosthetic extensions. Decommissioning procedures such as counting ammunition were experienced as a violation of the integrity of guerrilla embodiment. The process of dismemberment evoked by Macario did not apply just to the guerrilla: it was to fully engulf anthropology. The exchange between Macario and myself concluded thus:

> Silvia, you work with this tape recorder [Macario says to me], and I think you really love your tape recorder, and the day you will return to England, you will take it with you (*tú trabajas con esta grabadora, creo que la quieres mucho, y el dia que te vayas a Inglaterra te le la vas a llevar*).
>
> I reply that I have the tape recorder on loan from the university.
>
> Macario is very surprised and says, imagine that (*imagínate*)!
>
> I say, the tape recorder is not even mine.
>
> Macario says, that is too bad (*peor*). In any case, it is your work (*trabajo*), they gave it to you for that, like they gave me a rifle (*por eso te la dieron, como a mi me dieron el fusil*) and that is why you are very fond of it (*le tomas mucho cariño*), because the rifle I carried was not mine (*porque ese fusil que cargaba yo no era mio*), but handing it over,

> and in good condition (*buenas condiciones*), knowing that you were handing it over but you had grown fond of it. Like your spectacles, Silvia [he says to me], they are useful to you (*servir*) and it is not easy when someone tells you, look, I will give you a passport so that you may go (*a parte que por darte un pasaporte y que te vayas*), you give me your spectacles (*dame tus lentes*). When you know that those spectacles are being useful to you/you need them (*servir*), that they can be much more useful than that which they are offering to you, well, if you hand it over [the tape recorder, the spectacles, or the rifle] it is because you have no other option (*si lo vas a entegar es porque te encontrás obligada*), you have no other way out (*no tienes otra salida*). That is to give you an example of the situation we experienced/lived through (*eso es para ponerte un ejemplo, de la situación que vivímos*). With the *compañeros* we would say, *compas*, are we going to see each other again (*será compas que nos vamos a volver a ver*)? Will we (*será*)? *Compas*, what will become of us (*qué va a ser de nosotros*)?

Macario suggested that I think about the situation the *compañero/as* had experienced at demobilization by establishing a relation of equivalence between their rifles and my tape recorder. Macario had a rifle, I had a tape recorder. As I would want to take my tape recorder with me when I went back to England, they would have liked to keep their rifles, that is, the prostheses that had made guerrilla survival possible during the conflict. Endowed with the tools of our work, we had acquired prosthetic embodied subjectivity and grown fond of our respective prosthetic attachments. Macario was surprised to hear the tape recorder was not my own. This revelation perhaps unsettled the presupposition that *gringas* can own their own prostheses. With the knowledge that I had the tape recorder on loan, that is, that it belonged to others, Macario established a renewed sense of commonality between us. Both of us had to maintain our prostheses in good order, and this made parting from them the more painful. Handing over one's rifle would be as painful as leaving one's tape recorder behind. Macario emphasized the point by referring to another of my prostheses, and specifically, to my spectacles. He argued that they were useful to me to see the world and that anything that might be offered in exchange for them would not be satisfactory. Even a passport, the prosthesis of mobility across multiple borders, would not be acceptable, as one would only agree to such a transaction when given no other option. With no alternative, the guerrilla handed over their prostheses. Macario's powerful image did not just instate a relation of equivalence between his prosthetic embodiment and experience and mine. It also established the conditions of possibility for the guerrilla and anthropology to borrow each other's images in the phenomenology of the ethnographic encounter. The result was "a sense of excess [and] insufficiency, of lack of proportion and of connections being partial" (Strathern 1991, 115–6), as much as an extension of our perceptions.

Conclusion: The Aesthetics of Performative Knowledge Practices

The concept-metaphor of "prosthetics" conveys the complexities inherent in the aesthetics of social and cultural theory, and the practice and experience of ethnography. I have noted that during the course of my fieldwork I imagined the form of the accounts and narratives of ex-*guerrilleros/as* as prosthetically marked by the constant additions of more parts. Additions occurred through positive and negative relationalities of ex-guerrilla secrecy. Narrative parts took the form of unexpected revelatory additions, hastily added adjunctions and expressive tangible silences and retractions. Guerrilla narratives supplemented themselves and each other in secretive prosthetic articulations. I also began to think prosthetically about ethnographic subjects, in terms of both the prostheses that made our encounters possible and the aesthetics of the guerrilla subjects, revealed in the course of ethnographic exchanges. The ethnographic moment of realization of the complex naming practices relied upon by ex-combatants was underpinned by prosthetic aesthetics, in that subjects seemed to be contextually and temporally engaged in refashioning themselves anew, through the attachment of names, pseudonyms, and nicknames.[12] Thus they extended their agency, and gave form to guerrilla secrecy, while I learned to envision ethnographic prosthetic attachments, and to extend ethnography's capacities in the process. Further, guerrilla subjects, agency, and embodiments appeared in their prosthetic forms, as ex-combatants related their struggle, and their lives, performatively conjuring up all manners of attachments and connections. I have argued that prosthetics are implicated in the ethnographic encounter in complex ways, and that they also give a form to ethnography's aesthetics. In and through prosthetics, the *guerrilleros/as* and the ethnographer borrowed each other's images, to establish temporal and partial connections. Loosely paraphrasing Moore, and thus thinking prosthetically to an extent, prosthetics "is an aesthetic in the straightforward sense that it is a way of approaching the world, a perspective. Thus, it is simultaneously a *mode of knowledge* and an idiom, *a form* for the expression of knowledge" (Moore 1997b, 68–9; my emphasis). Prosthetics also give a form to post-plural knowledge practices, with constant deferrals, rearticulations, reinscription, and resignifications. Through the temporality of their form, the transience of their borrowings, "thrownness" (*Geworfenheit*) (Heidegger [1962] 2002), and historicity, prosthetics constitute a performative aesthetics. They give a form to ethnography's performativity.

Conclusion

In this book I set out to explore histories of violence and cultures of secrecy in Petén, northern Guatemala, in the aftermath of the 1996 Peace Accords signed by the Guatemalan government and guerrilla insurgents. Informed by ethnographic research among displaced constituencies with experiences of militancy in the guerrilla organization Fuerzas Armadas Rebeldes (FAR), I aimed to trace the contours of dispersed and intermittent guerrilla social relations; histories of governmentality in Petén, and their relation to state-sponsored violence, insurgency, and repression. I also dealt with the incitement and replication of ambivalence in social relations; the production of socialities and subjectivities marked by secrecy; guerrilla ethics and aesthetics of sociality established through generation and circulation of substance and multiple modes of relatedness; and phenomenologies of guerrilla prosthetic embodiment and subjectivity. In short, I set out to accomplish what Fardon (1990) deemed the ambitious and crisis-inducing program of writing ethnography.

Noting historical contextualizations of Guatemala provided through a range of interventions and perspectives, I pointed to instances of out-contextualization in the analytical and representational practices of social and cultural analysis. I argued that in the context(s) of Guatemala, social and cultural analysis, and its reliance on alignments of tropes of indigeneity, settlement, and place, produced normative and essentialist accounts of complex social realities and dynamics. They engendered habits of thought and approaches to the conceptualization of the research object that seemed to be ill-suited to an analysis of the subjects, processes, and dynamics that I encountered in the field and that are the focus of this work. In this review, I aimed to highlight processes through which ethnographic subjects out-contextualized the modes of accounting of social and cultural analysis during my fieldwork, at once exposing analytical presuppositions, bringing into stark relief the labor of fabrication that coincides with the ethnographic endeavor, and the ways in which social and cultural analysis may be consumed, reinterpreted, displaced—and indeed out-contextualized—by ethnographic subjects.

The emphasis on processes of out-contextualization seemed particularly relevant as I aimed to bring into view what I argued had been deemed "out of context" by multiple discourses—social scientific but also governmentally informed narratives—namely the region of Petén and related violent histories of displacement. Through the artifice of shifts in perspective and scale, I tried to reveal the (deferred) centrality of Petén to an understanding of histories of violence and conflict, experiences of insurgency and counterinsurgency, and related cultures of secrecy. With these devices, I furtively brought violence and conflict within the realm of perception, mimicking the partial, fragmentary, and secretive modes of disclosure and foreclosure that marked the revelation of experiences of the *conflicto armado* (armed conflict) during my fieldwork.

The partiality and splintering of the research object through movements between contextualization and out-contextualization are also powerfully felt in the way the Guatemalan conflict is framed in academic analysis and popular discourse. Such processes are most apparent when one reflects on the multiplication of names that are given to the Guatemalan conflict and the sheer variety of expressions used. These different ways of naming the conflict reference a plurality of understandings of what the violence that engulfed Guatemala actually was, the historical dynamics that led to it, and what the violence meant: *la lucha, La Violencia, el conflicto armado*, the variation *el conflicto armado interno*—with a differential emphasis on internal dynamics, rather than larger geopolitical process—war, *la guerra*, counterinsurgency war, genocidal war, *ch'a'oj, k'ayowal, época de la guerrilla, años de la represión, insurgencia*. The different names clearly also reflect different positions vis-à-vis the conflict and related politics of location, whether one is speaking in English or Spanish, from Guatemala, the United States, Europe, or elsewhere, from the position of communities that bore the brunt of state violence and repression, or from those whose lives were marked by a commitment to the revolutionary struggle. They refer to a range of processes of "reckoning," as Diane Nelson (2009) has poignantly argued. The book has approached the analysis under the sign of insurgency, to specifically connect histories of violence and conflict with the experiences of the combatants of FAR and directly reference their political figurations and investments. From all these perspectives, the plurality of names for the Guatemalan conflict articulate fundamentally performative dimensions that entail complex processes of restaging, reinscription, and resignification whose consequences for lived experience as well as for representation can never be fully anticipated but, rather, seem to always return one to a sense of excess, lack of proportion, and incommensurability. These in turn connect to a precarious openness—as a dimension of the deferred, the "not yet here," which, when framed in Derridean terms, points to the domain of justice. In some of my encounters in the field, this sense of possibility was powerfully ignited in conversations that seemed to provide a context in which to imagine and renew the prospects of revolutionary struggle, irrespective of the daily realities of disenfranchisement and marginalization, or the hostile and deteriorating political conditions. Far from an uncomplicated and stable appeal to futurity and revolution, the sense of excess and incommensurability at the heart of my ethnographic exchanges with the FAR combatants could just as easily be oriented toward the recognition of an impossibility to fundamentally grasp the nature of the events that were being recalled and performatively restaged in our dialogue.

In view of the complexity and plurality of ethnographic socialities, subjectivities, and their histories, and the recognition of a sense of excess and incommensurability at stake in lived experience and representation, in the book I resolved to confront analytical models and presuppositions. From the outset, I suggested that knowledge practices should be subjected to critical scrutiny. The task was critical and constructive in orientation and aimed to reimagine and rebuild, and to do so in ways that were deconstructive and performative. To some extent, my critical posture borrowed images from the guerrillas. The performative, Nietzschean analytical effort that I envisaged as the task of an ethnography of secrecy may seek to demolish the logocentrism and self-referentiality of Western metaphysics and its structure(s), as the guerrilla in Petén had sought to bring down a system of governance with its neo-imperial ties to rebuild sociality anew. In point of fact, FAR had not deferred the labor of reassembling the social realm to a post-revolutionary aftermath. Rather, the experience of the guerrilla had produced specific rearticulations of subjectivities and socialities during the insurgency. Guerrilla insurgent subjectivities were refashioned on a terrain marked by secrecy and traces lingered in the aftermath of the Peace Accords. The critical modes of social and cultural analysis thus intertwined in the realm of representation with guerrilla ethnographic modes through which subjectivities and socialities might be obliterated, suspended, refashioned, and reassembled anew. Histories of violence and conflict were shown to be deeply implicated in guerrilla secret socialities and subjectivities. In turn, the social and cultural field appeared as a site of ever-increasing secrecy-imbued plurality and partiality.

In the book, I have suggested that the experience of fieldwork made the interrelated questions of partiality, pluralization, and relativization appear critical to understanding *and* representing multiple and complex processes of contextualization and out-contextualization in Petén on my meandering routes through histories of violence and cultures of secrecy. Further, it was the ethnographic encounter and its partialities—in the form of retractions, refusals, foreclosures, disclosures, and revelations—that compelled me to confront the multiple, complex, and partial scales of guerrilla secrecy and to seek an adequate theoretical, hermeneutic, and representational frame through which shifts in perspectives might be apprehended *and* represented. This ethnography of secrecy is thus born out of the proliferation of partial perspectives of the ethnographic encounter. The ethnographic encounter is commonly construed as equivalent with the realm of the concrete, the practice of participant observation, the empirical vocation of anthropology, but, in fact, it is the most abstract and theoretical of "fields."

To understand and represent my encounters with the ex-guerrilla in Petén, I pointed to ethnographic moments of selective disclosure and foreclosure. I discussed guerrilla naming practices in the insurgency, and argued that these were critical to the articulation of partial guerrilla subjectivities and socialities. As I followed the proliferation of names and relationalities of guerrilla secrecy, I noted the ways in which subjectivities and socialities may be marked by the experiences of violence and conflict in complex ways. Violence, surveillance, and the control of secrets by state agents and neo-imperial powers instantiated ambivalence and indeterminacy in subjectivities and social relations. In turn, the revelation of complex practices of insurgent simulations, and counterinsurgent dissimulations, abated the coherence and distinctiveness of entities and the distinctions between them—as in the case of the categorical distinction between the Army and the guerrilla. In the scale of guerrilla secret socialities and relationalities, the guerrilla established merographic connections between and among entities, thus revealing entities to be similar and dissimilar, distant and adjunct. Furthermore, processes of augmentation and contraction were figured in accounts of the guerrilla whole as composed of three substances, namely "information," "supplies," and "combatants." Considering different perspectives on guerrilla substance, I noted distinct modes of expansion and diminishment, as well as differentiation and conjunction. Guerrilla sociality and relationality appeared to encompass multiple forms of relatedness and entailed multiple moral orders. The idiom of kinship permeated the guerrilla whole and produced orders of sameness and difference among combatants. In turn, guerrilla sociality developed distinctive modes of relations based on long-lasting principles of sameness, respect, equality, and *hermandad* (affinity/amity), enacted through practices such as commensality. While early attempts at regulating the scale of difference of gender and sexuality through the creation of institutions such as "marriages by arms" were short-lived, through modes of relatedness and moral orders, the guerrilla envisioned a long-lasting mirror image of the broader society. Guerrilla disassembling and reassembling of the social realm and the production of a guerrilla replica of society involved not just replication, but also reinvention. I have argued that partiality, complexity, and relativization, as they arose during my fieldwork, should be represented in post-plural scales, that is, in a mode of thought that focuses on connections and relations, thus forgoing appeals to discrete entities, unified subjects, and social wholes. Whether or not the scale of post-plurality may be said to underpin my account of guerrilla subjectivities and socialities—as they arose in the course and the contexts of my fieldwork—I have argued that they presuppose a form: that is, they are underpinned by prosthetic aesthetics. Out of the phenomenology of the ethnographic encounter, subjects revealed themselves in and through their prosthetic extensions. As we discussed the loss and acquisition of our prostheses, I, the ethnographer, and the guerrillas borrowed each other's images in and through our prosthetic extensions and prosthetic imaginings. Through the transience, tentativeness, and "thrownness" (Heidegger [1962] 2002) of these borrowings, we gave form to each other, and in this shift of partial perspectives, gave form to the scale of post-plurality.

Such shifts in partial perspectives precipitate reflections on knowledge practices and theoretical models, and reveal how to "centering" there may correspond specific "decentering," while contextualization and commensurability creation may be tied to forms of out-contextualization and incommensurability creation. Further, post-plurality is revealed to harbor destructuring and deconstructive possibilities, making the artifice of ethnographic accounting explicit, and inscribing its tentative and provisional character (Rapport 1997, 658) within a performative horizon. From the partial perspective of philosophy, performativity suggests a critique of models of subjectivity and sociality and the knowledge practices that sustain them. Deconstructive processes of resignification, rearticulation, and restaging at stake in such performative reinscription of the ethnographic enterprise entail welcoming—with anticipation, not fear—out-contextualizations of this partial, tentative, and provisional account.

Notes

Introduction

1. Peace negotiations were inaugurated by the "Procedures for the Establishment of a Firm and Lasting Peace" convened in Esquipulas, Guatemala, August 1987. A second phase of peace negotiations began in March 1990 and produced the "Basic Agreement on the Search for Peace by Political Means," known as the "Oslo Agreement." This was followed by the "Agreement on Procedures for the Search for Peace by Political Means," known as the "Mexico Agreement," and by the "Agreement on a General Agenda," both signed in April 1991. The "Framework Agreement on Democratization in the Search for Peace by Political Means," known as the "Querétaro Agreement," was signed in July 1991 and concluded the second phase of negotiations (Jonas 2000).

2. The Guatemalan Peace Accords encompass a framework, "Framework Agreement for the Resumption of the Negotiating Process between the Government of Guatemala and the *Unidad Revolucionaria Nacional Guatemalteca*," signed in Mexico, D.F., January 1994, and eleven Agreements: (i) "Comprehensive Agreement on Human Rights," signed in Mexico, D.F., March 1994; (ii) "Agreement on Resettlement of the Population Groups Uprooted by the Armed Conflict," signed in Oslo, Norway, June 1994; (iii) "Agreement on the Establishment of the Commission to Clarify Past Human Rights Violations and Acts of Violence That Have Caused the Guatemalan Population to Suffer," signed in Oslo, Norway, June 1994; (iv) "Agreement on Identity and Rights of Indigenous People," signed in Mexico, D.F., May 1996; (v) "Agreement on the Social and Economic Aspects and Agrarian Situation," signed in Mexico, D.F., May 1996; (vi) "Agreement on the Strengthening of Civilian Power and on the Role of the Armed Forces in a Democratic Society," signed in Mexico, D.F., September 1996; (vii) "Agreement on the Definitive Ceasefire," signed in Oslo, Norway, December 1996; (viii) "Agreement on Constitutional Reforms and the Electoral Regime," signed in Stockholm, Sweden, December 1996; (ix) "Agreement on the Basis for the Legal Integration of the *Unidad Revolucionaria Nacional Guatemalteca*," signed in Madrid, Spain, December

1996; (x) "Agreement on the Implementation, Compliance and Verification Timetable for the Peace Agreements," signed in Guatemala, December 1996; and (xi) "Agreement on a Firm and Lasting Peace," signed in Guatemala, December 1996 (Guatemalan Peace Accords 1996).

3. See Haraway 1989; 2003; Strathern 1988; 1999.

4. The use of vernacular in the book is inspired by, and pays homage to, the work of Ricardo Falla (1978; 1992).

5. See also Moore's discussion of a feminist anthropologist's "anthropological imagination" (Moore 1994, 129–50).

6. Taussig (1987, 121) notes, in the context of his analysis of the rubber boom in the early twentieth century in Colombia, that "[a]ll societies live by fictions taken as real. What distinguishes cultures of terror is that the epistemological, ontological and otherwise philosophical problem of representation—reality and illusion, certainty and doubt—becomes infinitely more than a 'merely' philosophical problem of epistemology, hermeneutics, and deconstruction. It becomes a high-powered medium of domination, and during the Putumayo rubber boom this medium of epistemic and ontological murk was most keenly figured and thrust into consciousness as the space of death."

7. According to Geertz, "[w]hat the ethnographer is in fact faced with . . . is a multiplicity of complex conceptual structures many of them superimposed upon or knotted into one another, which are at once strange, irregular, and inexplicit and which he must contrive somehow first to grasp and then to render" (Geertz 1973, 10). In sum, according to Geertzian thick description, the task involves "grasping" strange, irregular, and inexplicit conceptual structures, and "rendering" them adequately.

8. This point is also made by Valentine Daniel (1997). With reference to an interview with an Estate Tamil woman recounting the death of her father in war-torn Sri Lanka, Daniel (1997, 334) notes "the ambivalence of her charge to me, to tell and yet not to tell." However, Daniel's work is not concerned with exploring the connection between the charges to tell and not to tell, on the one hand, and secrecy, on the other hand.

9. The report did charge that genocide was perpetrated in four regions of Guatemala, namely the north of Huehuetenango, the Ixil and Joyabaj areas in Quiché, and Rabinal in Baja Verapaz. This declaration informed the genocide case against a number of defendants presented not in Guatemala, but rather before the Spanish Audencia Nacional, the National Court in Madrid endowed by Spanish law with transnational jurisdiction over such crimes (see Roht-Arriaza 2008) in 1999. The Spanish National Court accepted jurisdiction over the case in 2005 and later issued requests for extradition procedures and arrest warrants for Guatemalan military officials. These, however, were deemed unacceptable and were ultimately rejected by the Guatemalan Constitutional Court in 2007, a judgment that was corroborated by the Guatemalan Constitutional Court specifically by noting that Spain, as a country that had supported the work of the Commission for Historical

Clarification, was bound by the premise that any "official truth commission would have no judicial effects" (see Roht-Arriaza 2008, 80). In May 2013, the Guatemalan Constitutional Court overturned the verdict issued by a national court convicting army general Efraín Ríos Montt to eighty years in prison for genocide and crimes against humanity..

10. Guatemala is divided into twenty-two *departamentos* (administrative regions).

11. An extraordinary account of Turcios Lima's death was offered by "Tita," the woman who was traveling with Turcios Lima but who survived the crash (Montes 1968, 122–41). She noted that insurgents as well as Army officers attended the funeral.

12. *Campesinos* may be translated as "agricultural workers" but it refers more broadly to the rural population.

13. This was the result of more than an oversight. During the negotiations related to the relevant Peace Accord and in times of interim cease-fire, the guerrilla organization ORPA kidnapped a wealthy Guatemalan woman and asked for a conspicuous sum of money in return for her release (Jonas 2000, 52–3). The kidnapping greatly affected the URNG's bargaining power at the negotiating table, at the time when the Accord for and on behalf of their own combatants was at stake (Jonas 2000). Many FAR ex-combatants I spoke to in the course of my fieldwork thus deeply resented ORPA, and Gaspar Ilom in particular. In conversation with me, they argued that the lack of discipline and lax leadership of ORPA had been detrimental to them all and the cause of much hardship.

14. For a discussion of the context of the 1999 elections, notably the referendum of the same year, see Carey (2004) and Warren (2003).

15. This interview is discussed in Chapter 3.

16. The adjective "ladino" in Guatemala commonly refers to those who consider themselves to be of Spanish ancestry. The history of this category of ethnic difference is explored in Chapters 1 and 2. For a comprehensive account, see Grandin (2000) and Taracena Arriola (1999).

17. The Academia de Lenguas Mayas (Academy for the Study of Maya Languages) was founded by Maya writers and intellectuals with the aim to record, preserve, and foster Maya indigenous languages in Guatemala.

The Maya linguistic communities are Poqomchi', Achi', Q'eqchi', Ch'orti', Kaqchikel, Poqomam, Sipakapense, Tz'utujil, Mam, Ixil, Sakapulteka, Uspanteka, Awakateka, Chalchiteka, Akateka, Chuj, Jakalteka, Q'anjob'al, Tektiteka, K'iche', Itza', and Mopan (see www.almg.org.gt, last accessed in July 2012).

Chapter 1

1. Archaeological and anthropological research have particularly long histories in the country, but other disciplines such as, for example, history, sociology, and human geography have also made important contributions. In this chapter, I focus on knowledge practices that, while often germane to the discipline of an-

thropology, are nevertheless illustrative of social scientific knowledge practices more generally.

2. "Native knowledge was conventionally contextualised in terms of integrated local cultures, and anthropological knowledge was set against the background of western ethnocentrism and the Malinowskian-inspired vision of the 'detection of civilisation under savagery'" (Strathern 1987, 256; see also Dilley 1999, 3). Note, however, that Geertz (2000) has argued that the "discovery" of ethnocentrism is not rightfully anthropology's own.

3. See Grandin 2000; Wilson 1995.

4. Warren (1993, 25) notes that

> *la violencia* was a confrontation between military and guerrilla forces. From the military point of view, it was a battle against communism, against an armed and dangerous menace within. Guerrilla terror needed to be met with counterterror. The counterinsurgency war began with the successful routing of guerrilla forces in eastern Guatemala in the 1960s. In the late 1970s and early 1980s, during the regimes of General Lucas García (1978–1982) and General Ríos Montt (1982–1983), the situation intensified as guerrilla groups mounted attacks on military installations, took over towns, and threatened major landowners in the western highlands. . . . From the guerrilla's point of view, this was an armed struggle to challenge the legitimacy of the state and the exploitation of Guatemalan peasants by wealthy landowners and export-oriented commercial elites. They recruited combatants from the countryside and sought support from peasant populations. In their terms, this was a war of liberation to resolve brutally conflicting class interests in a country with the lowest physical quality of life index in Central America and the third lowest, after Haiti and Bolivia, in all of Latin America.

For a painstaking analysis of *La Violencia* from the perspective of the Guatemalan Army, see Schirmer (1998).

5. Smith and Adams (2011) note that ethnographies of Guatemala have tended to represent the events of 1954 through three key narratives, namely as a violent CIA-led chain of events; as a watershed moment understood as an interruption of the democratic reforms of the Árbenz and Arévalo decade and/or an inauguration of decades of military rule; as a more complex set of events described in terms that do not explicitly contradict the emphasis on the role of the CIA or the generalized sense of a dramatic historical break with deep and long-lasting repercussions. To highlight the implications of this argument, analyses of ethnographic narratives relating to the historical events of the 1954 coup reveal on the one hand the complexity of the ethnographic contexts and the significant implications of the events in question; on the other hand, they also offer an insight into the way in which certain narratives and framings have permeated and shaped ethnographic accounting of Guatemala for over fifty years. From the perspectives of my interlocutors in

the field, the Arévalo and Árbenz years were much less the focus of analysis and remembrance than the events of the 1960s. Some prominent individuals, such as Alfonso Bauer Paiz, were occasionally noted as examples of a direct connection between the progressive times of Árbenz and Arévalo and the guerrilla struggle that emerged in the early 1960s.

6. The notion of the "enemy within" rose to prominence in the context of the Doctrine of National Security devised by the United States government and implemented in Guatemala in the 1950s (CEH 1999, Chapter I, Items 120-36; Landau 1988).

7. Of the large body of relevant work, I would single out research carried out in Alta Verapaz (Grandin 2004; Wilson 1995), Quetzaltenango (Grandin 2000), Santiago Atitlán (Carlsen 1997), and Chimaltenango (Green 1999; 2002). Lovell (1992) and Taracena Arriola (2002) have cogently addressed these questions with reference to the western regions of the country, while research by Dary (2003), Dary, Elías, and Reyna (1998), and Pinto Soria (1993) are concerned with the eastern regions.

8. Ideologies of *mestizaje*, *blanqueamiento*, and *ladinización* in Guatemala are explored below. Different national histories of *mestizaje* and *blanqueamiento* in Latin America have also been cogently analyzed, see for instance Wade (1993; 1997, chapter 1) on Colombia and Kingman Garcés (2002) on Ecuador. Stepan (1991) focuses on nationalism and the eugenic movement in Argentina, Mexico, and Brazil. Radcliffe and Westwood (1993) consider the intersections between discourses of *mestizaje*, *blanqueamiento*, and gender in Latin American contexts.

9. Taracena Arriola (2002; see also 1999) highlights the fact that the creation of *castas* by the colonial administration engendered a considerable juridical problem for the colonial administration. The colonial project was predicated on the motto "Two Spains in America, a Republic of Spaniards and a Republic of *Indios*." It was therefore unclear what juridical space should apply to the new fashioned liminal categories of *ladino* and *pardo*.

10. *Diputación Provincial de Nicaragua y Costa Rica al Ministerio de Gobernacion de Ultramaar, sobre la dificultad de aplicar el sistema electoral constitucional en un medio dividido en 22 castas, 22 de noviembre de 1820*, cited in Taracena Arriola (2002, 4; my emphasis).

11. Practices associated with "passing" are discussed further in Chapter 4, and specifically with reference to the distinction between the guerrilla and the Army.

12. For Martínez Peláez, criollos are Guatemala-born people of Spanish descent. As cogently summed by Lovell and Lutz (2009, xxvi), "Severo [Martínez Peláez]'s basic thesis, for which he marshals a vast array of evidence, is that Guatemala remains a colonial society because conditions that arose centuries ago when imperial Spain held sway have endured. Neither Independence in 1821 nor liberal reform following 1871, Severo alleges, altered economic circumstances that assure prosperity for a few and deprivation for the majority."

13. For an excellent analysis of the complexity, fluidity, and relational character

of ladino identity and the historically shifting racialized hierarchies in Guatemala, see Hale 2006.

14. See also www.almg.org.gt, last accessed in July 2012.

15. Of relevance here are the publications of the Instituto Indigenista Nacional from 1946 to the late 1970s. See, for example, Instituto Indigenista Nacional (1948a; 1948b; 1969). The Instituto Indigenista Nacional issued a periodical, *Guatemala Indígena*, and a Bulletin. The Seminario de Integración Social Guatemalteca publications were also under the Instituto's remit (see, for example, Carmack 1979; Goubaud Carrera 1964; Méndez-Domínguez 1967; Wagley 1957).

16. Petén is one of the twenty-two departments (*departamentos*) in Guatemala.

By "substantive disappearance" I mean that texts may mark Q'eqchi' presence on maps while simultaneously excluding them from the analysis (see Schwartz 1990). Up to very recently, there has been no record of work on Petén that considered Q'eqchi' culture to be Petenero, or to pertain to the social and cultural life of the *departamento* in however abject a position, although Liza Grandia's (2006) research makes an important contribution toward redressing this.

17. The "*municipio* as social unit" is also amenable to further classification. In Tax's work (1937) the key distinctions are between closed-corporate and open communities.

18. For an account of the relatively untroubled careers of Sol Tax and Robert Redfield in the 1940s and 1950s, notably during McCarthyism, see Price (1998; 2004). The FBI held a file on Robert Redfield (Price 2004, 171), but both Redfield and Tax continued to work in the years of anticommunist witch-hunts. Work at the Instituto Indigenista Nacional also continued during successive administrations and into the years of *La Violencia* (see note 4).

19. Anthropologists were literally engulfed in the histories of *La Violencia* in Guatemala. Guatemalan anthropologist Myrna Mack was killed in 1991. Victor Montejo was a schoolteacher who was forced to flee the country in the 1970s. In the United States he trained as an anthropologist and has written extensively about his experience of the violence (Montejo 1987; 1991; 1999).

20. Ricardo Falla (Manz 1995) argues that social scientists should not be only superficially committed or sympathetic to their respondents. Rather, Falla's six-year-long fieldwork with the Communities of Population in Resistance Ixcán (CPR Ixcán), that is, a civilian population escaping army repression and hiding in the Ixcán forest, is an example of how it is possible to address directly the needs of the community and involve one's respondents in the research process.

21. For literature on returnees, see Rousseau et al. (2001) and van der Vaeren (2000), while González (2000) and Stepputat (1999) follow movements from local perspectives. Stølen (2007) provides an admirable account of experiences of the conflict, exile, and return from the perspective of Petén and Ixcán. Other works explicitly concerned with tracking transnational movements and dimensions include Foxen (2006), Nolin (2006), Rodman Ruiz (2006), and Taylor et al. (2006).

22. For example, it is interesting to note that *Forest Society* was, until recently, hardly ever cited by anthropologists working in Guatemala, although it constitutes a key reference for geographers (Carr 2001; Sundberg 1997; 1998; 2003; 2004) and NGO staff working in Petén.

23. A notable exception is the work of Charles D. Thompson (2001) on the Jacaltecos and their relation to borders that "bleed."

24. On the politics of indigenous movements see Warren 1995; 1996; 1998.

25. Social scientists and researchers are fully historical subjects and, as such, they are participants and observers to the fullest of extents (Price 2000; 2004). This history has just begun to be unraveled, and for Petén, it is yet to be written.

26. For an interesting discussion of the multiplicity of genres of ethnographic writing on Guatemala, see Smith and Offit (2010).

27. "If different knowledge practices produce different forms of incommensurability, then their foundational or transcendent concepts (their instruments) will also have different work to do" (Strathern 1995b, 11).

Chapter 2

1. Juxtaposition is a textual strategy that is not deployed here with the intent of providing a solution to the problem of context. As I explained in Chapter 1, the problem of context has preeminently epistemological dimensions that cannot be settled by simply adjusting representational conventions. The latter can, however, be deployed to highlight epistemological questions and it is to this end that I rely on juxtaposition here.

2. Accounts are drawn from memoirs that FYDEP personnel have produced (see Samayoa Rivera n.d.) as well as from interviews and conversations with ex-FYDEP employees I conducted in the field.

3. A comprehensive history of archaeological campaigns in Petén is yet to be written. The most well-known institutional presence in the *departamento* was the fifteen-year-long archaeological investigation (1956–1970) undertaken by the University of Pennsylvania Museum at the ancient Maya site of Tikal. Important research was also carried out by the Mesoamerican archaeology teams at Tulane University and Vanderbilt University. For an account of the work of Arthur Demarest, see Demarest (2004).

4. The view of Petén as a remote and inaccessible region is found in accounts of FYDEP employees (Samayoa Rivera n.d.) and Guatemalan historians (Soza 1970). These representations are mirrored in Norman Schwartz's social history of the region (Schwartz 1990). I visited Petén for the first time in 1978. Access by land from Guatemala City was an arduous journey that took longer than twenty-four hours. Fokker planes would also transport goods, people, and information from Guatemala City to the airstrip on the shores of the lake Petén Itzá, central Petén.

5. Schwartz (1990, 32) notes that the Itzá were "a Mayanized people of non-

Maya origin who had migrated to settle in Yucatán. Between 1200 and 1450 Itzá groups moved south from Yucatán to Petén, where they dominated previously established people." I retain the orthography deployed by Schwartz (1990) in this section. Thus, when referring to Schwartz (1990), I use the spelling "Itzá."

6. During the course of my fieldwork, the resistance of Tayasal was discussed by many Peteneros living on the shore of the lake Petén Itzá. While the processes of constitution of remembrance of the past are plural and complex, the fact that the Peteneros in question resided on the very site where Tayasal is said to have been located may be important. After a heavy rainfall, children perused the soil searching for fragments of pottery and obsidian and commented on Tayasal periodically resurfacing.

7. It should be noted that the Spanish conquest of Yucatán was undertaken between 1527 and 1546 and control of much of Guatemala and Verapaz had been achieved by 1527 (Schwartz 1990, 33; see also Jones 1998). Although uprisings were frequent, the fierce resistance put up by the Itzá of Tayasal is noted with pride by the present-day inhabitants of the towns and villages on the shore of the lake Petén Itzá.

8. This is consistent with many historical accounts of the movement of Mexicanized Maya moving into Petén in the postclassic period and to the highlands (see, for example, Carmack 1981; Fox 1987; Hill and Monaghan 1987).

9. The repression against chicle workers did not end in the period following the overthrow of Jacobo Árbenz in 1954. In 1980 Peckenham noted that "SUCHILMA, the chicle workers' and woodcutters' union, has made significant progress in the past year, enough to threaten the bosses' power base. In April 1979 SUCHILMA's leader, Alfonso Torres Castro was violently seized from his house in San Benito by the police. His wife and children were beaten in the process. His arrest had been ordered by Waldemar Amador, a local resident with a reputation for exploiting chicle workers" (Peckenham 1980, 176).

10. For studies of governmentality in other regions of Guatemala see, for example, McCreery (1990), Sieder (2000), Stepputat (2001), and Watanabe (1995b). These authors deal with different historical periods and geographical locations and may not explicitly frame their respective analyses in terms of a study of "governmentality." Nevertheless, I take their contributions to inform a focus on local histories of governmentality in Guatemala.

11. In 1980 Fiedler (1980, 120–1) noted that "Petén colonization is not a new concept; thirty years ago, for example, the Árbenz government implemented a program. But even if we restrict ourselves to looking only at the legacy of the current effort, the starting date is 1964." Colonization of Petén in the twentieth century therefore did not begin with FYDEP, but rather with the progressive administrations of Arévalo and Árbenz, when it was linked primarily to nationalist political strategies, and only tangentially to substantive land reforms. The mid-1960s are discussed in the next section.

12. Clark (2000, 423) defines FYDEP as "a military sub-unit that governed Pe-

tén from 1959 to 1989," but does not elaborate as to the reasons for and modalities of the relation between FYDEP and the military.

13. For an example of studies of governmentality in Latin America, see Poblete (2001).

14. In the section below, I note the ambivalent status of *Promotores* through the account of a FYDEP employee.

15. Schwartz (1987) considers the role of FYDEP in the process of colonization of Petén and notes Handy's suggestions that FYDEP may have fostered a "latifundia style development" (Handy 1984, 216–7) in the region. With reference to the role of the military in the process, Schwartz notes that

> military officers have benefited from FYDEP's programs. Many officers, coming from upwardly mobile middle, rather than traditional elite, sectors, wish to acquire land, but opportunities to do so in the highlands have been preempted by established nonmilitary elites . . . The Petén and the Northern Transversal, where traditional oligarchies have not established complete preeminence, are well suited to officers' ambitions; land is available and inexpensive . . . Given the increasing "regnancy" of the military (Adams 1970) from the late 1960s to 1985, there was little chance than an agency that helped officers realize their goals would be easily dismantled (Schwartz 1987, 176).

Schwartz (1987, 176) concludes that "[m]ilitary interests need not prohibit reform *within* FYDEP, as opposed to radical change" and lists a number of regional factors that are reasons for the complex intersection of FYDEP interests and the Army's. With regard to this, I wish to highlight that Schwartz's account is given from the perspective of the military. In its appeasement and defense of upwardly mobile military/FYDEP personnel vis-à-vis the influence of established elites, Schwartz's analysis reveals its partiality and situatedness.

16. The title of this section is inspired by the account of the colonization of Petén offered by Romeo O. Samayoa Rivera in his memoir *Colonización de El Petén: Paralelo 17.* His recollections of his time in office with FYDEP are gathered in a book that I found on the shelves of a bookstore in La Antigua, Guatemala. No details regarding the publisher or date of publication are indicated, thus suggesting that Samayoa Rivera may have financed and overseen the publication and distribution of his work.

17. See the quotation from Samayoa Rivera immediately above, as an example.

18. It is unclear from Samayoa's prose what exactly may be at stake in the processes through which villages are made to appear and disappear through the art of magic. Whether this is a flight of fancy, foreboding of violence to come, or a meditation over the violent character of colonization is an open hermeneutic question.

19. I singled out the formation of Colpetén under direct instruction of the government and practical overseeing of FYDEP because in the early 1980s, Col-

petén was one of the villages that produced a substantial number of members of the Fuerzas Armadas Rebeldes. As my interlocutors in the field explained, most of the FAR combatants who originally settled in Colpetén were brutally killed.

20. For a history of Protestantism in Guatemala, see Garrard Burnett (1998) and essays in Garrard Burnett and Stoll (1993). Following a review of ethnographies of Guatemala, Smith and Adams (2011, 4–5) have pointed out that the Arévalo administration sought to maintain the clear distinction between church and state previously introduced by Ubico in the Constitution of 1944. This played out differently in different areas of the country, but the anticlerical climate intensified during the Árbenz administration. This included the curtailment of access to the country for US missionaries. Following the coup and during the Castillo Armas years, this stance softened and Catholics were treated as allies by the regime and missionaries returned to the country (Smith and Adams 2011, 5).

21. In Petén, many rural communities and urban neighborhoods have a *salón social*, that is, a space dedicated to community meetings and community activities. A *salón social* usually consists of a thatched building with four posts.

22. *Zapote* is the fruit of a tree of the Sapotaceae family.

23. Liberation Theology developed in Latin America via a fusion of Marxism and readings of theological texts from "below," that is, from the perspective of the poor. Gutierrez, author of *A Theology of Liberation* ([1971] 1988), argued that theology should be reinterpreted in local contexts and praxis, and in the struggles for social change and social justice.

24. For in-depth analysis of the movements of the populations living in the cooperatives on the Usumacinta River in the early 1980s, see excellent accounts provided by Stølen (2007) and Van der Vaeren (2000).

25. *Asaltos* entail stopping vehicles and stealing travelers' belongings under the threat of weapons. During the conflict, *asaltantes* were said to be FAR *guerrilleros/as* gathering funds for the struggle, an accusation always robustly rejected by ex-*guerrilleros/as* themselves. Following the Peace Accords, *asaltos* in Petén have not decreased. Routes to the archaeological sites are prime targets, but the roads to El Naranjo and Guatemala City are not immune. While I was in Petén, *asaltantes* stopped two buses on their way back from Tikal, kidnapped two foreign tourists, and killed a Guatemalan tourist guide. *Asaltos* and kidnappings on these routes are commonplace (*Prensa Libre*, 5 January 2005; *Prensa Libre*, 9 August 2006). *Asaltos* and violent activities of *maras* (youth gangs) are possibly two of the most feared types of crime in post–Peace Accords Petén (for a discussion of contemporary perceptions of violence, see Smith and Offit 2010).

26. The new disputed internal borders in question are those of the Maya Biosphere. The relation between the creation of this Natural Reserve in 1990 and the agency of empire, in the incarnation of USAID (United States Agency for International Development), is explored later in this chapter.

27. *Lavado*, literally "washing, laundry," refers to the laundry hand-washed by women in exchange for a small payment. Regarding "widows" and narratives of

displacement, see Zur (1998) and Green (1999) for ethnographically rich and interesting accounts.

28. *Aguadas* are naturally occurring water basins of varying dimensions, scattered across the Petenero landscape.

29. *Q'eqchi' revuelto*: literally, "scrambled Q'eqchi'."

30. *Mayejak* refers generally to religious offerings and celebrations.

31. *Gringa* implies foreignness in Guatemala. I explore the complex relationalities at stake in the term *gringa* in Chapter 3.

32. For a discussion of contemporary practices relating to Pan-Maya inspired spirituality, see, for example, Little (2009).

33. As one of the ex-combatants pointed out, the head of CONAP in 2000 was a *capitán*, an Army captain. The local institutions of Petén were in the process of being remilitarized. As the combatant argued, "el ejército no se desmovilizó, hicieron la pantomima, pero el ejército no se desmovilizó [the Army did not demobilize, they did the pantomime, but the Army did not demobilize]."

34. Grandia (2000) argues that the population of Petén has grown exponentially in recent years and may have surpassed the half million mark.

35. The law that regulated the activities of Fondo de Tierra had just been published and circulated in 2000 and was still provisional. In 2001 a full "*reglamento*" was expected, to make the operations of the Fondo de Tierra work in practice. As it happens, this community was finally granted access to some land and relocated to a *finca*. The new settlement had no transport links of any sort, and people had to proceed on foot to reach the community, or any neighboring settlement. In May 2004, I was told that land had been granted to the community in conjunction with a project to grow plantain. Despite the generally insalubrious conditions of the site, the quality of the soil was extremely good, and the plantain crop had yielded an extremely satisfactory harvest. However, given the location of the settlement, it had been impossible to trade the crop.

Chapter 3

1. This agreement was later superseded by a certain "randomness" brought on by the protractedness and mutuality of exchanges. Randomness may be an effect of ex-guerrilla secretive post-plural scales and modes of relationality; see below in the text.

2. I read Nelson's book assiduously during the course of my fieldwork.

3. The substantive analytical question here relates to the place granted to positionality in social and cultural analysis. For example, for Nelson, positionality of a specific relational kind is central and it is related to the practice of "fluidarity" (Nelson 1999, 48). Concerning "fluidarity," Nelson writes that

> all identity is formed through articulation, a notion that problematizes traditions of solidarity that lean on "solid" identities and clear-cut divisions

> between victim and victimizer. Taking the articulatory notion of identity seriously, along with the relationality of gringa identity, I develop the concept of *fluidarity* as a practice of necessarily partial knowledge—in both the sense of taking the side of, and of being incomplete, vulnerable and never completely fixed . . . This neologism plays with the idea of *solid*arity in an attempt to keep its vitally important transnational relations open and at the same time question its tendency toward rigidity, its reliance on solid, unchanging identifications, and its often unconscious hierarchizing (Nelson 1999, 43–4).

An analytical focus on secrecy in post–Peace Accords Guatemala reorients the notion of "fluidarity" (see Nelson 2009). One way to figure the specific relationalities and related partialities of guerrilla secrecy in post–Peace Accords Guatemala is through Strathernian theoretical idioms.

4. I had very short hair at the time. In Mexico, La Pelona is an ironic and irreverent nickname for La Muerte, or Death. Others are *huesuda, pelada, la flaca, dientona*.

5. Sundberg (2004) makes similar observations with regard to issues of positionality and location in the context of her research on the cultural politics of nature and conservation in Petén.

6. Pedrito and Mosquito, ex-combatants whose articulations of secret relationalities with me I discuss below, may be taken as examples of over-agentic subjects. Prosthetic agency is discussed in Chapter 6, although echoes of prosthetic agentic subjectivities can already be discerned in the discussion of practices of naming that follows.

7. Here I use the term *scale* in reference to its epistemological dimension (Strathern 1991; 1999), that is, I understand scales to refer to different "orders of knowledge." Corsín Jiménez exemplifies this point clearly when he states that scales as *orders of knowledge* refer to instances "where particular orders of relations (of economy, or religion, or kinship, etc.) are mobilized and measured up against other scales, e.g. what image of 'the family' is conjured up when thinking about 'the miner' as the emblem of 'modernity'" (Corsín Jiménez 2005, 158). This meaning of scale and scale switching is closer to Wittgenstein's notion of "family resemblances" in *Philosophical Investigations* (Rapport, personal communication, 2004) than to disciplinary specific understandings of scale, as, for example, a spatial category in human geography.

8. The expression "low-intensity conflict" refers to a military strategy widely deployed in Guatemala and geared toward the preemptive elimination of dissent. Schirmer has documented how the Guatemalan Army General Gramajo, for instance, viewed "low-intensity" conflict and the exertion of minimum rather than maximum force to be the product of carefully crafted interventions that might curb conflict before its escalation (Schirmer 1998, 244). In practice this translated into sweeping terror campaigns, "[b]ut 'more sophisticated' . . . not just killing and massacre" (Schirmer 1998, 244).

9. Plurality of connections to the insurgency and different forms of militancy characterized association to the guerrilla. Many never erased the connection to their first and second names and surnames. A case in point is given in my discussion of guerrilla secret relationalities and other relationalities; see below.

10. Details of the administrative independence of the region of Petén are discussed in Chapter 2.

11. Pseudonyms are partly also prosthetic extensions of subjectivity that allow subjects to negotiate conflict situations (see Chapter 6).

12. *Apodos* deserve further analytical attention. I am, however, subordinating the detail and holographics of each part (each *apodo*) in order to make a point about the whole and hoping to demonstrate that the whole is an effect of scale, and that through scale switching the whole is shown not to be whole or complete.

13. "La Blanca" means "of light complexion," "fair haired."

14. *Tapiscar* is the activity of harvesting maize, beans, and other crops.

15. *Carros juleteros* are pickup trucks or other vehicles that provide a service similar to the bus, that is, they transport people for a relatively small fee.

16. In Spanish the subject of the sentence is the Army.

17. Romualdo possibly means "in ruins" here.

18. *Hombre punta*, literally "tip man."

19. "*Hechando verga*" in this context means the shooting went on.

20. "They just make one up" may be taken to mean "they make someone up," not just "they make someone's name up."

21. This is the first question I ask Mosquito since he decided to speak to me about his secret.

22. *Cobanera* means from the town of Cobán. The term is also used as a synonym for Q'eqchi' by non-Q'eqchi' persons in Petén. This usage has a derogatory inflection.

23. "Moscú" means Moscow. I was told that the inspiration for Moscú's name came from listening to Radio Moscow while *en la montaña*, in hiding in the jungle of northwestern Petén.

24. In Chapter 1, I discussed how specific ways of imagining relations between notions of "indigeneity" and "place" have produced nativist and essentialist accounts of ethnic identity in Guatemala. Nativism is part of a broader representational register that reduces indigenous identity to essentialist tropes—including narrow understandings of "origin"—and therefore obstructs understandings of indigenous subjects as coeval. To unsettle nativist representations in no way hinders indigenous struggles, including political projects and claims that rest on notions of indigenous sovereignty, as these need not be articulated on essentialist identitarian grounds, but on historical and political analyses of processes of uprooting, plunder, and dispossession. Thus, a critical perspective on nativism contributes to these struggles by expanding the analytical registers and representational frames through which indigeneity may be understood and the political project associated with them.

25. This section is inspired by the work of Michael Taussig (1999). The present analysis differs from Taussig's in two substantial ways. First, it does not replicate Taussig's emphasis on the visual apparent in his definition of secrecy as entailing masking and unmasking. Second, and perhaps more importantly, in his discussion of secrecy and initiation rituals, Taussig maintains that behind elaborate practices of secrecy, there is no actual secret. Conversely, in Guatemala, *guerrilleros/as* were not masked as Zapatista Subcomandante Marcos may have been, but what was kept secret in most cases did matter, both in terms of the relationalities that the secret engendered and the partialities it created. There were, and there still are, secrets. Relationalities of secrecy and the secrets on which they rest are not formalistic and, rather, are substantial. Substantive guerrilla secrecy nevertheless had a *form*. Aesthetic dimensions of guerrilla secrecy are examined in Chapter 6.

26. Partiality creates ambivalence, analyzed in relation to the repressive state; see Chapter 4.

27. I owe this insight to Sarah Pinto.

28. Fractal geometry is the scale of post-plurality.

Chapter 4

1. *Oriente* refers to the eastern region of Guatemala, namely to the *departamentos* of Zacapa and Chiquimula. The *Costa Sur* is the southern coast, on the Pacific Ocean.

2. See Note 12 in the Introduction for the meaning of *campesino.*

3. As discussed in Chapters 1 and 2, the indigenous population in Cobán, Alta Verapaz, is Q'eqchi'.

4. "*Indita*" literally means "young indigenous girl." The diminutive form of *indio* is usually derogatory in that it implies a demeaning and/or paternalistic attitude toward indigenous people.

5. Army counterinsurgency activities deliberately deployed imagery related to the devil. For instance, the military elite group Kaibiles stationed in Petén between 1974 and 1989 trained in a military compound called *El Infierno*, or Hell, in the vicinity of Melchor de Mencos (CEH 1999, Volume II, Chapter 2, 56). The term "Kaibil" derives from K'abowiil (God K), the pre-Columbian Maya deity associated with souls and lightening (see Freidel et al. 1993, 46).

6. Archaeologists would argue (Golden and Borgstede 2004) that no direct relation exists between the ancient Maya culture of the archaeological site of Tikal in Petén and contemporary Q'eqchi' culture in Alta Verapaz or elsewhere. This, of course, does not preclude Luis imagining a relation between the two.

7. The Federal Bureau of Investigation (FBI) is the agency of the United States Department of Justice and principal federal investigative agency. Its functions include the investigation of espionage, sabotage, organized crime, drug trafficking, and terrorism (see www.fbi.gov).

8. *Comisionados* refers to *comisionados militares*, that is, civilian populations enlisted to guard against guerrilla activities and keep fellow villagers under sur-

veillance as part of the process of militarization of the countryside (CEH 1999; see also Schirmer 1998).

9. See the account provided by a FAR *comandante*, Chapter 5.

10. *La milicia*, that is, civilian supporters.

11. *Parcela* is a plot of cultivated land.

12. *Ándale* is a colloquial expression that indicates assent.

13. For important discussions of the significance of Janus-faced figures in Guatemala, notably with regard to representations of indigeneity, see Fischer 2004; Nelson 1999; 2009, chapter 5.

14. *Botas de hule* were distinctive of guerrilla attire.

15. Nebaj, in the *departamento* of Quiché, is one of the three *municipios* of the Ixil region (Stoll 1993). The area was the site of the most virulent counterinsurgency campaigns of the conflict. The guerrilla group operating there was the Ejército Guerrillero de los Pobres (Guerrilla Army of the Poor; EGP).

16. Tojil was one of the principal deities of the K'iche' and Kaqchikel nations at the beginning of the sixteenth century (Carmack 1981). It appears in the Kaqchikel Chronicles (Maxwell and Hill 2006) and the Popol Wuj. Like K'abowiil, Tojil was coopted by the Guatemalan Army and deployed as a name of Army units.

17. *Oriente* refers to the eastern regions of the country.

18. *Cabal* is an expression meaning "precisely."

19. An example of Carlos' subtle sense of the absurd unraveled as we discussed *formación militar*, that is, the military training he had received *en la montaña*. During our conversation, I asked the most audacious of questions: "did you ever know where the arms you were given in 1981 came from?" Carlos politely said, "never, never, these were very delicate matters, you understand, so we would endeavor not to even ask where they were from." I suddenly became very conscious of the blunder, and added that the reason for the question was to ascertain who supported and indeed who did not support FAR. Although this was not in any way redeeming, Carlos ever more graciously replied that, of course, he understood what I meant, but reiterated that as far as he was concerned, he never dared inquire about the source of the arms he handled. I was mortified, but not sufficiently so, and to avert disgrace, I resorted to referring to something another ex-combatant had said. I pointed out that I had been told the very first arms of FAR, the very first that were handled, came from Vietnam. When I said this, I used a peculiar expression. I referred to the weapons in the diminutive and endearing form, *las primeritas que se manejaron*, as if arms were tender, precious beings. Here I was literally repeating what I had been told on a different occasion by an ex-combatant who had envisaged the first inflow of arms to come from Vietnam. Carlos chuckled at my remark and with sarcastic composure said, "*sí pues, sin duda alguna pues*! [yes, of course, no doubt about it!]." I learned eventually that if he never asked, I should not ask either.

20. This guerrilla, El Moreno Méndez, Rodolfo Sanchéz, is identified by nickname, pseudonym, name, and surname.

21. "Manolo" is another pseudonym of Rodolfo Sanchéz.

22. This reflects the composition of the Guatemalan Army during times of routine forced conscription.

Chapter 5

1. Comandante Manolo is referring to the FYDEP-related legislation of the mid-1960s discussed in Chapter 2 that prohibited logging north of *paralelo 17.*

2. "Fulano" means "so and so."

3. One *libra* is 0.454 kilos.

4. *Masa* is maize cooked in water with a pinch of slaked lime (calcium hydroxide), and then ground.

5. *Tamal* is a prized food in Petén. It is made out of maize, and contains meat, *achiote* (Bixaceae; *Bixa orellana*), and/or beans. The *tamal* is wrapped in banana leaves and boiled or steamed. "*Tamales peludos*" is an ironic and euphemistic expression that places emphasis on the meager quality of the *tamales guerrilleros.*

6. *Cabrón* in this context may be translated as "fool."

7. Discussion of marriage practices in insurgent movements is commonly related to broader analyses of gender relations. Bhebhe and Ranger (1991) and Kriger (1992) deal with gendered experiences of soldiers in Zimbabwe's liberation war. Barnes (1999) addresses gender dynamics and the articulation of oppositional responses in colonial Zimbabwe in the early to mid-twentieth century, while Kesby (1996) addresses gender relations in the context of experiences of insurgency and counterinsurgency in Zimbabwe between 1972 and 1980. Urdang (1979) documents the experiences of women in the PAIGC ranks (African Party for the Independence of Guinea-Bissau and Cape Verde) and in liberated villages in Guinea-Bissau. West (2000) addresses women's experiences in FRELIMO (Liberation Front of Mozambique) and interdictions concerning sexual relations with men in Mozambique. Kampwirth (2002) discusses women's experiences and marriage practices in revolutionary movements in Nicaragua, El Salvador, and Chiapas, complementing earlier analyses such as Randall's (1981) work with *Sandinista* women. This literature draws attention to both the articulation of gender relations in the context of the development of guerrilla movements and the management of gender relations during times of conflict. The marriage practices and related moral orders articulated at different points in the respective histories of struggle discussed in this literature are as heterogeneous as the different contexts of struggle. In Guatemala's case, the accounts by Colom (1998), Harbury (1995), Comandate Lola, Marta Estela Maldonado (González 2000; Kampwirth 2002, 196–7), Solórzano (1986), and Grandin (2004, Chapter 5) are concerned with women's experiences in the Ejército Guerrillero de los Pobres (Guerrilla Army of the Poor; EGP), not FAR.

8. *La pedida*, literally meaning "the request," is the formal request made by a groom, or the groom's parents, to marry a woman. The request is put to the woman's parents during a formal visit made by the groom or his parents to the woman's family home.

9. In Petén, "to converse" implies intimacy.

10. Here again, "speaking" or "conversing" implies intimacy.

11. *Compañerita* is the diminutive form of *compañera* and may be taken to imply either youth or simple-mindedness.

12. *Aldeas de resistencia* refers to the Comunidades de Población en Resistencia (CPR), literally, Communities of Population in Resistance. There were four different bodies of CPR in Guatemala: *CPR Costa*, located on the Pacific Coast and associated with ORPA (Organización del Pueblo en Armas, Organization of People in Arms); *CPR Sierra*, in the mountains of Quiché and associated with the EGP (Ejército Guerrillero de los Pobres, Guerrilla Army of the Poor); *CPR Ixcán*, also in Quiché and connected to the EGP; and *CPR Petén*, associated with FAR. The CPR always presented themselves as civilian populations under army persecution.

13. The person Rubén referred to in his concluding remarks was a prominent gay activist. In 2000, with the Grupo Promotor Colectivo Gay-Lésbico (Coordinating Group, Gay and Lesbian Collective), that person had organized the first public rally for "*el respeto a la diversidad sexual*," that is, "respect for sexual diversity," in Guatemala City. Rubén noted with appreciation the *compañero*'s radicalism, adding: "I may not identify, but I do not accuse you (*acusar*), nor do I vilify you (*agrear*) and least of all attack you (*atacar*)."

14. "Those who can drink more, drink more."

15. This point was made explicitly by Macario, whose thoughts are discussed in Chapter 6.

Chapter 6

1. For a definition of "the ethnographic moment," see the Introduction herein. The ethnographic moment described here is discussed in Chapter 3.

2. "To incorporate": Middle English *incorporaten*, from Late Latin *incorporare, incorporat-*, "to form into a body" (OED 2004).

3. Rubios is a brand of cigarettes produced in Guatemala. They are cheaper than imported brands. Cigarettes of whatever brand and label are viewed as superfluous items in Petén. Men often go to the local *tienda* (shop) and purchase one or two at a time. Most men *and* women, however, smoked with me.

4. A *chiclero* is a worker in the chicle industry; *lona* in Petén is a thick cotton fabric.

5. *Compas* is short for *compañeros*. *Dengue* is an illness similar to malaria.

6. *Milpa* is any stretch of land where maize has been planted.

7. It is unclear why the man was in no position to refuse to take the *guerrilleros/as* to the other side. It may have been a matter of politeness, but it could also have to do with the fact that because Alma said the man had no idea whom he was talking to, in fact this very (certainty or) uncertainty, and hence fear, may have precluded the possibility to refuse the favor.

8. The fact that the boots were made of leather is important. Resources were so

scarce in the guerrilla that most combatants wore rubber boots, or *botas de hule*. As discussed in Chapter 4, *botas de hule* were a signifier of insurgency.

9. A *manaquea* is a stretch of land where one finds *manaca*, that is, a type of palm with narrow branches very common in Petén. *Manaca* is used for roofing nowadays, as the more long-lasting leaves of *guano* palms become increasingly hard to find.

10. Surprise at seeing someone barefoot suggests that this episode must have happened relatively close to a main town with a ladino population, such as Melchor de Mencos. In the rural areas people, especially women, are often barefoot.

11. Macario is referring to the right-wing government that was elected in the first elections following the Peace Accords. While the FRG won the presidency in 1999 along with many of the leadership positions in the Guatemalan Congress, the URNG won a large number of seats both in the Parliament and at the municipal level.

12. See Chapter 3.

Bibliography

Adams, A. E. (1997) Los Cosechadores de Órganos y Harbury: Relatos Transnacionales de Impunidad Y Responsabilidad en Guatemala Después de la Guerra. *Mesoamérica* 34(Dec): 595–632.

Adams, A. E. (2005) ¿Diversidad cultural en la nacionalidad homogénea?: Antonio Goubaud Carrera y la fundación del Instituto Indigenista Nacional de Guatemala. *Mesoámerica* 50(Jan-Feb): 66–95.

Adams, A. E. (2011) Antonio Goubaud Carrera: Between the Contradictions of the Generación de 1920 and U.S. Anthropology. In: *After the Coup: An Ethnographic Reframing of Guatemala 1954*, Adams, A. E. and Smith, T. J. (Eds.). Urbana: University of Illinois Press.

Adams, R. N. (1965) *Migraciones Internas en Guatemala: Expansión Agraria de los Indígenas Kekchies Hacia El Petén*. Guatemala: Centro Editorial "José de Pineda Ibarra," Ministerio de la Educación.

Adams, R. N. (1970) *Crucifixion by Power: Essays on Guatemalan National Social Structure, 1944–1966*. Austin: University of Texas Press.

Ahmed, S. (1999) "She'll Wake Up One of These Days and Find She's Turned Into a Nigger": Passing Through Hybridity. *Theory, Culture and Society* 16(2): 87–106.

Asad, T. (Ed.) (1973) *Anthropology and the Colonial Encounter*. London: Ithaca.

Austin, J. L. (1962) *How to Do Things with Words*. London: Clarendon.

Barad, K. (2003) Posthumanist Performativity: Toward an Understanding of How Matter Comes to Matter. *Signs* 28(3): 801–31.

Ball, P., Kobrak, P., and Spirer, H. F. (1999) *State Violence in Guatemala 1960–1996: A Quantitative Reflection*. Washington, DC: AAAS.

Barnes, T. A. (1999) *"We Women Work So Hard": Gender, Urbanisation and Social Reproduction in Colonial Harare, Zimbabwe, 1930–1956*. Portsmouth, UK: Heinemann.

Barth, F. (Ed.) (1969) *Ethnic Groups and Boundaries: The Social Organizatisation of Culture Difference*. London: George Allen and Unwin.

Barth, F. (1975) *Ritual and Knowledge among the Baktaman of New Guinea*. Oslo and New Haven, CT: Universitetsforlaget and Yale University Press.

Baudrillard, J. (1988) *Selected Writings*, edited by Mark Poster. Stanford, CA: Stanford University Press.

Bell, J. P. (1993) El Proyecto Arevaliano Para El Petén. *Anuarios de Estudios Centroamericános* 19(1): 23–35.

Bhabha, H. K. (1995) In a Spirit of Calm Violence. In: *After Colonialism: Imperial Histories and Postcolonial Displacements*, Prakash, G. (Ed.). Princeton, NJ: Princeton University Press.

Bhebhe, N., and Ranger, T. (Eds.) (1991) *Society in Zimbabwe's Liberation War.* Oxford: James Currey.

Braidotti, R. (1994) *Nomadic Subjects: Embodiment and Sexual Difference in Contemporary Feminist Theory.* New York: Columbia University Press.

Burchell, G., Gordon, C., and Miller, P. (Eds.) (1991) *The Foucault Effect: Studies in Governmentality.* Chicago: Chicago University Press.

Butler, J. (1990) *Gender Trouble: Feminism and the Subversion of Identity.* New York: Routledge.

Butler, J. (1993) *Bodies That Matter: On the Discursive Limits of "Sex."*. New York: Routledge.

Butler, J. (1997) *Excitable Speech: A Politics of the Performative.* London: Routledge.

Caplan, P. (Ed.) (2003) *The Ethics of Anthropology.* London: Routledge.

Carey, D., Jr. (2004) Maya Perspectives of the 1999 Referendum in Guatemala: Ethnic Equality Rejected? *Latin American Perspectives* 31(6): 123–41.

Carlsen, R. S. (1997) *The War for the Hearts and Souls of a Highland Maya Town.* Austin: University of Texas Press.

Carmack, R. M. (1979) *História Social de los Quichés.* Guatemala City: Seminario de Integración Social Guatemalteca.

Carmack, R. M. (1981) *Quiché Mayas of Utatlán: The Evolution of a Highland Guatemala Kingdom.* Norman: University of Oklahoma Press.

Carmack, R. M. (Ed.) (1988) *Harvest of Violence: The Maya Indians and the Guatemalan Crisis.* Norman: University of Oklahoma Press.

Carmack, R. M. (1995) *Rebels of Highland Guatemala: The Quiche-Mayas of Momostenango.* Norman: University of Oklahoma Press.

Carr, D. L. (2001) Población, Uso del Suelo y Deforestación en El Parque Nacional Sierra de Lacandón, Petén, Guatemala. In: *Población del Istmo 2000: Familia, Migración, Violencia y Medio Ambiente*, Bixby, L. R. (Ed.). Costa Rica: Universidad de Costa Rica.

Carsten, J. (Ed.) (2000) *Cultures of Relatedness: New Approaches to the Study of Kinship.* Cambridge: Cambridge University Press.

Casaús Arzú, M. (1995) *Linaje y Racismo.* Guatemala: FLACSO.

Casaús Arzú, M. (2005) De la Incógnita del Indio al Indio como Sombra: El Debate de la Antropología Guatemalteca en Torno al Indio y la Nación: 1921–1938. *Revista de India* 234(May-Aug): 376–403.

Castree, N. (2005) The Epistemology of Particulars: Human Geography, Case Studies and "Context." *Geoforum* 36: 541–4.

Chant, S. with Craske, N. (2003) *Gender in Latin America*. New Brunswick, NJ: Rutgers University Press.

Clark, C. (2000) Land Tenure and Social Mobility in Tropical Petén. *Human Organization* 59(4): 419–27.

Clifford, J. (1980) Fieldwork, Reciprocity and the Making of Ethnographic Texts: The Example of Maurice Leenhardt. *Man* 15(2): 518–32.

Clifford, J. (1988) *The Predicament of Culture: Twentieth-century Ethnography, Literature, and Art*. Cambridge, MA: Harvard University Press.

Clifford, J. (1992) Traveling Cultures. In: *Cultural Studies*, Grossberg, L., Nelson, C., and Treichler, P. A. (Eds.). New York: Routledge.

Clifford, J. (1997) *Routes: Travel and Translation in the Late Twentieth Century*. Cambridge, MA: Harvard University Press.

Clifford, J. and Marcus, G. E. (Eds.) (1986) *Writing Culture: The Poetics and Politics of Ethnography*. Berkeley: University of California Press.

Colby, B. N. and van den Berghe, P. (1969) *Ixil Country*. Berkeley: University of California Press.

Colom, Y. (1998) *Mujeres en la Alborada: Guerrilla y Partecipación Femenina en Guatemala, 1973–1978*. Guatemala: Artemis and Edinter.

Comaroff, J. and Comaroff, J. L. (1992) *Ethnography and the Historical Imagination*. Boulder, CO: Westview Press.

Comisión para el Esclarecimiento Histórico (CEH) (1999) *Guatemala: Memoria del Silencio Tz'inil Na'tab'al*. Guatemala: UNOPS.

Coordinación de Organizaciones del Pueblo Maya de Guatemala (COPMAGUA) (1995) *Acuerdo Sobre Identidad y Derechos de los Pueblos Indígenas*. Guatemala City: Cholsamaj.

Corsín Jiménez, A. (2005) Changing Scales and the Scales of Change: Ethnography and Political Economy in Antofagasta, Chile. *Critique of Anthropology* 25(2): 155–74.

Csordas, T. J. (Ed.) (1994) *Embodiment and Experience: The Existential Ground of Culture and Self*. Cambridge: Cambridge University Press.

Csordas, T. J. (1999) The Body's Career in Anthropology. In: *Anthropological Theory Today*, Moore, H. L. (Ed.). Malden, MA: Polity.

Cullather, N. (1999) *Secret History: The CIA's Classified Account of Its Operations in Guatemala 1952–1954*. Stanford, CA: Stanford University Press.

Daniel, V. E. (1996) *Charred Lullabies: Chapters in an Anthropography of Violence*. Princeton, NJ: Princeton University Press.

Daniel, V. E. (1997) Mood, Moment and Mind. In: *Violence and Subjectivity*, Das, V., Kleinman, A., Ramphele, M., and Reynolds, P. (Eds.). Berkeley: University of California Press.

Dary, C. (1994) "Ladino: Apuntes para la Historia de un Término." *Ethnos, Boletín del Instituto de Estudios Interétnicos de la Universidad de San Carlos* 2(April/May): 1, 2, 10.

Dary, C. (2003) *Identidades Étnicas y Tierras Comunales en Jalapa*. Guatemala: Instituto de Estudios Interétnicos [IDEI].

Dary, C., Elías, S., and Reyna, V. (1998) *Estrategias de Sobrevivencia Campesina en Ecosistemas Frágiles: Los Ch'orti' en las Laderas Secas del Oriente de Guatemala*. Guatemala: FLACSO.

Das, V., Kleinman, A., Ramphele, M., and Reynolds, P. (Eds.) (2000) *Violence and Subjectivity*. Berkeley: University of California Press.

Day, S. (2007) Threading Time in the Biography of London Sex Workers. In: *Ghosts of Memory: Essays on Remembrance and Relatedness*, Carsten, J. (Ed.). Oxford: Blackwell.

Demarest, A. (2004) *Ancient Maya: The Rise and Fall of a Rainforest Civilization*. Cambridge: Cambridge University Press.

Derrida, J. (1970) Structure, Sign and Play. In: *The Languages of Criticism and the Sciences of Man: The Structuralist Controversy*, Macksey, R. and Donato, E. (Eds.). Baltimore, MD: John Hopkins University Press.

Derrida, J. (1972) *Limited Inc.* Evanston, IL: Northwestern University Press.

Derrida, J. (1974) *Of Grammatology*. Baltimore, MD: John Hopkins University Press.

Dilley, R. M. (Ed.) (1999) *The Problem of Context*. New York and Oxford: Berghahn Books.

Dilley, R. M. (2002) The Problem of Context in Social and Cultural Anthropology. *Language and Communication* 22(4): 437–56.

Downey, G. L., Dumit, J., and Williams, S. (1995) Cyborg Anthropology. *Cultural Anthropology* 10(2): 264–9.

Effatin, R. A. and Elías, G. S. (2002) Del Avance de la Frontera Agrícola al Manejo Forestal Comunitario: Petén, Guatemala. *Caravelle* 79:43–68.

Fabian, J. (1983) *Time and the Other: How Anthropology Makes Its Object*. New York: Columbia University Press.

Fabian, J. (1999) Ethnographic Misunderstanding and the Perils of Context. In: *The Problem of Context*, Dilley, R. M. (Ed.). New York and Oxford: Berghahn Books.

Falla, R. (1978) *Quiché Rebelde: Estudio de un Movimiento de Conversión Religiosa, Rebelde a las Creencias Tradicionales, en San Antonio Ilotenango, Quiché, 1948–1970*. Guatemala: USAC.

Falla, R. (1992) *Masacres de la Selva: Ixcán, Guatemala*. Guatemala: USAC.

Fardon, R. (1990) *Localizing Strategies: Regional Traditions of Ethnographic Writing*. Edinburgh: Scottish Academic Press.

Federación de Cooperativas Agrícolas de Guateamala (FEDECOAG) (1993) *Las Relaciones de Poder en las Zonas del Retorno en El Petén*. Guatemala: FEDECOAG.

Felman, S. (1983) *The Literary Speech Act: Don Juan with J. L. Austin, or Seduction in Two Languages*. Ithaca, NY: Cornell University Press.

Fernández, O. (1968) Su Biografía. In: *Turcios Lima: Biografía y Documentos*, Montes, C. (Ed.). La Habana, Cuba: Ediciones Tricontinental.

Fiedler, J. L. (1980) Commentary on Land Settlement in the Petén, Response to Nancy Peckenham. *Latin American Perspectives* 7(2/3): 120–3.

Fischer, E. F. (1999) Maya Identity and Cultural Logic: Rethinking Essentialism and Constructivism. *Current Anthropology* 43(4): 473–99.

Fischer, E. F. (2001) *Cultural Logics and Global Economics: Maya Identity in Thought and Practice*. Austin: University of Texas Press.

Fischer, E. F. (2004) The Janus Face of Globalization: Economic Production and Cultural Reproduction in Highland Guatemala. In: *Pluralizing Ethnography: Comparison and Representation in Maya Cultures, Histories and Identities*, Watanabe, J. M. and Fischer, E. F. (Eds.). Santa Fe: SAR Press.

Fischer, E. F. and Hendrickson, C. (2002) *Tecpán, Guatemala: A Modern Maya Town in a Global and Local Context*. Boulder, CO: Westview.

Fischer, E. F. and McKenna Brown, R. (Eds.) (1996) *Maya Cultural Activism*. Austin: University of Texas Press.

Fleming, C. (2002) Performance as Guerrilla Ontology: The Case of Stelarc. *Body and Society* 8(3): 95–109.

Flores, J. (1995) *La Estrella Falaz*. Guatemala: Editorial Estudiantil FENIX.

Flores, J. (1997a) *Ciudades Bajo los Arboles*. Guatemala: Editorial Estudiantil FENIX.

Flores, J. (1997b) *Sombras de Selva*. Guatemala: Editorial Estudiantil FENIX.

Flores, J. (n.d.) *El Verde Purpura*, no publication details available.

Fluehr-Lobban, C. (Ed.) (2003) *Ethics and the Profession of Anthropology: Dialogue for Ethically Conscious Practice*. Walnut Creek, CA: AltaMira Press.

Foucault, M. ([1978] 2004) Governmentality. In: *Michel Foucault: Power, Essential Works of Foucault 1854–1984*, Faubian, J. D. (Ed.). London: Penguin.

Foucault, M. (1980) *Power-knowledge: Selected Interviews and Other Writings, 1972–1977*. Brighton: Harvester.

Foucault, M. (1988) Technologies of the Self. In: *Technologies of the Self: A Seminar with Michel Foucault*, Martin, L. H., Gutman, H., and Hutton, P. H. (Eds.). London: Tavistock.

Fox, J. (1987) *Maya Postclassic State Formation*. Cambridge: Cambridge University Press.

Foxen, P. (2006) *In Search of Providence: Transnational Maya Identities*. Nashville: Vanderbilt University Press.

Freidel, D., Schele, L., and Parker, J. (1993) *Maya Cosmos*. New York: Harper and Collins.

Fuerzas Armadas Rebeldes (FAR) (1988) *Documentos Históricos*. Guatemala: FAR.

Gálvez Borrell, V. (Coordinator) (1997) *Qué Sociedad Queremos? Una Mirada desde el Movimiento y las Organizaciones Mayas*. Guatemala: FLACSO.

Gálvez Borrell, V. and Esquit Choy, A. (1997) *The Mayan Movement Today: Issues of Indigenous Culture and Development in Guatemala*. Guatemala: FLACSO.

Garrard Burnett, V. (1998) *Protestantism in Guatemala: Living in the New Jerusalem*. Austin: University of Texas Press.

Garrard Burnett, V. (2010) *Terror in the Land of the Holy Spirit: Guatemala*

Under General Efrain Rios Montt, 1982–1983. Cambridge: Cambridge University Press.

Garrard Burnett, V. and Stoll, D. (Eds.) (1993) *Rethinking Protestantism in Latin America*. Philadelphia: Temple University Press.

Geertz, C. (1973) *The Interpretation of Cultures*. New York: Basic Books.

Geertz, C. (2000) *Available Light: Anthropological Reflections on Philosophical Topics*. Princeton, NJ: Princeton University Press.

Gillin, J. (1952) Antonio Goubaud Carrera, 1902–1951. *American Anthropologist* 54(1): 71–3.

Gingrich, A. and Fox, R. (Eds.) (2002) *Anthropology, by Comparison*. London: Routledge.

Golden, C. W. and Borgstede, G. (Eds.) (2004) *Continuities and Changes in Maya Archaeology*. London: Routledge.

González, M. (2000) The Man Who Brought the Danger to the Village: Representations of the Armed Conflict in Guatemala from a Local Perspective. *Journal of Southern African Studies* 26(6): 317–35.

Goubaud Carrera, A. (1946) Distribución de las Lenguas Indígenas Actuales de Guatemala. *Boletín del Instituto Indigenista Nacional* 1(2/3): 1–16.

Goubaud Carrera, A. (1964) *Indigenismo en Guatemala*. Guatemala City: Guatemala Seminario de Integración Social Guatemalteca.

Goubaud Carrera, A., Rosales, J. D. D., and Tax, S. (1944) *Reconnaissance of Northern Guatemala*. Chicago: University of Chicago Library.

Grandia, L. (2000) ¿Cuántas Personas Quiere Usted Que Vivan en Petén? In: *Memorias del Encuentro Internacional de Investigadores: Nuevas Perpectivas de Desarrollo Sostenible en Petén*, Grünberg, G. (Ed.). Guatemala City: FLACSO.

Grandia, L. (2006) Unsettling: Land Disposession and Enduring Inequity for the Q'eqchi' Maya in the Guatemalan and Belizean Frontier Colonization Process. PhD Dissertation, Department of Anthropology, University of California, Berkeley.

Grandin, G. (2000) *The Blood of Guatemala: A History of Race and Nation*. Durham, NC: Duke University Press.

Grandin, G. (2004) *The Last Colonial Massacre: Latin America in the Cold War*. Chicago: Chicago University Press.

Gray, C. H. (Ed.) (1995) *The Cyborg Handbook*. New York: Routledge.

Green, L. (1999) *Fear as a Way of Life: Maya Widows in Rural Guatemala*. New York: Columbia University Press.

Green, L. (2002) Structures of Power, Spaces of Violence: Everyday Life in Post-Peace Accords Rural Guatemala. *FOCAAL European Journal of Anthropology* 39: 117–35.

Grünberg, G. (2001) Social and Environmental Consolidation of the Maya Biosphere Reserve, Peten, Guatemala. In: *Integrated Conservation and Development in Tropical America: Experiences and Lessons in Liking Communities,*

Projects and Policies, Rohades, R. E. and Stalling J. (Eds.). USA: SANREM CRSP and CARE-SUBIR.

Grünberg, G. and Ramos, V. H. (1999) *Base de Datos Sobre Población, Tierra y Medio Ambiente en la Reserva de la Biósfera Maya: Petén, Guatemala*. Petén, Guatemala: Cooperación Austriaca para el Desarrollo, USAID, and Project CATIE-CONAP.

Guatemalan Peace Accords (1996) Guatemalan Peace Accords. Guatemala City: Friedrich Ebert Stiftung.

Gupta, A. and Ferguson, J. (1997) *Culture, Power, Place: Explorations in Critical Anthropology*. Durham, NC: Duke University Press.

Gutierrez, G. ([1971] 1988) *A Theology of Liberation*. Maryknoll, New York: Orbis Books.

Gutmann, M. (1996) *The Meanings of Macho: Being a Man in Mexico City*. Berkeley: University of California Press.

Halberstam, J. (1998) *Female Masculinity*. Durham, NC: Duke University Press.

Hale, C. R. (2006) *Más Que un Indio (More Than an Indian): Racial Ambivalence and Neoliberal Multiculturalism in Guatemala*. Santa Fe, CA: SAR Press.

Handy, J. (1984) *Gift of the Devil: A History of Guatemala*. Toronto: Between the Lines.

Hannerz, U. (2003) Being there . . . and There . . . and There! Reflections on Multi-site Ethnography. *Ethnography* 4(2): 2001–216.

Haraway, D. J. (1989) *Primate Visions: Gender, Race and Nature in the World of Modern Science*. New York: Routledge.

Haraway, D. J. (1991) *Simians, Cyborgs and Women: The Reinvention of Nature*. London: Free Association Press.

Haraway, D. J. (1997) *Modest-Witness@Second-Millennium.FemaleMan-Meets-OncoMouse: Feminism and Technoscience*. New York: Routledge.

Haraway, D. J. (2003) *The Companion Species Manifesto: Dogs, People, and Significant Otherness*. Chicago: Prickly Paradigm.

Harbury, J. (1995) *Bridge of Courage: Life Stories of the Guatemalan Compañeros and Compañeras*. Monroe, ME: Common Courage Press.

Hardt, M. and Negri, A. (2000) *Empire*. Cambridge, MA: Harvard University Press.

Hastrup, K. (1990) The Ethnographic Present: A Reinvention. *Cultural Anthropology* 5(1): 45–61.

Hastrup, K. (1995) The Ethnographic Present: On Starting in Time. In: *A Passage to Anthropology: Between Experience and Theory*, Hastrup, K. (Ed.). London: Routledge.

Hayes, D. J., Sader, S. A., and Schwartz, N. B. (2002) Analyzing a Forest Conversion History Database to Explore the Spatial and Temporal Characteristics of Land Cover Change in Guatemala's Maya Biosphere Reserve. *Landscape Ecology* 17: 299–314.

Heidegger, M. ([1962] 2002) *Being and Time*. London: Blackwell.

Hendrickson, C. E. (1995) *Weaving Identities: Construction of Dress and Self in a Highland Guatemala Town.* Austin: University of Texas Press.

Hervik, P. (2001) Narrations of Shifting Maya Identities. *Bulletin of Latin American Research* 20(3): 342–59.

Hill, R. and Monaghan, J. (1987) *Continuities in Highland Maya Social Organization: Ethnohistory in Sacapulas, Guatemala.* Philadelphia: University of Pennsylvania Press.

Hogle, L. F. (2003) The Anthropology of Bioengineered Futures. *American Anthropological Association Anthropology News* 44(4): 14.

Huggan, G. (1994) Anthropologists and Other Frauds. *Comparative Literature* 46(2): 113–28.

Husserl, E. (1964) *The Idea of Phenomenology.* The Hague: Martinus Nijhoff.

Instituto Indigenista Nacional (1945) Editorial. *Boletín del Instituto Indigenista Nacional* 1(1): 5–10.

Instituto Indigenista Nacional (1948a) *Chuarrancho: Síntesis Socio-económica de una Comunidad Indígena Guatemalteca.* Guatemala: Instituto Indigenista Nacional.

Instituto Indigenista Nacional (1948b) *San Juan Sacatepéquez: Síntesis Socio-económica de una Comunidad Indígena Guatemalteca.* Guatemala: Instituto Indigenista Nacional.

Instituto Indigenista Nacional (1969) *Santa Eulalia, Tierra de Nuestros Antepasados y Esperanza Para Nuestros Hijos: Ecrito Por el Comité de Vecinos.* Guatemala: Instituto Indigenista Nacional.

Jaarsma, S. R. and Rohatynskyj, M. A. (Eds.) (2000) *Ethnographic Artifacts: Challenges to a Reflexive Anthropology.* Honolulu: University of Hawai'i Press.

Jackson, M. (Ed.) (1996) *Things as They Are: New Directions in Phenomenological Anthropology.* Bloomington: Indiana University Press.

Jameson, F. (1991) *Postmodernism, or the Cultural Logic of Late Capitalism.* London: Verso.

Jonas, S. (2000) *Of Centaurs and Doves: Guatemala's Peace Process.* Boulder, CO: Westview.

Jones, G. D. (1998) *The Last Maya Kingdom.* Stanford, CA: Stanford University Press.

Kampwirth, K. (2002) *Women and Guerrilla Movements: Nicaragua, El Salvador, Chiapas, Cuba.* University Park: Pennsylvania State University Press.

Kesby, M. (1996) Arenas for Control, Terrains of Gender Constestation: Guerrilla Struggle and Counter-Insurgency Warfare in Zimbabwe 1972–1980. *Journal of Southern African Studies* 22(4): 561–84.

Kingman Garcés, E. (2002) Identidad, Mestizaje, Hibridación: Sus Usos Ambiguos. *Proposiciones* 34(Oct): 1–8.

Knauft, B. M. (1996) *Genealogies for the Present in Cultural Anthropology.* New York: Routledge.

Kriger, N. J. (1992) *Zimbabwe's Guerrilla War: Peasant Voices*. Cambridge: Cambridge University Press.

Kristeva, J. (1982) *Powers of Horror: An Essay in Abjection*. New York: Columbia University Press.

Kuper, A. (1999) *Culture: The Anthropologists' Account*. Cambridge, MA: Harvard University Press.

Kurzman, S. L. (2001) Presence and Absence: A Response to Nelson and Wright. *Cultural Anthropology* 16(3): 374–87.

Lancaster, R. N. (1992) *Life Is Hard: Machismo, Danger and the Intimacy of Power in Nicaragua*. Berkeley: University of California Press.

Landau, S. (1988) *The Dangerous Doctrine: National Security and U.S. Foreign Policy*. Boulder, CO: Westview.

Landau, S. (1993) *The Guerrilla Wars of Central America*. London: Weidenfeld and Nicholson.

Limón, J. E. (1994) *Dancing With the Devil: Society and Cultural Poetics in Mexican-American South Texas*. Madison: University of Wisconsin Press.

Little, W. (2009) Maya Daykeepers: New Spirital Clients and the Morality of Making Money. In: *Economics and Morality*, Browne, K. E. and Milgram, B. L. (Eds.). Plymouth: Altamira Press.

Little, W. and Smith, T. J. (Eds.) (2009) *Mayas in Post-war Guatemala: Harvest of Violence Revisited*. Tuscaloosa: University of Alabama Press.

Lovell, W. G. (1992) *Conquest and Survival in Colonial Guatemala: A Historical Geography of the Cuchumatan Highlands, 1500–1821*. Montreal: McGill-Queen's University Press.

Lovell, W. G. and Lutz, C. H. (2009) Introduction. In: *La Patria del Criollo: An Interpretation of Colonial Guatemala*, by Martínez Peláez, S. Durham, NC: Duke University Press.

Lury, C. (1998) *Prosthetic Culture*. London: Routledge.

Manz, B. (1988) *Refugees of a Hidden War: The Aftermath of Counter-insurgency in Guatemala*. Albany: State University of New York Press.

Manz, B. (1995) Reflections on an *Antropología Comprometida*: Conversations with Ricardo Falla. In: *Fieldwork Under Fire: Contemporary Studies in Violence and Survival*, Nordstrom, C. and Robben, A. C. G. M. (Eds.). Berkeley: University of California Press.

Manz, B. (2004) *Paradise in Ashes: A Guatemalan Journey of Courage, Terror, and Hope*. Berkeley: University of California Press.

Marcus, G. E. (1998) *Ethnography Through Thick and Thin*. Princeton, NJ: Princeton University Press.

Martin, E. (1992) The End of the Body? *American Ethnologist* 19(1): 121–40.

Martínez Peláez, S. (1970) *La Patria del Criollo*. Guatemala: USAC.

Maxwell, J. M. and Hill, R. M., II (2006) *Kaqchikel Chronicles: The Definitive Edition*. Austin: University of Texas Press).

McCreery, D. (1990) State Power, Indigenous Communities, and Land in

Nineteenth-Century Guatemala, 1820–1920. In: *Guatemalan Indians and the State 1540 to 1988*, Smith, C. (Ed.). Austin: University of Texas Press.

Méndez-Domínguez, A. (1967) *Zaragoza: La Estratificación Social de una Comunidad Ladina Guatemalteca*. Guatemala City: Seminario de Integración Social Guatemalteca.

Méndez-Domínguez, A. (1975) Big and Little Traditions in Guatemalan Anthropology. *Current Anthropology* 16(4): 541–52.

Méndez-Domínguez, A. (1980) Evaluación de la Antropología en Guatemala. *América Indígena* 40(2): 341–53.

Merleau-Ponty, M. ([1962] 2002) *Phenomenology of Perception*. London: Routledge.

Mignolo, W. (2000) *Local Histories/Global Designs: Coloniality, Subaltern Knowledges, and Border Thinking*. Princeton, NJ: Princeton University Press.

Mirandé, A. (1987) *Gringo Justice*. Notre Dame, IN: University of Notre Dame Press.

Mirandé, A. (1997) *Hombres y Machos: Masculinity and Latino Culture*. Boulder, CO: Westview.

Misión de Verificación de las Naciones Unidas en Guatemala (MINUGUA) (1997) *Informe del Secretario General Sobre el Grupo de Observadores Militares Anexo a La Minugua*. Guatemala: United Nations.

Montejo, V. (1987) *Testimony: Death of a Guatemalan Village*. Willimantic, CT: Curbstone.

Montejo, V. (1991) *The Bird Who Cleans the World and Other Mayan Fables*. Willimantic, CT: Curbstone.

Montejo, V. (1999) *Voices from Exile: Violence and Survival in Modern Maya History*. Norman: University of Oklahoma Press.

Montejo, V. (Ed.) (2005) *Maya Intellectual Renaissance: Identity, Representation and Leadership*. Austin: University of Texas Press.

Montes, C. (1968) Prólogo. In: *Turcios Lima: Biografía y Documentos*, Montes, C. (Ed.). La Habana, Cuba: Ediciones Tricontinental.

Moore, H. L. (1994) *A Passion for Difference: Essays in Anthropology and Gender*. Cambridge, UK: Polity.

Moore, H. L. (1997a) Interior Landscapes and External Worlds: The Return of Grand Theory in Anthropology. *Australian Journal of Anthropology* 8(2): 125–44.

Moore, H. L. (1997b) Sex, Symbolism and Psychoanalysis. *Differences*, 9(1): 68–94.

Moore, H. L. (Ed.) (1999) *Anthropological Theory Today*. Malden, MA: Polity.

Moore, H. L. (2004) Global Anxieties: Concept-Metaphors and Pre-theoretical Commitments in Anthropology. *Anthropological Theory* 4(1): 71–88.

Moore, H. L. (2007) *The Subject of Anthropology: Gender, Symbolism and Psychoanalysis*. Cambridge, UK: Polity.

Morales, M. R. (2000) Problemática de la Identidad Ladina: Una Propuesta Política. *Revista de Estudios Interétnicos* 13(4): 4–13.

Nelson, D. M. (1999) *A Finger in the Wound: Body Politics in Quincentennial Guatemala*. Berkeley: University of California Press.

Nelson, D. M. (2001a) Phantom Limbs and Invisible Hands: Bodies, Prosthetics, and Late Capitalist Identifications. *Cultural Anthropology* 16(3): 303–13.

Nelson, D. M. (2001b) Stumped Identities: Body Image, Body Politic, and the Mujer Maya as Prosthetic. *Cultural Anthropology* 16(3): 314–53.

Nelson, D. M. (2003) "The More You Kill the More You Will Live": The Maya, "Race" and Biopolitical Hope in Guatemala. In: *Race, Nature and the Politics of Difference*, Moore, D. S., Kosek, J., and Pandian, A. (Eds.). Durham, NC: Duke University Press.

Nelson, D. M. (2009) *Reckoning: The Ends of War in Guatemala*. Durham, NC: Duke University Press.

Nolin, C. (2006) *Transnational Raptures: Gender and Forced Migration*. Aldershot, UK: Ashgate.

Nordstrom, C. and Robben, A. C. G. M. (Eds.) (1995) *Fieldwork Under Fire: Contemporary Studies of Violence and Survival*. Berkeley: University of California Press.

Oficina de Derechos Human del Arzobispado de Guatemala (ODHAG) (1998) *Guatemala: Nunca Más*. Guatemala City: Litografía e Imprenta LIL SA.

O'Neill, K. L. and Thomas, K. (Eds.) (2011) *Securing the City: Neoliberalism, Space and Insecurity in Postwar Guatemala*. Durham, NC: Duke University Press.

Ortner, S. B. (1995) Resistance and the Problem of Ethnographic Refusal. *Comparative Studies in Society and History* 37(1): 173–93.

Ortner, S. B. (Ed.) (1999) *The Fate of "Culture": Geertz and Beyond*. Berkeley: University of California Press.

Otzoy, I. (1996) Maya Clothing and Identity. In: *Maya Cultural Activism in Guatemala*, Fischer, E. F. and McKenna Brown, R. (Eds.). Austin: University of Texas Press.

Peckenham, N. (1980) Land Settlement in Petén. *Latin American Perspectives* 7(25–26): 169–77.

Pedroni, G. (1990) *Territorialidad Kekchi. Una Aproximación al Acceso a la Tierra: La Migración y la Titulación*. Guatemala: FLACSO.

Perera, V. (1993) *Unfinished Conquest: The Guatemalan Tragedy*. Berkley: University of California Press.

Pinto Soria, J. C. (1993) *História General de Centroamérica, II: El Régimen Colonial (1524–1750)*. Madrid: FLACSO.

Pitt-Rivers, J. A. (1954) *The People of the Sierra*. London: Weidenfeld and Nicolson.

Poblete, J. (2001) Governmentality and the Social Question: National Formation and Discipline. In: *Foucault and Latin America: Appropriations and Deployments of Discursive Analysis*, Trigo, B. (Ed.). New York: Routledge.

Posocco, S. (2004) Passing. In: *Sexuality: The Essential Glossary*, Eadie, J. (Ed.). London: Arnold.

Posocco, S. (2008) Zoning: Environmental Cosmopolitics in and around the Maya Biosphere Reserve, Guatemala. *Nature and Culture* 3(2): 206–24.

Prakash, G. (1992) Can the "Subaltern" Ride? A Reply to O'Hanlon and Washbrook. *Comparative Studies in Society and History* 34(1): 168–84.

Prakash, G. (1994) Subaltern Studies as Postcolonial Criticism. *American Historical Review* 99(5): 1457–90.

Prensa Libre (2005) A Merced de Asaltos, 5 January.

Prensa Libre (2006) Lamentan Trágico Deceso, 9 August.

Price, D. H. (1998) Cold War Anthropology: Collaborators and Victims of the National Security State. *Identities* 4(3–4): 389–430.

Price, D. H. (2000) Anthropologists as Spies. *The Nation*. 2 November.

Price, D. H. (2004) *Threatening Anthropology: McCarthyism and the FBI's Surveillance of Activist Anthropologists*. Durham, NC: Duke University Press.

Radcliffe, S. and Westwood S. (1993) *"Viva": Women and Popular Protest in Latin America*. London: Routledge.

Randall, M. (1981) *Sandino's Daughters: Testimonies of Nicaraguan Women in Struggle*. London: Zed.

Rapport, N. (1997) The Morality of Locality: On the Absolutism of Landownership in an English Village. In: *The Ethnography of Moralities*, Howell, S. (Ed.). London: Routledge.

Rapport, N. (2002) "The Truth Is Alive": Kierkegaard's Anthropology of Dualism, Subjectivity and Somatic Knowledge. *Anthropological Theory* 2(2): 165–83.

Rapport, N. (2003) *I Am Dynamite: An Alternative Anthropology of Power*. London: Routledge.

Redfield, R. (1956) The Relation Between Indians and Ladinos in Aguaescondida, Guatemala. *América Indígena* 16: 253–76.

Reina, R. E. (1964) The Urban World View of a Tropical Forest Community in the Absence of a City, Petén, Guatemala. *Human Organization* 23: 265–77.

Reina, R. E. (1967a) Milpas and Milperos: Implications for Prehistoric Times. *American Anthropologist* 69: 1–20.

Reina, R. E. (1967b) Annual Cycle and Fiesta Cycle. In: *Handbook of Middle American Indians*, Vol. 6, *Social Anthropology*, Nash, M. (Ed.). Austin: University of Texas Press.

Reina, R. E. and Schwartz, N. B. (1974) The Structural Context of Religious Conversion in Petén, Guatemala: Status, Community and Multicommunity. *American Ethnologist* 1(1): 157–91.

Rodman Ruiz, D. H. (2006) Gender, Migration, and Transnational Identities: Maya and Ladino Relations in Eastern Guatemala. PhD Dissertation, Department of Anthropology, University of Florida, Gainesville.

Roht-Arriaza, N. (2008) Making the State Do Justice: Transnational Prosecutions and International Support for Criminal Investigations in Post-Conflict Guatemala. *Chicago Journal of International Law* 9(1): 79–106.

Rosales, J. d. D. (1959) Indígenas de Guatemala. *América Indígena* 19(2): 115–24.

Rousseau, C., Morales, M., and Foxen, P. (2001) Going Home: Giving Voice to Memory Strategies of Young Mayan Refugees Who Returned to Guatemala as a Community. *Culture, Medicine and Psychiatry* 25: 135–68.

Rowe, W. and Schelling, V. (1991) *Memory and Modernity: Popular Culture in Latin America*. London: Verso.

Rubin, G. (1975) The Traffic in Women: Notes Towards a Political Economy of Sex. In: *Toward an Anthropology of Women*, Reiter, R. R. (Ed.). New York: Monthly Review Press.

Rubinstein, R. A. (Ed.) (1991) *Doing Fieldwork: The Correspondence of Robert Redfield and Sol Tax*. Boulder, CO: Westview.

Ruiz Puga, C. L. (1994) Las Migraciones y la Incorporación Socio-Económica de las Familias del Grupo K'ekchi, el la Aldea Indian Creek, Distrito de Toledo, Belice, Centroamérica. Thesis, Escuela de Historia, Área de Antropología, Universidad San Carlos de Guatemala, Guatemala City.

Samayoa Rivera, R. O. (n.d.) *Colonización de El Petén: Paralelo 17*. Guatemala.

Sanjek, R. (1994) Review of *Doing Fieldwork: The Correspondence of Robert Redfield and Sol Tax*. *American Ethnologist* 21(4): 929–31.

Schackt, J. (2000) La Cultura Q'eqchi' y el Asunto de la Identidad Entre Indígenas y Ladinos en Alta Verapaz. *Revista de Estudios Interétnicos* 8(13): 125–35.

Schackt, J. (2002) Los Mayas: El Origen del Término y la Creación de un Pueblo. *Revista de Estudios Interétnicos* 16(Aug): 7–26.

Schirmer, J. (1998) *The Guatemalan Military Project: A Violence Called Democracy*. Philadelphia: Pennsylvania University Press.

Schlesinger, S. and Kinzen, S. (1982) *Bitter Fruit: The Untold Story of the American Coup in Guatemala*. Garden City, NY: Doubleday.

Schwartz, N. B. (1971) Assimilation and Acculturation: Aspects of Ethnicity in a Guatemalan Town. *Ethnology* 10(3): 291:310.

Schwartz, N. B. (1983) San Simón: Ambiguity and Identity in Petén. *Sociologus* 33(1): 152–73.

Schwartz, N. B. (1987) Colonization of Northern Guatemala: The Petén. *Journal of Anthropological Research* 43(2): 163–83.

Schwartz, N. B. (1990) *Forest Society: A Social History of Petén, Guatemala*. Philadelphia: University of Pennsylvania Press.

Secretaría General del Consejo Nacional de Planificación Económica (1965) *Programa de Inversión Pública y Agricultura Para la República de Guatemala (1965–1969)*. Guatemala City: Secretaría General del Consejo Nacional de Planificación Económica.

Siebers, H. (1999) *"We Are Children of the Mountain": Creolization and Modernization Among the Q'eqchi'*. Amsterdam: Centre for Latin American Research and Documentation, CEDLA.

Sieder, R. (2000) "Paz, Progreso, Justicia y Honradez": Law and Citizenship in Alta Verapaz During the Regime of Jorge Ubico. *Bulletin of Latin American Research* 19(3): 283–302.

Simmel, G. (1906) The Sociology of Secrecy and Secret Societies. *American Journal of Sociology* 11: 441–98.

Sjöholm, C. (2005) *Kristeva and the Political.* London: Routledge.

Smith, C. A. (Ed.) (1990) *Guatemalan Indians and the State: 1540 to 1988.* Austin: University of Texas Press.

Smith, M. (2005) *Stelarc: The Monograph.* Cambridge, MA: MIT Press.

Smith, T. J. and Adams, A. E. (Eds.) (2011) *After the Coup: An Ethnographic Reframing of Guatemala 1954.* Urbana: University of Illinois Press.

Smith, T. J. and Offit, T. A. (2010) Confronting Violence in Postwar Guatemala: An Introduction. *The Journal of Latin American and Caribbean Anthropology* 15(1): 1–15.

Solórzano, S. (1986) *Mujer Alzada.* Barcelona: Sendai Ediciones.

Soza, J. M. (1970) *Monografía del Departamento de El Petén*, Vols. I and II. Guatemala: Editorial "José de Pineda Ibarra".

Spivak, G. C. (1988) *In Other Worlds: Essays in Cultural Politics.* New York: Routledge.

Spivak, G. C. (1999) *A Critique of Postcolonial Reason: Towards a History of the Vanishing Present.* Cambridge, MA: Harvard University Press.

Stavenhagen, R. (1975) *Social Classes in Agrarian Societies.* Garden City, NY: Anchor Books.

Stepan, N. L. (1991) *The Hour of Eugenics: Race, Gender and Nation in Latin America.* Ithaca, NY: Cornell University Press.

Stepputat, F. (1999) Politics of Displacement in Guatemala. *Journal of Historical Sociology* 12(1): 54–80.

Stepputat, F. (2001) Urbanizing the Countryside: Armed Conflict, State Formation, and the Politics of Place in Contemporary Guatemala. In: *States of Imagination: Ethnographic Explorations of the Postcolonial State*, Blom Hansen, T. and Stepputat, F. (Eds.). Durham, NC: Duke University Press.

Stevens, E. P. (1973) Marianismo, the Other Side of Machismo. In: *Male and Female in Latin America: Essays*, Pescatello, A. (Ed.). Pittsburgh, PA: University of Pittsburgh Press.

Stocking, G. J. (1983) The Ethnographer's Magic: Fieldwork in British Anthropology from Taylor to Malinowski. In: *Observers Observed: Essays on Ethnographic Fieldwork*, Stocking, G. W., Jr. (Ed.). Madison: University of Wisconsin Press.

Stoll, D. (1993) *Between Two Armies in the Ixil Towns of Guatemala.* New York: Columbia University Press.

Stølen, K. A. (2007) *Guatemalans in the Aftermath of Violence: The Refugees' Return.* Philadelphia: University of Pennsylvania Press.

Stone, R. A. (1996) *The War of Desire and Technology at the Close of the Mechanical Age.* Cambridge, MA: MIT Press.

Strathern, M. (1987) Out of Context: The Persuasive Fictions of Anthropology. *Current Anthropology* 28(1): 251–81.

Strathern, M. (1988) *The Gender of the Gift: Problems with Women and Problems with Society.* Berkeley: University of California Press.

Strathern, M. (1991) *Partial Connections.* Savage, MD: Rowman and Littlefield.

Strathern, M. (1992a) *After Nature: English Kinship in the Late Twentieth Century.* Cambridge: Cambridge University Press.

Strathern, M. (1992b) Parts and Wholes: Reconfiguring Relationships in a Post-plural World. In: *Conceptualizing Society,* Kuper, A. (Ed.). London: Routledge.

Strathern, M. (Ed.) (1995a) *Shifting Contexts: Transformations in Anthropological Knowledge.* London: Routledge.

Strathern, M. (1995b) Foreword: Shifting Contexts. In: *Shifting Contexts: Transformations in Anthropological Knowledge,* Strathern, M. (Ed.). London: Routledge.

Strathern, M. (1995c) The Nice Thing About Culture Is That Everyone Has It. In: *Shifting Contexts: Transformations in Anthropological Knowledge,* Strathern, M. (Ed.). London: Routledge.

Strathern, M. (1995d) *The Relation: Issues in Complexity and Scale.* Cambridge, UK: Prickly Pear.

Strathern, M. (1999) *Property, Substance and Effect: Anthropological Essays on Persons and Things.* London: Athlone.

Sundberg, J. (1997) NGO Landscapes: Conservation and Communities in the Maya Biosphere Reserve, Petén, Guatemala. *Geographical Review* 88(3): 388–412.

Sundberg, J. (1998) Strategies for Authenticity, Space and Place in the Maya Biosphere. *Conference of Latin Americanist Geographers Yearbook* 24: 85–96.

Sundberg, J. (2003) Conservation and Democratization: Constituting Citizenship in the Maya Biosphere Reserve, Guatemala. *Political Geography* 22: 715–40.

Sundberg, J. (2004) Identities in the Making: Conservation, Gender, and Race in the Maya Biosphere Reserve. *Gender, Place, and Culture* 11(1): 43–66.

Taracena Arriola, A. (1999) *Invención Criolla, Sueño Ladino, Pesadilla Indígena: Los Altos de Guatemala: De Región a Estado 1740–1850.* Guatemala City: CIRMA Ediciones.

Taracena Arriola, A. (2002) Guatemala: Del Mestizaje a la Ladinización 1524–1964. Visiting Professors Seminar Series, Teresa Lozano Long Institute of Latin American Studies, University of Texas, Austin.

Taussig, M. (1980) *The Devil and Commodity Fetishism in South America.* Chapel Hill: University of Carolina Press.

Taussig, M. (1987) *Shamanism, Colonialism, and the Wild Man: A Study in Terror and Healing.* Chicago: Chicago University Press.

Taussig, M. (1999) *Defacement: Public Secrecy and the Labour of the Negative.* Stanford, CA: Stanford University Press.

Tax, S. (1937) The Municipios of the Midwestern Highlands of Guatemala. *American Anthropologist* 45(1): 1–21.

Tax, S. (1942) Ethnic Relations in Guatemala. *América Indígena* 2: 43–8.

Tax, S. ([1953] 1963) *Penny Capitalism: A Guatemalan Indian Economy*. Chicago: Chicago University Press).

Taylor, M., Moran-Taylor, M., and Ruiz, D. R. (2006) Land, Ethnic, and Gender Change: Transnational Migration and Its Effects on Guatemalan Lives and Landscapes. *Geoforum* 37(1): 41–61.

Thompson, C. D. J. (2001) *Maya Identities and the Violence of Place: Borders Bleed*. Aldershot, UK: Ashgate.

Thornton, R. J. (1988) The Rhetoric of Ethnographic Holism. *Cultural Anthropology* 3(3): 285–303.

Turcios Lima, L. A. (1968) Documentos. In: *Turcios Lima: Biografía y Documentos*, Montes, C. (Ed.). La Habana, Cuba: Ediciones Tricontinental.

Urdang, S. (1979) *Fighting Two Colonialisms: Women in Guinea-Bissau*. New York: Monthly Review Press.

van der Vaeren, P. (2000) *Perdidos en La Selva: Un Estudio del Proceso de Rearraigo y de Desarrollo de la Comunidad–Cooperativa Unión Maya Itzá, Formada por Campesinos Guatemaltecos, Antiguos Refugiados, Reasentados en el Departamento de El Petén, Guatemala*. Amsterdam: Tela.

Villegas Rodas, M. (1953) El Ministro Brol en Jira por El Petén. *Revista Agrícola* 1(3/4): 52–9.

Vinegrad, A. (1998) From Guerrillas to Politicians: The Transition of the Guatemalan Revolutionary Movement. In: *Guatemala After the Peace Accords*, Sieder, R. (Ed.). London: ILAS.

Wade, P. (1993) *Blackness and Race Mixture: The Dynamics of Racial Identity in Colombia*. Baltimore: Johns Hopkins University Press.

Wade, P. (1997) *Race and Ethnicity in Latin America*. London: Pluto.

Wagley, C. (1957) *Santiago Chimaltenango: Estudio Antropológico-Social de una Comunidad Indígena de Huehuetenango*. Guatemala City: Seminario de Integración Social Guatemalteca.

Warren, K. B. (1978) *The Symbolism of Subordination: Indian Identity in a Guatemalan Town*. Austin: University of Texas Press.

Warren, K. B. (1993) Interpreting "La Violencia" in Guatemala: Shapes of Mayan Silence and Resistance. In: *The Violence Within: Cultural and Political Opposition in Divided Nations*, Warren, K. B. (Ed.). Boulder, CO: Westview.

Warren, K. B. (1995) Transforming Memories and Histories: The Meaning of Ethnic Resurgence for Mayan Indians. In: *America: New Interpretive Essays*, Stepan, A. (Ed.). New York: Oxford University Press.

Warren, K. B. (1996) Reading History as Resistance: Maya Public Intellectuals. In: *Maya Cultural Activism in Guatemala*, Fischer, E. F. and McKenna Brown, R. (Eds.). Austin: University of Texas Press.

Warren, K. B. (1998) *Indigenous Movements and Their Critics: Pan-Maya Activism in Guatemala*. Princeton, NJ: Princeton University Press.

Warren, K. B. (2003) Voting Against Indigenous Rights in Guatemala: Lessons from the 1999 Referendum. In: *Indigenous Movements, Self-Representation, and the State in Latin America*, Warren, K. B. and Jackson, J. E. (Eds.). Austin: University of Texas Press.

Watanabe, J. M. (1992) *Maya Saints and Souls in a Changing World*. Austin: University of Texas Press.

Watanabe, J. M. (1995a) Unimagining the Maya: Anthropologists, Others, and the Inescapable Hubris of Authorship. *Bulletin of Latin American Research* 14(1): 25–46.

Watanabe, J. M. (1995b) Entitling Ethnicities: Land, Locality, and Identity in Two Maya Land Titles from Western Guatemala, 1879–1891. In: *Indigenous Perceptions of the Nation-State in Latin America*, Giordani, L. and Snipes, M. (Eds.). Williamsburg, VA: Department of Anthropology, College of William and Mary.

West, H. G. (2000) Girls with Guns: Narrating the Experience of War of FRELIMO's "Female Detachment." *Anthropological Quarterly* 73(4): 180–95.

Wilson, R. (1991) Machine Guns and Mountain Spirits: The Cultural Effects of State Repression Among the Q'eqchi' of Guatemala. *Critique of Anthropology* 11(1): 33–62.

Wilson, R. (1995) *Maya Resurgence in Guatemala: Q'eqchi' Experiences*. Norman: University of Oklahoma Press.

Wilson, R. (1998) The Politics of Remembering and Forgetting in Guatemala. In: *Guatemala After the Peace Accords*, Sieder, R. (Ed.). London: ILAS.

Wright, M. W. (2001) Desire and the Prosthetics of Supervision: A Case of Maquiladora Flexibility. *Cultural Anthropology* 16(3): 354–73.

Zur, J. N. (1998) *Violent Memories: Mayan War Widows in Guatemala*. Boulder, CO: Westview.

Zylinska, J. (Ed.) (2002) *The Cyborg Experiments: The Extensions of the Body in the Media Age*. London: Continuum International Publishing Group.

Index

Page references in italics indicate an illustration.